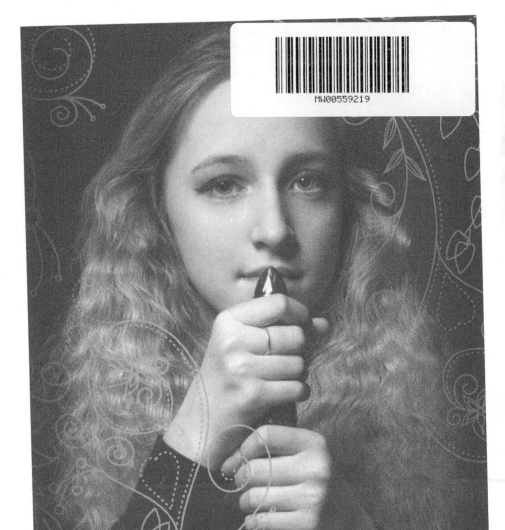

POLLYANNA'S
REVENGE

HOW MEMORY
& EMOTION
FOSTER HAPPINESS

W. RICHARD WALKER
Winston-Salem State University

CORY SCHERER
Pennsylvania State University

JESSICA HARTNETT
Gannon University

Kendall Hunt
publishing company

Kendall Hunt
publishing company
www.kendallhunt.com
Send all inquiries to:
4050 Westmark Drive
Dubuque, IA 52004-1840

Copyright © 2014 by W. Richard Walker, Cory Scherer, and Jessica Hartnett

ISBN 978-1-4652-4869-5

Printed in the United States of America
10 9 8 7 6 5 4 3 2 1

Dedications and Thanks

For Coralee,

For Jen, Emelia, Allison, and Elijah,

For Dom and Nico,

We would like to thank the following individuals for their help and support in this endeavor.

Harold Aurand, Gary Bond, Ashley Burrow, Stephen Couch, Matt Crawford, Nicole Currence, Amber DeBono, Jeff Gibbons, Dawn Henderson, Diana Lemus, Harry MacLean, Shawnda Marsh, Joseph Peterson, Tim Ritchie, Michael Sabb, Jeff Sable, Chuck Thompson, Rod Vogl, and Cecile Yancu.

We would especially like to thank John J. Skowronski for his invaluable role as mentor, colleague, and friend.

CONTENTS

About the Authors

W. Richard Walker is an associate professor of psychology at Winston-Salem State University, where he has taught since 1998. He is the author of approximately 40 research articles and scholarly book chapters on the topics of autobiographical memory and emotion, the effects of technology use in the classroom, and skepticism and pseudoscience. He and his wife are avid wildlife lovers and enjoy spending time working with birds of prey at the Carolina Raptor Center.

Cory R. Scherer is an associate professor of psychology at Penn State University–Schuylkill, where he has taught since 2007. His research area is in the topics of person memory, sex differences in jealousy, and positive psychology. He enjoys playing Wii with his three children and taking walks in the hills of Schuylkill county with his wife.

Jessica L. Hartnett is an assistant professor of psychology at Gannon University. She enjoys studying novel methods for teaching statistics and research methods, affective forecasting, and positive psychology. In her spare time, she reflects upon how lucky she is to have a philosopher husband who understands the demands of an academic career and a beautiful son who doesn't care about the demands of her academic career in the least.

INTRODUCTION

Pollyanna Wounded

Pollyanna. The word conjures up an image of a person with their head in the clouds and nary a care in the world. In the modern usage, the name is often lobbed as an insult to describe the naïve, the stooge, the rube who doesn't know any better. A person who is hopelessly unprepared for the harsh reality that waits for them. Real life is filled with pain and disappointment. Heartbreak. Death. No place for a Pollyanna.

The term *Pollyanna* comes from a best-selling children's book written by Eleanor H. Porter published in 1913. The story is, admittedly, simplistic and employs a number of standard plot devices typical of such books of the period. The story is about an 11-year-old girl who is raised in poverty by her missionary father, a widower who has forsaken material wealth. Pollyanna was named for two of her siblings—Polly and Anna—both of whom died as infants. After her father's sudden death, Pollyanna is sent to live with her estranged aunt, the stern and sour spinster, Miss Polly Harrington. Miss Harrington begrudgingly takes in Pollyanna out of a sense of duty to her deceased sister, a task that she considers "disagreeable." Much of this is described in the first pages of the book. So, to review, here is what Pollyanna faced: Two dead parents, two dead siblings, a life of poverty, and the prospect of being raised by a bitter, lonely woman she did not know. To a modern reader, this may sound like the beginning of a story in which Pollyanna would turn to some combination of drugs, abusive romantic partners, teen pregnancy, and perhaps even violence.

But Pollyanna did none of those things. Instead, she did something even more bizarre: She was *glad*. She was glad for the life and circumstances that were presented to her. She accepted the life of poverty chosen for her by her father. She accepted the deaths of her parents. She accepted her new living arrangements and the rules set by her strict aunt. Indeed, being glad was part of the game—the glad game. Her father had taught her to view each set of circumstances in the best, most positive light. The game had started when, after writing to the mission for a new doll, she had received a pair of crutches instead. Her father pointed out that she should be glad that she did not need the crutches. Rather than focusing on the disappointment, the glad game emphasized the positive. Pollyanna certainly isn't perfect: She does get into mischief by breaking some of her aunt's rules and by being very, very foolish. In one instance, after her aunt warns her against sleeping with the windows open, she impulsively decides to sleep out on the roof so that she can enjoy the cool night air. She realizes neither the inherent danger of her actions nor the fact that walking on the roof would wake others. As she is just nodding off to sleep, she is discovered and ordered to sleep in her aunt's bed so that she can be better supervised. For all of the trouble she causes, the little girl accepts responsibility and the punishment for her mistakes and misdeeds. And she looks on the bright side. It is fine to be punished for tardiness with a dinner of bread and milk, as long as you have an interesting dinner companion. Even after a period of depression following a car accident that causes the temporary paralysis of her legs, she eventual becomes "glad" to still have her legs.

To the modern cynic, the story of Pollyanna seems too sweet and perfect. Consider the moment in which the little girl receives the crutches rather than the doll she had wanted. Most children would not have accepted this as graciously as Pollyanna. The genius of Eleanor Porter's book is that the title character does not dwell on the what-ifs of life, only the realities placed before her. Porter created a character that was a fixed constant around which all of the other characters experience transformation. Her outlook and spirit is never more than temporarily dampened by even the most traumatic of life experiences, like the car accident. This makes Pollyanna different from most protagonists, who learn and grow from their experiences and interactions with others. There is no transformation for Pollyanna; she remains steadfast in the beliefs instilled in her by her father and her resilience inspires the people around her. Even the bitter Aunt Polly is finally won over by the gladness inspired by her niece's positive outlook as she finally allows others into her sheltered world.

This was not the end of Pollyanna and her "glad game." Not by a long shot. *Pollyanna* was a best seller in 1913 and was soon translated into more than a dozen languages. The original novel spawned 14 sequels, known as "glad books." The latest sequel was written in 1995 (obviously, not by the original author). The original book also inspired several movies (1920, 1960, 1989, 2003). Perhaps strangest of all, a 51-episode TV series called *Ai Shoujo Pollyanna Monogatari (The Story of Pollyanna, Girl of Love)*, which has a legion of Japanese anime enthusiasts. The town of Littleton, New Hampshire celebrated the 100th anniversary of the original book's publication on June 8, 2013 by holding the Official Pollyanna Glad Day.

Fast forward 100 years later from the original publication date and you would have to look rather hard to find another hero like Pollyanna. The popular culture trend is for the antihero. Don Draper, Dexter Morgan, and Walter White are the antihero stars of some of the most critically acclaimed television shows in our era (*Mad Men, Dexter,* and *Breaking Bad*, respectively). These characters cheat on their partners, exact vigilante justice via murder, and cook meth (again, respectively) and yet the television viewing public cheers them on. These anti-heroes seem to reflect a pop culture zeitgeist that states that happiness is for suckers and that we should always expect the worst from life. Popular books like *The Gift of Fear* and *The Wisdom of Psychopaths* have gained notoriety, exulting anxiety and antisocial behavior as keys to surviving and thriving in the world. *The New York Times'* Jonah Lehrer talked about "depression's upside"[1] and *Slate.com's* Joshua Kendall described how bipolar disorder inspires genius.[2] The consistent message seems to be that embracing our darker impulses is the pathway to many a life goal. As such, the idea of Pollyanna seems increasingly antiquated. Pollyanna has even become an eponym. This is a rarity and would be an honor if it was not for the definition of Pollyanna found in most dictionaries: "A person regarded as being foolishly or blindly optimistic." This is precisely opposite of the character envisioned by the author. Pollyanna accepted the reality of her circumstances, which meant that she was not blind to the world around her. And, while it is true that she was occasionally foolish, it was her optimism that usually got her out of trouble rather than placing her in it. So how is it that a character that is loved by millions, who faces the challenges of life with a smile and positive outlook, has been reinvented as a clueless, hopeless dupe? How can she clear her name and restore her honor? How can she claim her revenge?

Sweet Revenge

The twisting of Pollyanna's story is one that is more about psychology than it is literature. It is a misunderstanding about the human condition that is so widely accepted that it is rarely challenged with any serious conviction. It is a belief about how the mind copes with the hardships of life. The common belief is that most people are damaged goods. Those of us that do manage some semblance of happiness must be doing so via a stockpile of drugs and an army of physicians and therapists. To be clear, many people do need help, both clinical and pharmaceutical. Many groups, like veterans returning home from war, victims of domestic violence, and victims of devastating natural disasters, are grossly underserved when it comes to their emotional needs. In fact, they probably need *more* opportunities for medical and clinical intervention. But mainstream society has the mindset that all emotional setbacks are insurmountable traumas that paralyze the mind. As the first draft of this chapter was written, the mass shooting at a movie theatre in Aurora, Colorado took place, taking the lives of 12 innocent victims.[3] In the aftermath of the event, many of the 58 surviving shooting victims chose to share their stories with the media. A common line offered to summarize the heartache often resembled the following: "while the physical wounds will heal, the emotional wounds will not." The notion that people can overcome such tragedies and move on with their lives is an idea that is seen as foolishly optimistic. Unrealistic. Pollyanna.

Would the sweet and innocent Pollyanna really want revenge? The answer is yes, but not in the traditional sense. Vengeance is typically associated with seeking justice through direct physical confrontations that are both personal and violent. The wrongdoers are singled out, publically shamed, and sometimes harshly punished. Such vulgarity does not suit Pollyanna. That is not to say that she wouldn't seek justice, but she would probably wish even her harshest critics well and hope to inspire them to playing the "glad game" in their own lives. She would be likely to exact her revenge in the spirit of the poet George Herbert who wrote "Living well is the best revenge" (1651, *Jacula Prudentum,* line 520).

For Pollyanna to exact her brand of vengeance, many of the popular beliefs that people have about positive and negative emotions and events will have to be challenged: The belief that more people are unhappy than happy; the belief that negative events are more common life than positive events; the belief that negative emotions are stronger and last longer than positive emotions; and the belief that painful life events rarely resolve in recovery, reconciliation, or redemption. The belief that positive emotions blind people to reality, which sets them up for failure or something much worse, heartache. And, finally, that the norm after a traumatic experience is a life of unyielding festering emotion. These beliefs will not be blindly or foolishly challenged. Indeed, the reality of life's pain must be acknowledged and confronted. Negative events and emotions can sometimes be powerful, long-lasting, and overwhelming. Emotions can linger for decades and recovery is not always possible. But the exceptions can serve to help prove the rule: Life *is* pleasant, the human mind *is* resilient, and the world *is* what you make it.

The revenge that is fitting of Pollyanna is one of understanding and truth about how the mind actually is able to cope with negativity. To be sure, the approach that will be taken to seek Pollyanna's Revenge will be a largely empirical one. It will rely upon psychological research gathered from the last 80 years by a variety of researchers. Some of this research will involve massive surveys of public opinion while others will include much smaller studies conducted in controlled laboratory settings. A good portion of the research cited in this text will involve studies of autobiographical memory that we have conducted with the help of our colleagues and friends. Autobiographical memory, as one might surmise from the term, refers to the personal recollections of events that people have experienced. Psychologists have been studying autobiographical memories using a variety of techniques for several decades. These memories are often rich in details that give insight into the mental and emotional lives of the participants for whom they belong. Taken separately, these data represent approximately 500,000 unique events from more than 10,000 individuals collected over the last three decades. The samples include traditional college students, working adults, older adults, Caucasians, African-Americans, Native Americans, Irish, Danish, Germans, English, New Zealanders, and Ghanaians. The events themselves range from humorous anecdotes to deeply personal tragedies, from the mundane to the extraordinary.

However, the empirical approach is incomplete. While it provides analysis, it lacks context. Many of the points that will be made on Pollyanna's behalf will be driven home with narratives culled from a variety of sources, including historical documents, personal narratives, works of fiction and myth, and from personal interviews. These stories include: A town bully who terrorized a Midwestern community with acts of arson, child molestation, thievery, and attempted murder for a decade with impunity; a graduate student who found himself in the midst of a terrifying shooting spree that claimed the lives of five students he was teaching; a man who plotted an attack that killed his stepfather and severely injured his mother but who has found redemption after a 20-year prison sentence; a town that has been desiccated by an underground fire that has been burning for more than half a century; and finally, a 50-year-old African-American man and self-described Pollyanna who has had to cope with health problems since birth which necessitated the amputation of both of his legs, and who believes that confronting life's hardships has made him stronger. Together, this combination of data and drama tell a story about the human experience that is profoundly different from the narrative provided by the cynics, the one believed by nearly everyone.

At last, Pollyanna will have her revenge.

CHAPTER 1

Pollyanna's Gifts

Mount Airy, North Carolina sits an hour north of Winston-Salem, right off Interstate 77 near the Virginia border. The town has a unique distinction: It served as the inspiration for "*The Andy Griffith Show.*" The show ran on CBS from 1960–1968. It portrayed the life of Andy Taylor and his son, Opie, and the people they interacted with in the town of Mayberry, where Andy was the sheriff. The show was incredibly popular and is still shown in reruns with a devoted following. Mount Airy has become a tourist destination for fans of the television show. Tourists travelling through these parts will point at shops that seem familiar and stop for a haircut at a barbershop that they have never visited but they feel as if they know. If they are hungry, they might even stop for a pork chop sandwich and chat with total strangers about their favorite childhood memories from the time they had spent in Mayberry.

Image © spirit of america, 2013. Used under license from Shutterstock, Inc.

The real life Mayberry located in Mount Airy, North Carolina, the town featured in *The Andy Griffith Show*.

These people are not delusional; they are fans of Andy and Opie. Mayberry was a quirky, yet ideal place that served as the perfect backdrop for light comedy served up for a 1960s family television audience. The characters were simple but dignified in their own ways. The problems were minor and easily solved with folk wisdom and gentle humor. It is hard to imagine that such a place had any basis in reality. But it did.

Present-day Mount Airy, while having all of the trappings of modernity, is still a lot like its fictional counterpart. Part of this comes from the homage to all things Andy Griffith. The downtown area is made up for the tourists with spots like the Bluebird Café and Floyd's City Barbershop. Gift shops sell memorabilia, but it's more than that. The town is small and genuinely friendly. It is surrounded on all sides by country roads and can be crossed in ten minutes flat. A particularly fond set of memories held by the author (RW) include frequent trips to the Bright Leaf drive-in movie theatre, which closed just a few years ago. The double feature started with the national anthem accompanied by obligatory horn honking and was followed by a series of corny commercials enticing people to the concession stand. The image on the screen was intermittently blocked by the shadows of children playing near the screen. No doubt the town faces its share of problems, but the town is wholesome and friendly, a true slice of Americana.

There aren't many places like Mount Airy anymore. Or are there? If such places were truly rare, then opinion polls would find most people fearful in their homes and looking for a better place to live. But most people aren't fearful and they aren't looking to move. If you ask people about politicians in Washington, they will call them incompetent or corrupt (or both!). Ask people about their local representatives and you get a different story. The responses will generally be neutral or positive. Ask people about the national economy and the responses are neutral to pessimistic. Ask people about their personal economic prospects, the response are generally positive. Why? The reason is because most people are generally happy with their lives. Their moods are positive, they experience more ups than downs, and they see themselves as capable of handling most setbacks on their own. These attitudes are the result of a positive mindset that is found across the general population, in most circumstances, most of the time. The reasons why this mindset is so often overlooked will be discussed later. For now, consider two aspects of everyday life that most people take for granted: Good moods and good times, or as they will be referred in this text, Pollyanna's gifts.

The Gift of Good Moods

Moods are tricky things. They change at the smallest of circumstance. Can't find a parking space? Bad mood. Get an unexpected compliment? Good mood. Moods are not as prominent as emotions. They are more subtle, like background music. Think of an emotion as the lead guitar in a band and a mood as a bass guitar. The lead guitar gets a solo midway through many rock and roll songs. Everyone knows the lead guitarist. All the while, the bass guitar strums out a steady rhythm that forms the basis of most songs. Emotions are punctuated by brief bursts of frenetic energy and are hard to maintain for any length of time. Moods are more understated, expend less energy, and can be maintained indefinitely without much effort or thought. The moods that people typically find themselves in are happy moods. In fact, a happy mood is the norm.

The first piece of evidence that suggests that life is filled with happiness comes from research on positive and negative moods. The participants in this research were college students. At this point, you may roll your eyes and think to yourself, "Well, of course college students are happy, what with parties, sleeping in, and delayed adulthood." But what about a group of college-aged people confined to wheelchairs due to spinal cord injuries? In 1988, Chwalisz, Diener, and Gallagher studied the happiness levels of normal, healthy students and the happiness levels of the wheelchair-bound students. Both groups were asked to estimate the proportions of happy, unhappy, and neutral moods they experienced on a day-to-day basis. At first blush, the expected results seem obvious: Healthy students should be happier than their wheelchair-bound counterparts. Being disabled comes with a variety of physical challenges, not to mention the unfair social stigma associated with being in a wheelchair. In fact, one might go so far as to expect increased levels of depression and anxiety in the disabled sample. But that's not what happened. Both healthy and disabled students reported that they were happy 50% of the time, unhappy 22% of the time, and in a neutral mood 28% of the time. Two important points come out of this study: 1) Disabled students were just as happy as healthy students; 2) Happiness was experienced *twice* as often as unhappiness in both samples.

It's one thing to demonstrate happiness in a small study of college students, even disabled ones; it is quite another to demonstrate that widespread happiness is the norm. Perhaps more convincing data can be found outside the ivory tower of academe. The first stop in the journey will be the idyllic city of San Francisco, the city by the bay. San Francisco is the home of the Golden Gate Bridge, Chinatown, a vibrant gay and lesbian culture, and perhaps one of the best cityscapes in America. The city is beautiful and iconic. It is also one of the most expensive cities in the United States. It is routinely rated as having one of the highest costs of living, a distinction it has held for more than 30 years. Not surprisingly, the people who live there tend to make substantially more than the average American. Living the good life in a beautiful city requires a certain level of wealth. It would surprise few people if they found out that the citizens of San Francisco were happy. But it might be surprising to find out how happy. Rebekah North and her colleagues (2008) examined the happiness levels of 274 married couples who were surveyed four times over a 10-year period from 1981 to 1991. They assessed income (adjusted to 2006 dollars); family social support using the Family Relationship Index, which produces a score between 0 (no support) and 9 (high support); and happiness using a simple 5-point scale from 0 (very unhappy) to 4 (very happy). Over the 10-year period, income went up quite substantially for these people, from about $63,000 in 1981 to almost $78,000 in 1991. Family support was quite high across all four assessments, showing little movement, ranging in scores from 6.6 to 6.8. Happiness remained essentially fixed, ranging from a low of 2.86 to a high of 2.99, averages well above the midpoint of the scale.

Being happy in San Francisco is probably fairly easy, especially when a person has an income well above the national average and good family ties. How about going to the streets of one of America's toughest working cities? A place that has seen more than its share of crime and economic suffering over the last three decades. In 1976, Detroit was a city on the verge of decline. Everyone knew it. The weak post-Nixon economy was suffering from stagflation, a term coined to describe the confluence of a stagnant economy and inflation. International gas embargoes had led to higher gas prices and consumers were buying fewer cars. Although foreign cars were still the exception, Ford, Chrysler, and General Motors had seemed to run out of ideas. Former muscle cars like the Ford Mustang and Chevy Nova were being re-imagined as shadows of their former selves. They were now branded as being "sensible" and "economical." All of these factors were bad news for the Motor City. And the problems experienced in 1976 Detroit were not merely economical: This was a city so crime ridden that it had the highest murder rate in the country. Each Halloween Eve, gangs would burn down entire neighborhoods in a ritual of violence and arson known as "Devil's Night." In the midst of this existential crisis, a public opinion poll was conducted by Andrews and Withey (1976) using citizens of Detroit. They were shown a series of seven faces, ranging from ☺ (very happy) to ☹ (very unhappy), to describe how they felt about their life as a whole. The results were clear: 93% of the sample described themselves as happy or very happy while only 7% of the sample described themselves as "Neutral" or "Unhappy."

What do these samples of college students, upscale citizens of San Francisco, and denizens of Detroit have in common? They were all Americans. Maybe you are thinking that this penchant for happiness is an American phenomenon. Americans are known for thinking highly of themselves and their abilities. The importance of the pursuit of happiness is written into the American Declaration of Independence. Perhaps things are different elsewhere. To address this issue, consider the work of Ruut Veenhoven. Dr. Veenhoven is a sociologist who has studied the phenomenon of happiness since the early 1980s. He has observed that there is a wide variety in the kinds of experiences that people describe as being "happy". In his view, happiness is better described as several related phenomena, rather than a single phenomenon. Two factors that help give rise to these phenomena are 1) how many domains of a person's life are affected by the experience; and 2) how long the experience lasts. By crossing these factors, four distinct experiences of happiness emerge: Pleasure, Domain Specific Happiness, Peak Experiences, and Life Satisfaction. *Pleasure* is the experience that is most often associated with happiness. Pleasure is short lived and domain specific. Eating dessert or having sex are examples of experiences that create pleasure for most people. *Domain Specific Happiness* refers to the kind of satisfaction that a person experiences when considering a single aspect of life. This kind of experience is more long-lasting, but limited in scope. A professional considering her career might find herself happy with her accomplishments and her status. *Peak Experiences* refer to those brief yet all-encompassing experiences of pleasure that touch every aspect of a person's existence. For a moment, everything is connected, and it all makes sense. The final experience of happiness is probably the most important: *Life Satisfaction.* Life Satisfaction is the experience of happiness that is not derived from a single episode; it is the happiness that comes from totality of the life experience. This is a combination of a person's psychological state of mind, their physical health, economic and social welfare, and whether or not they are hopeful about the future.

Alright, let's get back to laying to rest the counterargument that Americans are a happy bunch of people. Veenhoven has gathered data on happiness from around the world and is the scholar most directly responsible for creating the World Database of Happiness[1], an online register for all sorts of data related to quality of life. The website is remarkable to navigate and should be examined to fully capture the enormity of the project. As of 2014, there were just over 3,900 empirical studies using accepted measures of life satisfaction and happiness and about 6,000 distributional findings from around the world. There is data available for almost every country on Earth. It is a treasure trove for researchers and an avalanche for the uninitiated. Data is easily found and can be compared in units that can be equated. No apples to oranges.

Consider a simple comparison between the two countries that the United States shares a border: Canada and Mexico. Canada, the "Great White North," is the home of free healthcare and hockey. The climate can be very cold and has several sparsely populated regions. It is also fairly crime free, fairly wealthy, well-governed, and has a citizenry of educated people. Mexico is more of a mixed bag. Sunny beaches and ancient pyramids are great tourist destinations. However, the ongoing war between the government and the drug cartels is a major cause of anxiety. The war has led to an escalating cycle of violence and corruption. Estimates of civilian deaths are wildly unreliable and range from a few thousand to tens of thousands. Additionally, the people and land of Mexico have been exploited by international industry in order to take advantage of cheap labor and loose environmental standards. Which country is happier? On a normalized scale ranging from 0–10, Canadians score a 7.8 while Mexicans score a 7.9. With all due respect to any statisticians who may care to disagree, most observers would call the contest a tie. The United States scored just below its neighbors with a 7.4.

The site is also interesting in another kind of data it presents. Not only does it look at how happy people are, but it also provides estimates of how much of their lives they spend being happy. Think about that for a moment: How many years does the average person spend being happy? The question seems esoteric. Conventional wisdom suggests that people don't spend hardly any of their lives being happy, let alone years. The average Canadian is happy for about 62 years, the average Mexican is happy for 59 years, and the average American spends almost 58 years being happy.

Before these results are discounted as rogue data points, the website also allows a person to look at the data across time. Samples entered include data-sets going back more than 60 years. While it is true that there are more samples for places like the United States, there is no attempt to distort the results by cherry-picking the samples. In 2014, Canada had 8 representative samples from the years 1946 to 2000, with all of the scores hovering between 7 and 8. Likewise, Mexico had 7 samples between the years 1975 and 2012, none falling below 6.2. That is not to say that some countries aren't below the midpoint of the scale (5), but they aren't that much below the midpoint.

Take Iraq as an example. In the last 10 years, one of the most volatile places in the world has been Iraq. The U.S. invasion in 2003 and the subsequent sectarian violence have been simultaneously heartbreaking and maddening. According to the Iraq Body Count project, between 105,000 and 115,000 civilians were killed in the conflict. That is more than 30 times the people killed in the attacks of September 11, 2001. Moreover, the post-Saddam period was rampant with widespread looting and kidnappings, which only served to deepen the sectarian divides and strengthen opposition to American forces, who were more often seen as occupiers than liberators. Faced with such devastation of country and culture, it is not surprising that the Iraqi people were unhappy. They scored a 4.7—just 0.3 below the midpoint of the scale.

A review of the countries that have data available show a consistent pattern: Most of them are above the midpoint of the scale. Wealthy countries tend to be happier, but that is not the only factor predicting life satisfaction. To be clear, there are countries far below the midpoint of the scale—countries that have been devastated by political corruption, widespread poverty, and natural disasters. Haiti fits this description with savage accuracy. The ongoing suffering in Haiti is simply unacceptable and the global community should be ashamed for casting its gaze away from the obvious needs of the Haitian people. Critics of research on global happiness suggest that these data provide intellectual cover for such tragic cases of pain and injustice. The argument suggests that by describing most of the world as "overwhelmingly happy," the research on global happiness allows people to turn a blind eye to the many instances of social and economic injustice that exist around the world. But the critics have it wrong. Any kind of data can be used or misused to support a variety of political agendas. Indeed, we would argue that more data is typically better than less data when trying to capture the essence of the human experience.

Admittedly, the approach taken by Veenhoven and others is a markedly different way of thinking about happiness than most people are used to. To some critics, the measures that are being employed are soft and unknowable. Usually, when one compares the lives of people living in various countries to one another, terms like Gross Domestic Product (GDP) are trotted out by sober-faced economists. After all GDP is real. Or is it? Perhaps this solid indicator of national well-being is not as solid as one might imagine. The GDP can be calculated by a simple equation, $GDP = C + I + G + (X - M)$, where C = household consumption expenditures, I = gross private domestic investment, G = government consumption and investment, X = gross exports of goods and services, and M = gross imports of goods and services. A room full of skilled economists can use the exact same data and the exact same equations to produce wildly different results and to proffer diametrically opposing solutions to whatever they see as the problem.

Perhaps GDP is too complex. Consider a 'simpler' number to calculate: Unemployment. This seems easy to figure by comparison. Simply take the number of unemployed divided by the total number in the labor force and multiply the result by 100. This can be done with a pocket calculator. And an Ouija Board. What the equation fails to consider is the operational definitions of "unemployed" and "labor force." How do you count people who are underemployed—that is, people who have jobs but are only working part-time? How do you count discouraged workers—people who are unemployed and have given up on their prospects of finding work? How do you account for temporary or seasonal employment? What about the impact of undocumented workers?

The point is not to deride economists who are doing their best to make sense of a complex and ever-changing marketplace, but to remind people that society is already accustomed to thinking about terms that are fuzzy using numbers that are hard to pin down. We are taught to think of these things as tangible when, in fact, they are just mental constructs rife with ambiguity and open for exploitation. Assigning a "happiness score" to an entire country or estimating the "number of happy years" may seem outlandish, but it is no more bizarre than calculating things like GDP and unemployment and assuming that these represent stable, completely knowable measures of economic health.

The results of this ongoing project are remarkably similar to the findings of researchers working in more traditional mediums that are grounded in more familiar methodologies. Using similar kinds of data, Ed Diener and David Myers (1995) combined the results of 916 surveys of life satisfaction and happiness. The combined analysis consisted of 1.1 million people from 45 countries around the globe. They performed a meta-analysis, a statistical tool that allows researchers to examine trends in data across multiple data sets with varying methodologies and samples. Such analyses are stubbornly conservative, meaning that the demonstrated effects have to be both powerful and widespread for this analysis to produce results that warrant attention. They calibrated the combined data to an easy-to-understand scale ranging from 0 (*very unhappy* or *completely dissatisfied*) to 10 (*very happy* or *completely satisfied*). The average result was 6.75. What the average result misses, however, is the overall distribution of scores: More than 90% of the responses were above the midpoint of the scale.

Ed Diener and his colleagues were not done yet. In 2010, with Ng, Harter, and Arora, Diener published the results of another massive survey on global happiness. Working with the Gallup Poll organization and employing techniques from telephone calls to door-to-door surveys to ensure a representative sample, they interviewed 136,839 participants across 132 countries. In 2006, when this survey was completed, it included 96% of the world's countries. Some countries, such as North Korea, were obviously not included in the study, and the emotional lives of its citizenry can only be guessed at. However, this was clearly not a sample composed only of wealthy, democratic countries. This was a sample of humanity. Among the many questions were those that probed the emotional lives of the people completing the survey. Specifically, they were asked to think about the previous day and whether or not they had experienced any positive emotions (enjoyment, smiling, laughing) or any negative emotions (depression, worry, sadness, anger). The positive and negative responses were scaled on two separate scales from 0 to 1, with 0 indicating they had not experienced any of the emotions during the previous day and 1 indicated they had experienced all of the emotions on the previous day. While there were cultural differences worth noting, particularly in countries that were lacking basic human rights like freedom of expression and freedom of religion, the overall results should not be ignored. The overall mean response for positive emotions was 0.71 while the overall mean response for negative emotions was 0.23. People reported having three times as many positive emotions as they did negative emotions. The world, as whole, was pretty happy.

The Gift of Good Times

The human experience is not just comprised of good moods; it is made up of individual episodes. These episodes are lined up one after another in a continuous string of events that help to create an unbroken stream of experience commonly referred to as *life*. As people stop to consider their own unique set of life events, whether through private reflection or boisterously sharing their experiences with others, they are forming their own personal narratives. In Western cultures, like the United States and Europe, these personal narratives tend to begin about the time we learn to tell stories, about the age 3. It is rare that autobiographical memories are recalled much earlier or later than this benchmark age. For the purposes of this discussion, studies of autobiographical memory offer a window into the day-to-day experiences of people of all walks of life. Some of the experiences are positive, some are negative, and many others are neutral. Casting aside the neutral events, which are often mundane and trivial, which events do people experience more often?

To help begin answering this question, consider the work of Willem Wagenaar (1986), a psychologist who employed a diary method to study his own memory. A diary method is exactly what it sounds like. He dutifully wrote down descriptions of various events that happened to him on a daily basis. He recorded 2,600 unique events over a span of 6 years. He later tested himself on the contents of his diary, a rigorous procedure that involved carefully presenting himself with a series of cues to help remind him of the event. Being a committed researcher, he never "cheated" by going back and reviewing the diary contents to boost his memory performance. His diary revealed much about his memory, but also much about his life. You see, while recording the event descriptions, he also made a quick rating of how pleasant or unpleasant the event was when it happened. This rating was made on a simple 5-point scale ranging from Very Pleasant to Very Unpleasant, with 0 being Neutral. Ever the scientist, Wagenaar made sure that he recorded a wide range of experiences in his diary, and he was keen to understand that *very* pleasant or *very* unpleasant events were few and far between. Indeed, only 120 of the 2,600 events were rated as being either very positive or very negative. Of those events, 73 were positive and 47 were negative. Positive events outnumbered negative events by a ratio of 1.5 to 1.

The findings of Wagenaar, while impressive, represent the experiences of a single man. Like any reasonable scientist, he wanted to contrast positive and negative events. To do this, the samples of positive and negative events should be approximately equal. Hence, he probably found himself looking for negative events to record. This observation certainly does not repute Wagenaar's work. Indeed, his efforts have helped to form the foundation of research in autobiographical memory. This observation is made to recognize a phenomenon that can be observed in many studies of autobiographical memory. When participants are asked to record positive and negative events in these studies, they often find the second part of the task harder. To record a reasonable number of negative events, they have to make a concerted effort to pay attention to the negative events. In other words, they have to overestimate their own life's negativity.

In order to address this observation, scientists will often give negative events an advantage, too. Not that it changes the story too much. Consider the 2008 study by Frijters, Johnston, and Shields. They examined the life data collected four times a year from 19,914 Australians between the years 2001 and 2006. Data was collected through a massive national survey called the Household, Income, and Labour Dynamics in Australia (HILDA) that is used to help make policy decisions on things like education, health, and economic development. Specifically, they wanted to examine the impact of various positive and negative life events on the overall happiness of the participants. Instead of sampling positive and negative events equally, they sampled 10 events: 6 negative and 4 positive. Positive events included things like getting married, having a child, and having finances improve. Negative events included things like separation, illness, and getting fired. Given this potential bias, it would be reasonable to assume that negative events substantially outnumbered positive events. They didn't. The results of the survey indicated that there were 12,181 positive events and 10,913 negative events experienced by participants in the sample, a ratio of 1.1. Remember, researchers are clearly overestimating negative events in a way that is far more explicit than Wagenaar. To remedy that, divide the number of positive events (12,181) by the number of positive categories (4) and divide the number of negative events (10,913) by the number of negative categories (6). You should have gotten 3045 (positive) and 1818 (negative). The result is that positive events outnumbered negative events by a rate of 1.7 to 1.

Another example of this tendency towards recording positive events comes from a sample of life experiences of high school students 25 years after Wagenaar's study. Lüdtke and his colleagues (2011) tracked 2000 German high school students over a period of 4 years. Some of these students went on to college, others trade or professional schools, and still others entered the world of work. Much like Wagenaar's work, this research also provided a window into the lives of the participants. The participants were given a survey to measure the occurrence of 34 specific significant life events (e.g., a significant personal loss, an important achievement, death of loved one) that may or may not occur in the life of a young adult. Participants were asked to indicate whether or not the event had occurred and to rate the event as very positive (5), positive (4), neutral (3), negative (2), and very negative (1). The event 'Traveled Abroad' was rated as the most positive event (4.59) while 'Death of a Friend' was rated as the most negative (1.38). Across all participants, there were approximately 24,000 event occurrences. Based upon the ratings provided by participants, 14,076 were positive and 10,653 were negative. Overall, positive events outnumbered negative events by a rate of 1.3 to 1.

One thing to remember is that some events occurred far more often than others. For instance, while getting married was rated as one of the most positive experiences in the survey, only 46 nuptials were recorded in Lüdtke's sample. Likewise, negative experiences, such as going to prison, happened a mere 14 times in the study. A better understanding of how often the participants experienced positive and negative events can be afforded by looking at the most frequently occurring life events. The top 10 most common events and their frequencies are presented in Table 1.1. Using the emotion ratings provided by participants, the individual events were coded as positive or negative. Items marked with an asterisk were rated by the participants as being positive events. Two things become obvious. First, six of the ten events are perceived as being positive in the lives of the participants. Second, look at the frequency of the events. The six positive events totaled 9,669 individual experiences while the four negative events totaled 5,204 individual experiences.

Life Event	Frequency
Travelled Abroad	2,075*
Changed Accommodations	1,588*
Started a New Job	1,572*
Moved Away from Home	1,549*
Change in Financial Situation (better)	1,457*
Illness or Injury of Family Member	1,454
Entered New Relationship	1,428*
Broke off Relationship	1,342
Convicted of Minor Offense	1,314
Change in Sleep Habits	1,094

*Indicates a positive life event.

TABLE 1.1 The top 10 most common events and their frequencies as recorded by German university students (adapted from Lüdtke, Roberts, Trautwein, & Nagy, 2011).

Of the most frequently occurring kinds of life events, positive events outnumbered negative events by a ratio of almost 2 to 1.

As you glance through these data, you might note that the most frequently occurring event for these students was travelling abroad. It's hard to imagine life being anything but good if a person has the financial resources to be able to do that, in some cases more than once. That's why it's important to temper these data with data collected from adolescents living more modest lives in a large metropolitan center. Conventional wisdom tells us that for a person living in the "wrong part of town," daily life can be anything but positive. Or can it? Lawrence Scheier, Gilbert Botvin, and Nicole Miller (1999) sampled 1420 students in a sample from a large northeastern metropolitan city that was quite ethnically diverse (most likely, New York City). Again, the participants provided information on the instances of positive and negative events in their lives. More than three quarters of the sample was African-American or Hispanic. Scheier and his colleagues were interested in the impact of neighborhood stress on alcohol use among the minority urban youth. They examined the content of event descriptions to see what kinds of experiences these students were reporting. Not surprisingly, they found that perceived neighborhood stress was high, particularly among male adolescents of the African-American and Hispanic groups. The students were cognizant of the pressures of poverty, bullying, and the very real presence of gangs. However, they also found that when they sampled the relative frequency of positive and negative life events, the ratio always favored positive events. The highest ratio was almost 4 to 1. The lowest ratio was almost 3 to 1. These teens recognized that their neighborhoods were troubled and that their immediate surroundings were less than ideal, but their lives were more positive than they were negative. Much more.

Another, much older study demonstrates a similar finding. Waldfogel (1948) conducted one of the earliest studies that investigated the emotional content of childhood memories. In a retrospective memory study, participants were given 85 minutes to write down all the events they could remember from the first eight years of childhood. Later, they were asked to give several ratings of these events, including whether each event was pleasant, unpleasant, or neutral. If this task sounds difficult, it wasn't. As it turns out, people liked writing and talking about themselves. The results provided more evidence for a positivity bias in everyday events. Waldfogel's participants rated about 50% of their events as pleasant, about 30% as unpleasant, and about 20% as neutral. The ratio of positive to negative events: 2 to 1.

A critic would correctly point out that Waldfogel's findings could have alternative explanations. One explanation is that participants in a standard recall task might be responding to subtle environmental cues that might trigger more pleasant memories than unpleasant memories. This concern was addressed in a study that was conducted using a sensory deprivation chamber. In one of their experiments, Suedfeld and Eich (1995) had 24 participants spend one hour in a sensory deprivation chamber. At the end of the hour, while still floating in the chamber, participants were asked to recall 12 memories and to make several ratings for each memory. If the bias in favor of pleasant events was caused by environmental cues, then sensory deprivation should eliminate that bias. It did not. Participants rated their recalled events as being pleasant (66%) more often than unpleasant (33%).

Another criticism that could be lodged against the bias in favor of pleasant events is that the Waldfogel (1948) and Suedfeld and Eich (1995) data come from events that were voluntarily recalled by participants. Perhaps the unconscious mind would reveal the true (dark) content of the human experience. This was clearly Sigmund Freud's thinking on the subject. In his view, the unconscious mind was a cauldron seething with repressed memories. These memories would rise to the surface from time to time and wreak havoc with people's lives. Of course, people would work hard to hide these gloomy events from themselves and others, such was the purpose of many of Freud's famous defense mechanisms. However, there is a relatively straightforward way to examine the notion that the unconscious mind is hiding a mountain of pain and anguish. Examine the content of event memories that spontaneously pop into people's minds. These memories are called involuntary memories, and there has been a steady line of research on this topic since the mid-1990s.

Dorthe Berntsen (1996) used a diary procedure in which Danish participants were asked to record their involuntary memories as they occurred. Participants recorded a brief description of each memory and the situation in which it came to mind. One might surmise that involuntary memory experiences are rare and fleeting, but that is not the case at all. Indeed, the data showed that participants were having several involuntary memory experiences each day. Berntsen's data showed that these involuntary memories were often triggered by stimuli in the immediate surroundings. It has long been known, or at least suspected that this is true. Proust pondered the role of smell in his memory recall experiences (Berntsen, 2005). If the bias for pleasant information was caused by a voluntary search for positive memories, then sampling involuntary memories should eliminate this bias. It did not. Consistent with the results of the Waldfogel and Suedfeld and Eich studies, the event memories recorded in Berntsen's study are positively biased: 49% of the events were positive, 32% were neutral, and 19% were negative.

Although the results of these studies are suggestive, they also are potentially tainted by retrospective memory biases. A source of data that bypasses this difficulty comes from diary studies of memory (Thompson, Skowronski, Larsen, & Betz, 1996). Participants in these studies usually recorded one event each day and were told to record only unique events. Event recording typically spanned an academic term. However, six participants kept diaries for periods ranging from 1.5 to 2.5 years. When participants recorded each event, they also rated the event's pleasantness, among other ratings. Hence, a person's perception of the pleasantness or unpleasantness of each event at the time it happened is exactly known. Across eight studies, these data sets include a total of 229 participants and a total of 23,202 diary entries. These diaries include a variety of participants, including participants of different racial and ethnic backgrounds and participants that ranged in age from the late teens to the early fifties. If the positivity bias obtained in the previous studies was the result of a retrospective bias, then the use of a diary methodology should eliminate the bias. It did not. Every study yielded more pleasant than unpleasant events. Summing across all eight studies, 60% of the events were positive and 25% of the events were negative.

As one might imagine, conducting diary studies can be very time consuming. The strength of the methodology, that you are capturing slices of life as they happen, is offset by the fact that a single study can take months to complete. Thankfully, modern technology has helped make this process a bit easier. Walker (2013) had 29 participants keep track of daily life events for a six-week period using their cell phones. Participants received three prompts per day between the hours of 9:00 a.m. and 8:00 p.m. on their cell phone via a simple text message. The recording task for participants was simple: Record 6–10 words that summarized what they were doing at that time of the prompt and provide a simple rating of how pleasant or unpleasant the event was. This rating was conceptually similar to the rating scales of Thompson, replacing the numeric scale with emoticons. Only data received within one hour of the prompt was kept, yielding about 95 events for each participant for a total of 2,731 events. The results were clear: 1,311 events were positive, 848 events were neutral, and 572 events were negative. These results are very similar to the results Thompson reported almost two decades before. In this case, the methodology captured more neutral events than the traditional paper and pencil diaries, but the ratio of positive and negative events was just over 2 to 1.

One might argue that the results of these studies are suspect because participants engage in self-editing of event entries, causing positive events to be over-represented in the diaries. There are at least two reasons to discount this concern. The first has to do with the nature of instructions provided to participants. Participants were explicitly told to try to record events such that the diaries would contain as many different combinations of these ratings as possible. If participants drew any conclusions about the kind of events that should be recorded, it would likely be to record equal numbers of pleasant and unpleasant events. The second reason to discount the self-editing concern lies in the diary entries themselves. If self-editing were widespread in these studies, one might suspect that relatively few diary entries would deal with very personal (and sometimes troubling) life events. Participants routinely included diary entries that described the intimate details of some extremely unpleasant events (e.g., deaths, romantic troubles, personal health problems, alcohol abuse, drug addiction). Some of the entries were embarrassing, others quite painful. One of the more humorous and embarrassing entries was one that was collected when one of the authors (RW) was at the Ohio State University in the early 1990s. The entry read in part "I had a very sexual experience with 8 other people." Indeed, having read many, many such entries, it is the view of the authors that the participants could have self-edited a bit more. The point is, if participants were trying to selectively edit their diaries, these events would be likely candidates for such editing. Those events were dutifully recorded, sometimes in graphic detail.

Now you know a LOT about the research that has been done in academia to study this ratio of good to bad. This may lead some to ask whether researchers can identify a point in time or a set of events that can distinguish happy, satisfied people from those who are less happy or dissatisfied? We wish that were the case, but to ask that question may be to miss the point about happiness. Happiness is an experience that is tied as much to the mindset of the individual as it is to the experiences of that individual. No single event can unequivocally characterize a person's life as "happy" or "successful" just as no single event can deem a person's life "miserable" or "a failure." But if one steps back from the individual events and considers the data as a composite, a very curious pattern begins to emerge. Figure 1.1 presents a summary of

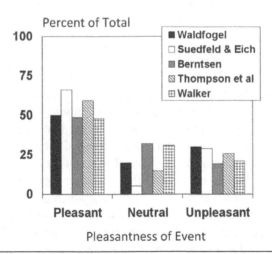

FIGURE 1.1   The percentage of pleasant, neutral, and negative events for childhood memories (Waldfogel), memories retrieved in a sensory deprivation chamber (Suefeld & Eich), involuntary memories (Berntsen), personal events recorded in daily diaries (Thompson), and randomly cued personal events reported via text messages (Walker).

many of the studies discussed in this (in order: Waldfogel, 1948; Suedfeld & Eich, 1995; Berntsen, 1996; Thompson, et al., 1996; Walker, 2014). A similar picture emerges in all these studies: 50% or more of the events or estimates are rated as pleasant, whereas roughly 25% are rated as unpleasant. It is the relative weight of positive and negative events that gives life its affective tone. As demonstrated by these studies, most people perceive life to be pleasant more often than they perceive life to be unpleasant. Good times outnumber bad times at ratio of just over 2 to 1.

Finding Mayberry

This chapter started with a trip to Mayberry, the idealized fictional town of Andy Griffith's youth. This place was based on the very real town of Mount Airy, North Carolina. While the real town is different from Mayberry in many important ways (the town has more than one deputy, and the deputies are armed with more than a single bullet), it is also quite similar in what is perhaps the most important way—it is a good place to live with good people who live their lives enjoying happiness and good times. To experience Mayberry firsthand is quite refreshing, and if one finds themselves nearby, a trip there is highly encouraged. This is especially true in late September, when the town hosts its annual Mayberry Days. Be on the lookout for David Browning, also known as "The Mayberry Deputy," who does a great job channeling the humor and mannerisms of Don Knotts. But as this chapter has demonstrated, making the trip is not necessary to experience the essence of Mayberry.

Pollyanna's gifts, the gifts of good moods and good times are what make a place like Mayberry so appealing. These things can come in many forms. As Ruut Veenhoven pointed out, some emotional experiences are intense and all-encompassing, but these experiences are rare and short-lived. Other experiences are more subtle but are no less important to the lives of the people who experience them. But don't take an academic's word for it—consider the wisdom of North Carolina's favorite son. When reminiscing about Mayberry and its inhabitants, Andy Griffith commented that the underlying theme of the *Andy Griffith Show* was the love the characters had for each other and what high regard they had for each individual. The script for each show was scrutinized to ensure that the integrity of the characters was not impugned. Yes, there was humor, but never ridicule. The show, which depicted a community of people who cared for each other, *was* a community of actors, writers, and producers who genuinely cared for each other. The fantasy of Mayberry was rooted in a very real and very common human experience of love and mutual respect. And that's the point.

Mayberry is found nearly everywhere in the world. It is found in the lives of college students in the United States and Germany. It is found in citizens of Australia and San Francisco. It can be found in war-torn countries like Iraq and Mexico and in tough cities like Detroit. Mayberry exists in the childhood memories of adults remembering their past and in the lives of inner-city teens living in troubled neighborhoods. It is found in the experience of happiness and life satisfaction that has been documented in countries around the world by a variety of researchers using an array of methods and samples. It is found in the daily events that people record in diaries or that they report to researchers conducting national surveys.

Where is Mayberry? Where is this place festooned with Pollyanna's gifts of gladness and good times? Mayberry isn't confined to the state of North Carolina; it is a state of mind. Mayberry can be found in a place that most people call home. Of course, going home can be hard, as the place that a person remembers is never quite what they find. The mind can play tricks on a person's perceptions and memories. We will now consider Pollyanna's gifts in the context of many well understood cognitive illusions to determine if they are real or if they reflect the wishful dreams of a biased mind.

CHAPTER 2

Cassandra and the Wolf

In Greek myth, Cassandra was the daughter of King Priam of Troy. Cassandra was considered to be the second most beautiful woman in the world, second only to Helen of Troy. A beautiful, mortal young woman descendant of royalty, she was destined to attract the attention of the gods. Apollo, the son of Zeus, was the idealized male deity: A baby-faced athletic youth in his prime. Apollo was the god of light, healing, poetry, and music. His most important role was as the patron of Delphi, which meant that he was a deity who inspired prophecy. According to Aeschylus' *Oresteia*, Cassandra promised to be his lover, and so Apollo granted her the gift of prophecy in return. In an alternate version, she spent a night at Apollo's temple, at which time the temple snakes licked her ears clean so that she was able to hear the future. However, after the union was consummated, she broke off the relationship. In his wrath, Apollo placed a curse on her so that she would retain the gift of foresight but that no one would ever believe her predictions. She prophesied the Trojan Horse, the fall of Troy, and her own eventual murder. The tale of Cassandra is rife with irony. She held the knowledge that could save her home and herself from harm, but the more she tried to provide counsel, the more she was rejected. Like Pollyanna, the name Cassandra has been retained in the English language as a word. A Cassandra is an individual that offers truth to others who refuse to listen.

The story of Cassandra bears some resemblance to one of the fables of Aesop. Aesop was a slave and a storyteller in ancient Greece. His stories, drawn from humble events, were intended to impart great truths. Consider the truth imbedded in one of his most famous tales, *The Boy Who Cried Wolf*. In this story, a shepherd boy repeatedly tricks his neighbors into thinking that a wolf is hunting his sheep. After a number of false alarms, a wolf actually appears, and the now genuine cries of the young shepherd are ignored by nearby villagers. His flock is eaten and, in some versions, the shepherd is killed as well. The moral lesson, of course, is that lying to others will ultimately result in being disbelieved. Like the word *Cassandra*, this tale has found a place in modern English. To "cry wolf" is to trumpet a falsehood. Taken together, these parables offer very different lessons. The tale of Cassandra warns us not to readily dismiss potential wisdom from those we are disinclined to believe. *The Boy Who Cried Wolf* suggests that we should always be sure to speak the truth to others, lest be discredited and disbelieved. Despite these warnings, we still tend to ignore, if not outright ridicule, truths that seem unlikely or go against conventional wisdom.

Take the case of Dr. Barry Marshall. Dr. Marshall dedicated much of his professional life to the study of the gastrointestinal tract. That's a fancy way of saying that he is interested in stomachs. He is most famous for his research studying stomach ulcers, painful sores that can kill a person by causing them to bleed out and are risk factors for developing stomach cancer. In particular, Dr. Marshall studies the relationship between the *h. pylori* bacteria and ulcers. Within gastroentological circles, this is a pairing as famous as peanut butter and jelly. This is because stomach ulcers are usually teeming with *h. pylori*. Conventional medical wisdom stated that, after the ulcer formed, the bacteria was attracted to and thrived in the ulcer. Gastroenterologists had been taught that stress causes ulcers and that ulcers attract *h. pylori* bacteria for so long that no one questioned it. Until Dr. Marshall. Dr. Marshall theorized that the relationship was the other way around: He proposed that the bacteria caused the ulcers.

And Dr. Marshall caught hell from his colleagues about it because he was denying an accepted truth (that no one could quite remember the source of and no one had hard evidence for). After speaking at a larger research conference in 1986, his wife overheard other attendees harshly criticizing his work, despite the fact that he was culminating evidence for his theory. He found that treating people with antibiotics did cure most people of their ulcers (early evidence for the causal relationship Marshal proposed). He was also able to demonstrate the causal relationship in pigs. But people were still tearing apart his research, mostly because it didn't fit conventional wisdom. Marshall decided that the only way to firmly establish this finding was through research using humans. However, ulcers hurt and can cause you to bleed a lot and can lead to cancer. It is hard to convince people going through these symptoms to try an experimental treatment, so Dr. Marshall's ability to do human research was limited to a sample size of one: Himself. One day in 1984, he had an endoscopy to check his stomach for both ulcers and *h. pylori* bacteria (he had neither). Then he doubled-down on his theory and drank a broth of *h. pylori* bacteria. What happened? He developed the first symptoms of ulcers within 3 days. After 14 days of devastating symptoms that included nausea, uncontrollable vomiting, and gastritis, a painful swelling in the lining of the stomach, he finally began a course of antibiotics. His harrowing self-study showed conclusively that the bacteria *caused* ulcers. His body of work was so paradigm shifting that he won the Nobel Prize for medicine in 2005. Along the way, he also revolutionized the treatment for ulcers (antibiotics, not antianxiety medication and yoga classes) and probably saved plenty of lives by doing so.

The lessons of these narratives mirror the paradox of positive psychology. Positive emotions and events can have powerful effects that often go unnoticed by social scientists, the media, and society at large. When data is presented and arguments are made about such effects, a question like "Doesn't a bias favoring positive emotions mean that people are being unrealistic?" invariably emerges. The implication is that, somehow, what looks like a healthy psychological process is really just more evidence of how feeble the mind really is. As researchers who have fielded such questions when presenting findings about positive aspects of the mind, we empathize with Cassandra's spirit. There is ample evidence that the human mind has the capacity to overcome hardship and thrive in the face of adversity. However, it is also important that the effects of positive emotions not be overstated. Positive emotions do not cure cancer, create wealth, or grant wishes. Thinking happy thoughts will not heal psychological illnesses any more than imagining a positive future will make it happen without effort. It is true that many claims made by positive psychologists have been overstated and some have been patently false. So, it is important that the claims that are made about positive emotions be substantiated and subjected to due skepticism. As dedicated scholars, we do not want to be mistaken for errant shepherds.

Two claims that have been made thus far in this book: First, most people are happy most of the time, regardless of their culture, income, and circumstance. This is a worldwide phenomenon that describes a little more than two-thirds of humanity. Second, people experience pleasant events about twice as often as they do negative events. This has been established in numerous national surveys, studies of event sampling, and tests of autobiographical memory. These claims may be difficult for some to accept, even with the empirical support that has been provided. This is understandable because the human mind is wired to evaluate new information, like the arguments and data presented in this text, through the lens of pre-existing beliefs. Once those beliefs are fixed in mind, the mind can then perform a magic trick worthy of Houdini: It can interpret evidence that clearly contradicts those beliefs as either irrelevant or as strengthening the very beliefs being challenged.

When it comes to beliefs about positivity and negativity, there is ample evidence that most people believe that negative emotions and events are more frequent and more powerful than positive emotions and events. These beliefs contradict what people report in their own lives. Yes, they say, negative emotions are more powerful, but not in *my* case. Negative events definitely outnumber positive events, but not for *me*. Even when their own experiences show that they may be wrong, people cling to this belief. Indeed, when Diener and Diener (1996) surveyed 29 working adults, 44 psychology majors, and 15 clinical psychology graduate students, they all overestimated the prevalence of clinical depression and underestimated the frequency of people that report positive life satisfaction. One might excuse the working adults and the undergraduates, but the clinical students should have known better. How can this cycle be broken? One way is to make an effort to understand the processes of the mind, including how it treats unique stimuli, how it gauges the potential impact of positive and negative events, and how it estimates the frequency of such experiences. These processes work cooperatively and invisibly to create a kind of emotional myopia that leads people to overestimate the frequency and power of negativity in spite of the contrary evidence in their own lives.

The von Restorff Effect

Hedwig von Restorff was a female postdoctoral graduate student at the Psychological Institute at the University of Berlin in the early 1930s. She would later become a psychiatrist and pediatrician, but for now she toiled away as an assistant to Professor Wolfgang Kohler, one of the key founders of Gestalt psychology. In her research, she presented her participants with a list of distinct words, mostly common nouns. One word was printed in a different color than the others. She then tested the memory of her participants by having them recall the words. She found that people overwhelmingly remembered the distinctly printed word because it was "isolated" from the rest of the list. It stood out. What she stumbled on was an effect so basic that it could be applied to a variety of psychological stimuli: Words, names, sounds, faces, objects, smells, tastes, and even tactile sensations. If something is distinct, unusual, or just different, it is more likely to be remembered.

The reason why this occurs has to do with a combination of the encoding and retrieval mechanisms in memory. First, unusual stimuli capture the attentional resources of the mind because they defy expectations and encourage additional study. Consider the following list of six words: CAT, DOG, FISH, MINOTAUR, BIRD, SNAKE. For most people, their eyes stop for a fraction of a second on the fourth word. In that moment, the brain checks its databases for the unusual term referring to a mythological creature that is half man and half bull. That additional half-second helps to imbed that exotic item in memory. Second, the retrieval strategies used to recall items from memory tend to favor recalling distinct items before more common items. Much research has been conducted on the von Restorff effect, with the balance of the results tending to favor the relative importance of retrieval over encoding. This means that very unusual and rare items tend to be recalled first as they are more accessible in memory, while more common and frequent items are recalled later. Again, think of the list presented just a few sentences ago. What word comes to mind first? If you happened to say "FISH," we respectfully reply "BULL!"

The von Restorff effect in memory has a potentially significant effect on how people tend to recollect their emotions and their experiences. If a person has a good day working at a department store as a cashier, when asked about her day, she might simply reply "ho-hum, nothing special." The day may have had included a few pleasant conversations or an unexpected compliment from a co-worker, but these events happen so frequently that they become the invisible, unnoticed norm. The same individual on a different day, a day on which she experiences similarly pleasant emotions and events but also had to deal with a particularly difficult customer, might respond to the same query with a reply like "Today sucked. Some people are just horrible." The unpleasant interaction is unusual and unexpected. It is exotic and more likely to be included in a review of the day's events. But the von Restorff effect is not the sole culprit for the emotional myopia expressed by most people.

The Availability Heuristic

Quick: Which kills more people each year, shark attacks or coconuts? The correct answer is shark attacks. It has been widely reported and repeated that coconuts routinely kill 10 to 15 times more people than sharks. That statistic, which has been used to defend the much persecuted shark is, alas, not true. While it is true that sharks are far less dangerous than conventional wisdom suggests, they are more dangerous than coconuts, but just barely. Sharks kill on average about eight people a year worldwide while coconuts kill about five. Like many statistics, the veracity of this number is usually judged on how right or wrong the number feels. Sharks are dangerous animals and reports of attacks and deaths often receive national media attention. Movies that depict sharks like *Jaws* and *Deep Blue Sea* come to mind. Coconuts are just harmless coconuts. They sit benignly in the produce aisle at the grocery store. But coconuts can weigh as much as 3–4 pounds and, from time to time, they fall from a height of 20–25 feet onto a person's head. Ouch! Ok, you might agree that a sizable coconut falling from a significant height might be dangerous, but it still feels like the shark should be much, much more deadly. Why?

The reason is because of a phenomenon called the Availability Heuristic. When examples of something come quickly to mind, say for instance a shark attack in the news, people judge the likelihood of that event as much greater than the likelihood of something else that takes longer to recall, say a report of a falling coconut killing an unlucky tourist. The more available the example is in a person's mind, the more often that example is judged to occur. This particular example, of course, is inherently biased by the tendency of mass media outlets to over report flashy stories like shark attacks and under report

ex. work w/ hands + eyes

mundane accidents like drupe-related injuries. Consider a much more academic example: Of all of the words in the English language, which is more common, words that begin with the letter R or words that have R as the third letter? No rational person would ever be expected to know the answer to this question, so they would be forced to guess. The answer is that there are more words with R as the third letter than there are words that begin with R. As you might imagine, most people get this question wrong. The reason is, like sharks and coconuts, people find it easier to think of instances of words that start with R than words with R as the third letter. The former is much more available in memory than the latter, in the same way that shark attacks are more available than coconut injuries.

Like the von Restorff effect, the Availability Heuristic can be applied to a variety of stimuli and circumstances. Much of the research has involved perceptions of risk. It should come as no surprise to find out that most people are bad at assessing risks in their daily lives. Even a brief amount of time spent on YouTube will demonstrate that some folks are prone to do very dangerous and very stupid things without seeming to think about the consequences of their actions. But real risk is not just found in the acts of the woefully dumb. Consider how Americans viewed risk in the weeks and months after the attacks of September 11th, 2001. The images of the collapsing World Trade Center Towers were visceral and frightening. Since the attacks employed commercial airplanes that were hijacked and used as makeshift missiles, it seems understandable that many Americans avoided commercial air travel and relied on what seems to be a safer mode of transportation, the automobile. Air travel would not return to pre-9/11 levels for almost a year. That meant there were more cars on the nation's highways during that year. More cars = more accidents = more deaths. Gerd Gigerenzer (2007) posed a very straightforward question: How many people were killed in automobile accidents as a result of 9/11? The answer was that there was a noticeable spike in traffic fatalities during the 12-month period after the terrorist attacks, totaling about 1,500 additional deaths. In the minds of these travelers, the images of 9/11 were so accessible that it seemed safer to drive rather than to fly. What they failed to consider was a statistic that has been widely disseminated since the mid-20th century, that driving a car is always more dangerous than flying on a commercial aircraft. Even if an event like 9/11 had been repeated every single month during 2001, it would have still been much safer to fly across the country than make the trip by car that year.

Now consider how the von Restorff effect dovetails nicely with the Availability Heuristic. Infrequent and exotic events are pushed to the head of the line when it comes to memory recall. Negative emotions are events that occur less often, in many cases much less often, than their positive counterparts. The human memory system treats them as rare and exotic specimens, spending a bit more time analyzing them and indexing them in the experiential database. When forced to consider the relative frequency of positive and negative emotions and events in our lives, the exotic nature of these incidents bring them to mind more quickly. The relative availability of negativity over positivity now begins to distort the perception of their relative frequencies. The negative begins to be overrepresented and the positive is subsequently marginalized. The very tendencies of the mind to seek out novel occurrences serve as one of the primary building blocks of the emotional myopia described previously. But these two psychological phenomena are not alone. Emotions and events are not experienced in a vacuum, they are inherently tied to the experience of time, a concept that the mind both creates and distorts.

Affective Forecasting Error

Time is a tricky thing to think about. Physicists claim that time is really just a manifestation of physical space and that the concept of time is created by the human mind. When one of Albert Einstein's dear friends passed away, he wrote a letter to his friend's family that eloquently expressed his grief and provided a pithy description of time. He stated that even though his friend's death had preceded his own, it mattered not "... for us physicists believe the separation between the past, present, is only an illusion, although a convincing one." One of the trickier facets of time to consider involves estimates about the future. How long will it take to lose 20 pounds? How long will it take for a broken bone to mend? How long will it take for a contractor to finish a construction project? To answer these kinds of questions, people rely upon their past experiences. They would likely think back to their last diet or a previous injury. They might have some documentation from a similar job performed by another company. In all of these cases, the person really wants to know "how long will this diet/injury/construction last?" How long will it take?

Peter F. Drucker famously said 'The only thing we know about the future is that it is going to be different' (Drucker, 1973, p. 43). His point was that the past is often a poor indicator of what the future holds. This is especially true when one is trying to gauge the potential longevity of an emotional event. How long will it take before the joy of driving a new car wears off? How long will the thrill of a new romance last? How long will it take to mend a broken heart? How long should a person mourn? These questions afford no simple answers. The emotional experiences of people are varied. There are circumstantial differences. First cars and first loves are not quick to fade in a person's heart. There are individual differences, of course. Some people simply bounce back after a setback faster than others. And there is the slippery question of what constitutes "normal and healthy." An otherwise psychologically healthy person may mourn the loss of a child or spouse for many years without being considered abnormal.

But still, there is a point at which a reaction to an emotional experience should, in most circumstances and most people, recede in intensity and relevance. Emotions have expiration dates, even if they are not always readily apparent. Daniel Gilbert, a Harvard psychologist who studies emotion, has conducted many studies looking at how well people are able to predict the longevity of their positive and negative emotional experiences (Gilbert & Ebert, 2002; Gilbert, Lieberman, Morewedge, & Wilson, 2004). The results suggest that people are usually pretty good at predicting which emotions they will experience (e.g., happiness, sadness) in response to future events. However, their ability to predict the duration and peak magnitude of these emotions is far from accurate. Generally speaking, people predict that the emotional impact of an event will last much longer that it actually does. If a person thinks that a new TV or computer will make them happy, they are probably right. It just won't make them as happy for as long as they think it will. But the predictions that people make about the duration of positive and negative emotions are lopsided. They routinely predict that negative emotions will last much, much longer than they actually do. Gilbert and his colleagues point out that people fail to recognize just how quickly they are likely to recover from a negative emotional experience. Even when their own experiences suggest otherwise, people cling to the idea that negative emotions have long-lasting effects.

Now consider these three phenomena all working together. We have already established that the combination of the von Restorff Effect and the Availability Heuristic can distort people's estimates of the relative frequency of positive and negative emotions and events. The result is that even though negative emotions and experiences occur less often, they are disproportionately represented in the human mind. Now, consider what happens when Affective Forecasting error is added to the now simmering pot. The mind, already having artificially inflated the frequency of negativity, is now confronted with the task of estimating how long the pain, anger, or sadness will last. It overestimates the long-term effects of the emotion by a mile. Remember, in this scenario, the individual being described is a "normal, psychologically healthy" person. This person is expected to see the world rationally, but instead is led to a belief that counters the experience of most people. They believe that negative emotions and events are more frequent than they actually are AND they believe that these negative emotions will have long-lasting effects.

The intersection of memory, availability, and future neglect nicely sets up the individual for a bias so wickedly subtle that most people do not even realize they are expressing it: The confirmation bias.

The Confirmation Bias

Any discussion where there are at least two viable points of view has likely caused a fight. Republican or Democrat? American Football or Football (aka Soccer)? Ketchup or Catsup? Sharp divisions in outlook can mean that two individuals who might agree on almost any given subject can see a single phenomenon in entirely different ways. Consider the stereotypical example of whether a glass of water is half-full or half-empty. This hackneyed example is worth mentioning because it is so telling. According to conventional wisdom, if you are the kind of person to see the glass as half-full, chances are very good that you are more optimistic, and if you see the glass as half-empty, you are pessimistic. Believe it or not, two psychologists named Craig McKenzie and Jonathan Nelson (2003) have tested this idiom. They presented participants with a 4-ounce glass. For half of the participants, they were shown a full glass that was then emptied in front of them to the halfway point. When asked to describe the glass as half-full or half-empty, only 31% of the people described the glass as half-full. For the other participants, they were shown an empty glass that was then filled right in front of them to the halfway point. Over 85% of these participants described the glass as half-full. The point of this study is that the participants used their initial exposure to the full or empty glass as reference point for how they viewed the subsequent change in water level. That reference point, which was viewed for only a few moments, helped to form a transient belief that significantly biased how people viewed the subsequent events. What they saw tended to confirm that belief. Having watched half of the liquid dumped out of the glass, the container was more 'empty' than it had been. Likewise, for those who watched liquid poured into the empty vessel, the glass was more 'full' afterwards.

The confirmation bias can significantly distort our perceptions of reality. Michael Shermer, the publisher of *Skeptic Magazine*, knows this all too well. For more than two decades, he has been arguing with the true believers of almost every crackpot theory one can imagine. Bigfoot, UFO's, conspiracy theories, he has seen and heard just about everything. In his 1997 book *Why People Believe Weird Things*, he described his visit to the Edgar Cayce Association for Research and Enlightenment (ARE). For those who may not be familiar with ARE, this is an organization that follows the teachings and traditions of Edgar Cayce, one of the most prominent psychics of the twentieth century. One of the highlights of Shermer's visit included a test of his own psychic ability with a classroom of other psychic pupils using a Zener machine. Zener cards are small cards with one of five random symbols written on them (a plus sign, a square, a circle, a star, and three wavy lines). The Zener machine shuffles the cards and presents them in various sequences. This is repeated 20–25 times. The person being tested cannot see the cards but is encouraged to guess the sequence of the five symbols. After the trials were scored, it was found that Michael Shermer scored a 7/25, which did not qualify him as a native psychic. The instructor administering the test told him not to worry, as psychic powers could improve *with training*. That was the cue for Shermer to pounce. He knew that the results of the Zener card test were the effects of random chance, and he wanted to see the instructor squirm. First, he pointed out the results of he and his fellow students were not that unusual and could be explained by simple random chance. The instructor responded with a cryptic response about how psychic powers were variable and difficult to study. Next, Shermer noted that the instructor, having taught this subject for many years, should have tremendous psychic ability. Certainly he could score much higher than average. Perhaps 15/25? He asked for a demonstration. The instructor declined.

Having just shown members of the audience that effects they were witnessing were not caused by anything more than random chance, you might imagine that Shermer had just scored a major coup in favor of skeptics everywhere. You would be wrong. The skeptic had made his point quite convincingly. But that didn't matter to the other psychic pupils or even to the instructor. In fact, the take home message that many of Shermer's fellow "students" had received from the minor confrontation was that psychic power was real, but that it just didn't work all the time. The reason they came to this conclusion is because any result that had been witnessed by the audience would have simply confirmed their preconceived beliefs. They were at ARE to cultivate their psychic powers. They already believed in ESP regardless of what evidence was marshaled for or against it. All the evidence could do was further strengthen that belief.

Once the belief that negativity is more common and more powerful than positivity is firmly in place, a feedback loop is created to nurture and grow that belief. The minor setbacks and hazards that are a normal part of life can begin to seem more significant and frequent. The simple and quiet pleasures of seeing an old friend or taking a relaxing walk are relegated to the corners of the life experience. And when real tragedy strikes—and it will for every person in every circumstance—the event appears as a gigantic iceberg in an already treacherous ocean.

Even given this distorted outlook, it is still likely that many people would begin to realize the truths of Pollyanna's gifts, the gifts of good moods and good times. They would begin to realize the fact that most people are happy and that most events in life are pleasant. But there is one more distortion that overwhelms the mind and forces it to see the world as being much darker and meaner than it really is.

An Aside on Relative Deprivation or "Why I Hate Justin Bieber"

The experience of relative deprivation is another phenomenon that can help explain why many people underestimate the frequency and power of positive life events in their own lives. Relative deprivation is a $10 word for a 25-cent idea: It is just another word for jealousy. Social psychologists have long known that social comparison plays an important role in how people think about themselves. Festinger (1954) hypothesized that people have a drive to continually evaluate their competencies in an effort to better understand their true abilities and limitations. When perceived weaknesses are detected, people are then motivated to make improvements. In a world where talent and success are normally distributed among lots of people, social comparison makes sense. But when distribution of talent and success are far from being normally or equitably distributed, social comparison becomes the engine for jealousy. Take the case of a middle-aged academic psychologist and a 130-pound teenage heartthrob. The academic works his way studiously through high school and then completes his undergraduate degree. His grades are good, but not stellar. He gets accepted to a graduate school, but does not receive financial support. Five years later, a PhD is conferred along with a substantial amount of student loan debt. He gets a tenure-track job, gets married to a fantastic woman, publishes a number of papers, and earns tenure. His life is pretty good.

Then comes along Justin Bieber. He is talented and lucky. His videos on Youtube become extremely popular with one of the hottest demographics in the world—young teenage girls. They cheer adoringly when he vomits on stage. He travels the world, "writes" a best-selling autobiography, and stars in his own movie. By the time he turns 18, he is worth an estimated $110 million dollars.

By comparison, the middle-aged academic's life looks pretty lame. Of course, the comparison that is being made is unfair. The academic's life is actually pretty awesome. On a whole, most musicians are less successful than most academics. Musicians work in seedy bars for tips and the chance to sell their homemade CD's while professors live a fairly comfortable life at colleges and universities. But still, the mind wants to make the comparison even though it has no right to do so. Like most adults, I don't really hate Justin Bieber as a person. I hate the **idea** of Justin Bieber as a cultural obsession: A really talented and lucky kid who became a superstar without ever having paid his dues.

The Cascade

January 1, 2000, was an ominous date on the calendar, indeed. The start of a new millennium was a time rife with possibilities, many of them terrifying. Less than a decade after "winning" the cold war against the Soviet Union, America stood as the world's primary superpower, with the biggest economy reliant on the most advanced technologies. Computers were everywhere and seemed tied into all the essentials needed for society to function. This was the case for many other countries as well, but the realization that modern society was dependent on computers seemed to strike a particular cord with some Americans. Could society degenerate into apocalyptic hellscape if these computer systems experienced a catastrophic failure all at once? To be sure, the American public had been primed to expect the end of civilization since the days of the Cuban Missile Crisis. Movie screenwriters had provided countless doomsday scenarios throughout the '70s and '80s, many of them playing on our fears of technology run amok (e.g., Omega Man, Mad Max). In the mid-1990s these fears seemed to the leap the chasm between outlandish science fiction and serious global threat in three short letters: Y2K.

Y2K was shorthand for the "year 2000" problem that was first identified in 1984 by Jerome and Marilyn Murray. The problem began with early computing systems developed in the 1950s. For their time, they were technological marvels, but they had the problem of being extremely limited in memory capacity. So limited, as it turns out, that saving two character's worth of data was enough of a savings that programmers created a quick and dirty shortcut when programs needed to store and use calendar date information. Instead of storing an entire date like 11/17/1961, they shortened it to 11/17/61. After all, the data being crunched OBVIOUSLY didn't come from earlier than the 1900s. There was no reason to worry about dates after 1999, so the programmers of the period thought, because as the memory capacities of computers expanded, future programmers would certainly fix the calculation. But no one did. It wasn't until 1996, at the urging of New York Senator Daniel Patrick Moynihan, that Congress sounded the alarm, producing its first report on the Y2K problem and establishing a commission to study its potential impact. In February 1998, President Clinton issued Executive Order 13073, "Year 2000 Conversion," which required all federal agencies to fix the Y2K problem in their systems.

The technical Y2K problem was real and did require diligent work on the part of many agencies and private companies. Without such efforts, there would have likely been some significant problems associated with this computer bug. But Y2K gave a certain class of fearmongers an opportunity to publish books, make TV and radio appearances, and generally do anything they could to scare the hell out of as many people as possible. Many followed the example of Michael Hyatt, author of *The Millennium Bug*, who provided three levels of scenarios of increasing despair. The "Brownout Scenario" would last from a few weeks to a few months and would include problems with the electrical grid, transportation, communication systems, banking, government, healthcare, and sporadic disruptions of social order. The "Blackout Scenario" would mean up to three years of "multiple system failures and social upheaval," including the complete loss of electrical power, rampant disease and starvation, martial law, and widespread riots. The "Meltdown Scenario" would last for many years and would entail the complete breakdown of the all aspects of a functioning government, economy, and society.

In everyday terms, a cascade is more than a mere waterfall. A waterfall might entail a few hundred gallons of water falling every few seconds from a precipice of 10 or 20 feet. A cascade is thousands of gallons of water falling each second from heights of 70 feet or more. Niagara Falls between Canada and the U.S. is a cascade. Angel Falls in Venezuela is a cascade. Cascades are thunderous and overpowering sites not to be simply enjoyed; they are places to be overwhelmed and awed. A belief cascade is much the same. A belief cascade is when a belief, or set of related beliefs, creates a chain reaction in the way a culture views an important aspect of reality (Kuran & Sunstein, 1999; Lemieux, 2003). It is more than a simple bandwagon effect, in which people are momentarily overwhelmed by the social cues around them. In a belief cascade, people adopt the new belief en masse because it offers many advantages over older beliefs: It is simple, plausible, and insightful. The idea gains currency not only for its intellectual merits, which may be rock solid or quite weak, but also for it social merits. Holding this belief helps people gain a certain amount of credibility in the eyes of their cultural peers. Belief cascades are not always bad or misleading, but they do have a habit of leading the masses away from obvious facts. In the weeks before the clock struck midnight and closed the door on the 20th century, there were not widespread panics or lines at the grocery stores. But most people did back up their computer files and stopped by their bank or ATM to get some extra cash. *Just in case.*

Now consider how a belief cascade could influence a society's perceptions of positive and negative emotions. We have already established that the individual mind can be tricked into overestimating the frequency and the emotional longevity of negative events via such mechanisms as the von Restorff Effect, the Availability Heuristic, and the Affective Forecasting error. Together, these form the basis of an individual's beliefs about how positive and negative emotions work. These beliefs distort not only how the individual views the experiences in their own lives, but how they interpret the events they see in the lives of people around them via the confirmation bias. Now, recognize that this same process is happening en masse to people throughout society. Some of these beliefs are repeatedly transmitted through mass media, social networking sites, and other forms of communication that garner large audiences with short attention spans. These messages are tailored to accentuate narratives that are exotic and dramatic and negative events and emotions are both. "If it bleeds, it leads" is a common phrase used to describe exploitative and fear-based media. Images of trauma, both physical and psychological, capture audiences and hold them hostage in a way the positive, uplifting stories can't.

And so the cascade completes the cycle started by the foibles of individual minds into beliefs so pervasive that it is accepted by nearly everyone without question: Negative emotions are more frequent and powerful than positive ones. As a corollary to this belief, a second belief also gains a foothold—that negative emotions help to clarify the mind, bringing it closer to truth while positive emotions cloud thinking, leading the mind astray. These beliefs have gained such widespread credibility through the mass media onslaught of the last 50 years that psychologists are now beginning to detect generational differences in the outlooks of younger people. The "can-do" attitude of the so-called Greatest Generation, the generation that endured the Great Depression and fought World War II has been replaced by the "why bother" attitude of Generation Y, those who were born after 1980.

Jean Twenge is a psychologist who has studied long-term personality trends in American society, and she has made some startling discoveries. Before we describe her findings, it is important that we understand exactly what she has done. Twenge and her colleagues have conducted several meta-analyses on personality studies that were conducted as far back as the 1940s. This involved hundreds of studies and tens of thousands of participants. Using comparable measures of personality, these studies provided snapshots of what personalities were like at different points in time. Differences between these studies, therefore, reflected genuine personality changes. The beauty of this approach is in its simplicity: The researcher is looking for long-term sustainable trends in the data. Twenge has found several things. She has learned that people are becoming more and more narcissistic in recent generations. This does not mean that people are becoming more positive and confident; instead it means more selfishness, more unrealistic thinking, and more disdain for the plight of others. The younger people in her studies, particularly those under the age of 40, are anything but positive and confident. They routinely experience higher levels of depression, anxiety, and loneliness than people from previous generations. They view friendships and romantic relationships as more provisional and temporary. They are less socially and politically engaged than previous generations and express apathy at much higher rates. They have much less faith in the societal institutions like courts and governments that have been put in place to set right some of the injustices of the world. They are prone to seeing the world as being harsher and crueler than it really is. That is the heartbreak of the belief cascade that has washed over people in the modern era. The cascade of pain, fury, and fear. By holding fast to the belief that negative emotions are all-powerful, people are learning that the only way to persevere in a cruel and hostile world is though selfishness and the derogation of the people around them.

Cognitive Dissonance: The Prestige

> Every great magic trick consists of three parts or acts. The first part is called The Pledge. The magician shows you something ordinary: a deck of cards, a bird or a man. He shows you this object. Perhaps he asks you to inspect it to see if it is indeed real, unaltered, normal. But of course...it probably isn't. The second act is called The Turn. The magician takes the ordinary something and makes it do something extraordinary. Now you're looking for the secret...but you won't find it, because of course you're not really looking. You don't really want to know. You want to be fooled. But you wouldn't clap yet. Because making something disappear isn't enough; you have to bring it back. That's why every magic trick has a third act, the hardest part, the part we call The Prestige.
>
> —Michael Cain as Cutter, *The Prestige* (2006)

The argument in this chapter thus far has been that many cognitive mechanisms invisibly work to create the belief that negativity is stronger than positivity in spite of the direct evidence to the contrary in their own lives. The astute reader is probably asking by now a very straightforward question: Can't these SAME mechanisms (e.g., availability, confirmation) contribute to people's perception that they and their lives are positive? The answer is yes. It is possible, but that's not usually what happens. To understand why, two things need to be kept in mind. First, rarity triggers many of the biases discussed in this chapter. That's why shark attacks and anthrax are more memorable and scarier than car crashes and heart disease. Because people actively seek out positive experiences and avoid negative ones, negative events are rare. Second, humans have the remarkable ability to hold two completely contradictory beliefs at the same time and use these competing beliefs to create an alternate view of reality. Psychologists call this phenomenon "cognitive dissonance," and it is the hardest part of the mental magic at the heart of this chapter: The more positive a person's life is, the more powerful negative events appear to be.

Dissonance is best understood through example. In 1956, Festinger, Riecken, and Schachter described the case of Dorothy Martin, a Chicago housewife who made some very unusual claims in the previous few years. She had been involved with a group that would eventually form the basis of L. Ron Hubbard's Scientology following. She accepted many of their basic tenants including, most importantly, the belief in intelligent alien life, and the ability of humans to contact these beings under certain conditions. She believed that she had achieved these conditions and that she was receiving messages from another planet. These messages warned of an impending flood that would destroy all terrestrial life on Earth on December 21st, 1954. These predictions attracted a number of potential believers. Festinger and his colleagues had a front row seat to all of the action by joining the group. She gathered a small following of believers who gave up their jobs or left college, gave away money and possessions, and in some cases even left their spouses in the hope of salvation. Dorothy had also prophesied at midnight on December 20th, an alien visitor would welcome the chosen few aboard a spacecraft that would rescue them from the impending devastation.

When the visitor failed to arrive at the appointed time, the group sat in stunned silence for more than four hours. They were confronted with two diametrically opposing facts: 1) they had believed the prophecy and had personally sacrificed to maintain that belief; 2) they had just witnessed incontrovertible proof that the prophecy had failed. How could they reconcile this? The logical thing would be to accept the error for what was, a case of very poor judgment. Some cried. Finally, at 4:45 a.m., only a few hours before Earth's final hour, Martin began receiving an otherworldly message. The message said "The little group, sitting all night long, had spread so much light that God had saved the world from destruction." Earth had been spared because of the efforts of Martin and her followers. How convenient. In spite of clear evidence to the contrary, the cult began to express their beliefs even more fervently and openly than ever before. Once a quiet group that shunned the media spotlight, they began to trumpet their views to anyone who would listen. After all, they had saved the world.

Of course they hadn't really saved the world. They had just experienced cognitive dissonance in a very dramatic way. Everyone experiences dissonance, but in much more subtle ways. Consider the classic "smoker's dilemma." A smoker in the 21st century surely knows that smoking is a significant health risk and that it has been causally linked to cancer, respiratory, and cardio-vascular problems. They continue to smoke, in part, because of the addictive nature of nicotine. But they also continue to smoke because they are usually very adept at ignoring the obvious facts before them. One of the authors of this text (RW) had the opportunity to witness this first hand when his brother died in early 2012. David had smoked almost two packs of cigarettes a day for four decades. Suffering from breathing problems that he thought were caused by bronchitis or flu, he went to the hospital on a Thursday morning. He went home Saturday morning and died on Tuesday. Five days. During this time, the family held a vigil by his bedside. Several would periodically step outside for a quick communal smoke. The questions and comments were always the same: "I wonder what happened?" (Puff, Puff) "I don't know, he was always healthy as a horse." (Cough, Cough). When pressed, they would admit that smoking *could* cause cancer and that it might have *contributed* to David's death, but it didn't cause it. There was certainly no reason for them to quit.

And so it is with positive and negative emotion. The trick is now complete. First, experience provides the Pledge. We experience a mix of positive and negative events during the course of our lives. Second, cognitive biases provide the Turn. Rare negative events capture our attention (von Restorff Effect) and become fixed in our memories (availability) while more frequent positive experiences fade into the background. We overestimate the power and longevity of negative events (affective forecasting error). This forms the basis of a belief that is counter to our own experiences (confirmation bias) that is reinforced by social forces beyond our control (belief cascade). Third, cognitive dissonance provides the Prestige. We are able to hold diametrically opposing beliefs about positive and negative emotion. When we are asked to examine our own lives in detail, we see the gentle, the kindness, and the joy. When asked about life in general, we see the hardship, the struggle, and the sorrow. We conclude that negative events are more common and that negative emotions last longer. Somehow, we see *our* happy lives as the exceptions and not the rule.

Cassandra and the Wolf

This chapter began with the mythological tale of Cassandra and Aesop's classic fable *The Boy Who Cried Wolf*. The point drawn from these thematically opposing narratives is that researchers in the psychological sciences must take great care to neither ignore truths presented before them nor serve as the heralds of lies and half truths. It is certainly the case that the new area of positive psychology has helped reveal aspects of the human condition that, up to now, few people have noticed. For instance, the work of Ed Diener, Ruut Veenhoven, and others has found that much of the world is happy, in spite of great differences in culture and wealth. Likewise the work of Dorthe Berntsen, Chuck Thompson, and others has shown that pleasant events outnumber negative events at a rate of two to one. These findings have been published in peer-reviewed journals and replicated by numerous researchers around the world. Scholars in psychology, clinicians in practice, and everyday people find these results difficult to accept. This is the tale of Cassandra updated for the modern world.

'African Art Dancer by Anthony Krikorian.'

But it is also true that authors closely tied to the positive psychology movement have made some claims that are questionable and some have crossed the line into the near delusional. And it almost seems that the more outrageous the claim, the more likely the public is to accept the claim. Consider the case of Rhonda Byrne, an Australian author who wrote the best-selling book *The Secret*, which was published in 2006. Central to the thesis of this text is a principle that she calls the law of attraction. This law suggests that the thoughts and behaviors of a person magnetically attract particular events, circumstances, and people that are similar in frequency to them. The practical upshot is that if a person thinks happy thoughts, that act alone will attract opportunities for things like wealth, romance, and friendship. To achieve a particular goal, the author encourages a three-step process: Ask, Believe, and Receive. This process draws its origin from the Bible, Matthew 21:22: "And all things, whatsoever ye ask for in prayer, believe, ye shall receive." Yet whether a person employs religious prayer or the more agnostic process of visualization, the idea is much the same: Imagine your goal and the opportunities for achieving that goal will materialize. But the law of attraction has its flip side. Thinking negative thoughts attracts similar events and circumstances as well. Sad thoughts encourage heartbreak while angry thoughts encourage confrontation. On the surface, many positive psychologists would agree about the potential effects of positive and negative thought patterns. Such thought patterns are part of a series of steps that can create powerful positive or negative spirals in people's lives. But where Byrne differs from most positive psychologists is that she describes a straight and unerring line between a person's attitudes and the consequences that result in their lives. No other steps, no overt changes in behavior, and no setbacks. This is unrealistic and encourages unhealthy wishful thinking. It also encourages people to blame the victims of tragedies, implying that they are somehow responsible for what happens to them. The path to success is as simple as thinking happy thoughts. Aesop's fable could be reimagined as "the author that cried hallelujah!"

The reason we revisit these tales is because we want to address the reader as honestly and directly as possible. In this chapter, we have argued that the beliefs held by most people about positivity and negativity are largely wrong. We have argued that these beliefs are the result of a combination of memory and decision-making biases combined with a cultural obsession with all things negative. We argued that the consequence is a belief system that is held by the vast majority of people that stands squarely in contrast to the very experiences those people report. They believe that life is harsh and that negative emotions are more powerful than positive emotions when their own lives reveal the opposite is more likely to be true. That is a provocative argument. And it might be wrong.

For the last 19 years, we have conducted more than 50 studies of emotion and memory. We have varied our methods and our samples to minimize the potential effects of bias in our results. We have tested thousands of participants varying in demographics. We have seen our results replicated by researchers around the country and around the world. Nothing gives a scholar a greater sense of pride and relief than to see that happen. Yet, it is always possible that we have missed something, maybe something big. We might be wrong. We make this statement out of humility because we do not want to impart the message that positivity is all-powerful. It is not. But neither, we would argue, is negativity.

The counterargument to optimistic thinking is always that optimism somehow inspires foolishness while pessimism encourages realism. Barbara Ehrenreich (2009) made the case that positive thinking is undermining America and that it was responsible for the financial meltdown of 2008. She suggests that years of unbridled optimism set up the economy for collapse. More pointedly, she singles out the research in positive psychology as part of an elaborate smokescreen that is being used to mask the economic disparities in the U.S. and widespread suffering around the world. She claims that the primary benefit of this research is to warm the hearts of the wealthy and the powerful. In reviewing her work, the aforementioned publisher of *Skeptic Magazine*, Michael Shermer, described positive psychologists as having "drank the kool-aid," a macabre reference to the mass suicide of Jonestown in the late 1970s. In some ways, we understand their arguments and honestly say that we empathize with the spirit in which they are made. However, we must take issue with what we see as significant flaws in their thoughts.

Where to begin?[1] First, it is important to remind ourselves that the true cause of the economic meltdown of 2008 was not the optimistic view of Americans. If this were the case, then America, being one of the most optimistic countries in the world, would be facing economic hardship alone. In fact, much of the rest of the world suffered setbacks far worse than America. Perhaps, if one extends the logic of Ehrenreich, the deleterious effects of optimism spread like a virus and influenced other countries as well. That would explain why the collapse was worldwide and not localized in the U.S. If that were the case, one would expect that more optimistic countries should have experienced more hardship than countries that were less optimistic. After all, the logical follows that →More optimism → More foolishness → More recession. This was not the case either. How optimistic the citizens of the countries were did not predict how greatly those countries were affected during the meltdown. Indeed, countries like Canada with life satisfaction higher than the United States are actually doing better in 2012 than the U.S. The average Canadian in 2012 had more wealth than the average American.

But the data disproving Ehrenreich's thesis is even more conclusive. Remember Ruut Veenhoven's database on worldwide happiness? These data suggest that the phenomenon of happiness is at least half a century old. During that time there have been many economic ups and downs throughout the world, but the happiness levels have stayed almost fixed. If Ehrenreich was right, then each economic up and down should have been accompanied by concordant spikes in happiness. Each downturn should have been preceded by an uptick in happiness. They were not. (See Figure 2.1 for U.S. happiness and recession data from 1948–2010) It is true that some countries fluctuated more than others in both happiness and in economic health. Consider the country of Romania in the decade after the collapse of the Soviet Union. Romania is geographically and culturally isolated from the rest of the world thanks to the Carpathian mountain range, its people largely poor and uneducated. The long-term effects of oppressive communist rule had left the people monetarily and emotionally bankrupt. Veenhoven's data support that observation. But as the 1990s came to a close, surveys of the Romanian people began to show a steady increase in their levels of happiness. The average happiness levels peaked just over the midpoint of the scale. Early in the 21st century, their country still faced very real hardships that will likely not be resolved for decades, but having endured widespread suffering for generations, the Romanian people were showing their resilience and the ability to strive for their futures. Happiness alone will not repair their economy nor undo the damage

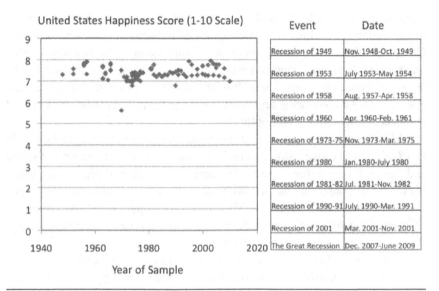

United States Happiness Score (1-10 Scale)

Event	Date
Recession of 1949	Nov. 1948-Oct. 1949
Recession of 1953	July 1953-May 1954
Recession of 1958	Aug. 1957-Apr. 1958
Recession of 1960	Apr. 1960-Feb. 1961
Recession of 1973-75	Nov. 1973-Mar. 1975
Recession of 1980	Jan.1980-July 1980
Recession of 1981-82	Jul. 1981-Nov. 1982
Recession of 1990-91	July. 1990-Mar. 1991
Recession of 2001	Mar. 2001-Nov. 2001
The Great Recession	Dec. 2007-June 2009

Year of Sample

FIGURE 2.1   Happiness levels do not appear to spike prior to economic recessions. Happiness data adapted from The World Database of Happiness. (http://www1.eur. nl/fsw/happiness). Recession data adapted from US Business Cycle Expansions and Contractions (http://www.nber.org/cycles/cyclesmain.html).

caused by generations of suffering, but it is an indication that the Romanian people have retained a substantial portion of their humanity not obliterated by their collective experience. And that's the point. In harping to her readers that happiness alone is not the solution to problems involving injustice and economic inequality, Ehrenreich has inadvertently vilified one of the most adaptive and important aspects of the human experience: Hope.

So, if optimism is not to blame for the economic collapse of 2008, what is? The answer is all of the things that pundits and news people have been talking about since the meltdown (e.g., Krugman, 2008). One legitimate cause of the meltdown was the lack of regulation in the financial sectors of much of the world economy. Banks were able to turn the once stable and secure mortgage market into a virtual casino through the use of credit default swaps based upon loans that were unlikely to be repaid. Profiteers like Bernie Madoff misled investors about the earning potentials of their investments by creating elaborate Ponzi schemes. It also been documented that major banks manipulated key interest rates by artificially raising and lowering the London Interbank Offered Rate (LIBOR) rates (Treanor, 2012). LIBOR rates are basically the rates at which banks charge for short-term loans between financial institutions. These loans keep the financial markets operating and usually are not prone to capricious fluctuations, thus making them stable foundations for many retirement funds. When the banks started gaming the LIBOR rates, their manipulations ruined the retirement plans of millions of American workers. Of course, there were many other significant issues: The housing bubble burst, many European countries were drowning in debt—the list is lengthy. However, when one boils down all of these factors into basic human drives, one can make a convincing argument that "The Great Recession" was caused by deception and greed. Not optimism.

Ehrenreich also suggests that the research is overwhelmingly biased in favor of "conservative values," which she equates to the philosophy of greed and power. It is true that some of the research does support one of the principle claims of conservatives, that religious faith is a cornerstone of happiness. The research of David Myers (2000) has shown that people with a meaningful religious life tend to be happier than people who do not hold such faith. But it doesn't matter what religion the person follows, Christianity or Islam or whatever, faith helps to create a platform for coping with adversity and allows for emotional flourishing. That would seem to partially support Ehrenreich's claim about a conservative agenda—most conservative Americans are very religious. But she does not emphasize that the same research suggests that more wealth does *not* result in more happiness. David Myers (2000) also showed that increasing wealth from the mid-1950s to the late 1990s did not lead to corresponding gains in life satisfaction. More recently, Elizabeth Dunn and Michael Norton (2012) recently analyzed Gallup polling data and found that the reported happiness of Americans did not substantially increase beyond income levels of about $75,000 a year. It should be pointed out that income levels for Americans in 2012 was about half that figure. Now consider what happened between income levels of $25,000 and $55,000. One might imagine that people at the higher income levels would be substantially happier than the people at the lower end. Happier? Yes. Substantially? No. People making $55k were only 9% happier than people making $25k. Below $25k a year, increased income does lead to substantial gains in happiness. These results could be used to support the idea of redistributing wealth more equitably throughout society, particularly to those individuals in poverty. Such an idea is decidedly not a conservative one. The point is that the data do not clearly support a conservative agenda or a liberal agenda. It just is what it is.

And for those skeptics who believe that it is appropriate to compare the study of positive emotions to one of the worst mass suicides in history? We would respectfully argue that Michael Shermer inadvertently crossed the line between rigorous skepticism and knee-jerk cynicism. As we mentioned before, there have been many false claims about the mystical effects of positive emotions. But we would remind Shermer and like-minded skeptics that negative emotions such as fear and anger can also be effectively employed to distort people's views of reality. Hucksters have used the prophecies of Nostradamus to scare people and sell merchandise for decades. The anxieties associated with the purported arrival of the end of the world (as foretold by Mayan prophecy) on December 21, 2012, spawned numerous books and a blockbuster movie that highlighted the end of the world (although, seriously, exactly how many times can an airplane barely escape a crumbling chasm?). The rule is simple: More fear = More profits. It's hard to get rich telling people that they are doing just fine. In Shermer's criticism of positive psychology, he has painted its research with such a broad brush that he seems to suggest that positive emotions are somehow *more* biasing than negative ones.

Indeed, Dr. Shermer is not alone. The most famous figure in psychology, Sigmund Freud, who founded the psychodynamic approach to psychology, has cast a very long shadow over Western culture. His ideas about the human mind, sexuality, and society resonate to this day. And they were far from positive. He thought, among other things, that most people had sexual attraction to their parents and held on to pent-up feelings about potty training. Freud's theories were used to label homosexuality a mental disorder. Many of his case studies were used to argue that women were morally and intellectually inferior to men. To be fair, a majority of psychologists have formally repudiated many of his ideas as repulsive, sexist, and un-testable. But, like an ex-lover that you just can't get out of your system, most psychologists secretly hold a flame for Freud's ideas. For one thing, he was quotable as hell. Consider this nugget on his impressions of humanity: "I have found little that is good about human beings on the whole. In my experience most of them are trash." His formal theory on the human condition was not much better. He proposed a host of mental processes known as defense mechanisms that essentially shielded the mind from the pain of reality. Chief among these mechanisms were the twin processes of denial and repression. Denial refers to the ability of people to ignore aspects of reality that they find upsetting or counter to their beliefs. An individual who fails to acknowledge global warming might be said to be in denial. Repression refers to the tendency for the mind to keep painful memories out of conscious awareness. An incest survivor who is unwilling to talk about her experience may have repressed the event.

Freud's message was simple: The mind is able to construct a fanciful version of reality that afforded it shelter in an otherwise harsh world. One of the goals of psychoanalysis was to identify these distortions and uncover the underlying pain they had allowed to fester deep in the unconscious mind. Dragging these experiences into the light of day would allow the individual to properly confront them and achieve a greater understanding of reality, which was a sign of psychological health. One of the consequences of this approach is that no one got off the hook. According to Freud, just about everyone was psychologically "damaged goods," the only difference between people who were happy and people who were miserable was that miserable people were no longer in denial. Acknowledging and accepting feelings of fear, depression, and anger could help to orient people to reality, help them foster their hidden talents, and allow them to flourish with a more realistic outlook.

But is this really true? Can embracing negativity actually make people more psychologically healthy? Perhaps it would be helpful to review the powerful and long-lasting effects that negative emotions and experience can wield. We argue that these emotions do not clarify thought or encourage realistic outlooks. Nor do they do foster great talent or grant a person a more rigorous and objective worldview. In fact, they do precisely the opposite. We argue that the overwhelming effects of negative emotions and experience are, in fact, *negative*. They distort thought, curb creativity, and create unhealthy and unrealistic worldviews. Remember, the primary argument of this text so far has been that negative emotions are less powerful than positive emotions. But that does not mean that negative emotions are powerless. Not by a long shot.

CHAPTER 3

"It's really a shame...that was a really nice truck"

Ken Rex McElroy was a bad man by almost every measure of which one can think. In the mid to late 1970s, he was the town bully of Skidmore, a small town of less than 500 in Nodaway County, Northwest Missouri. He was a bear of a man, estimated at just under six feet and weighing close to 250 pounds. He was known as a cattle rustler and small time thief who would physically intimidate people who tried to accuse him of a crime. Formal charges were brought against him 21 times, but witnesses always backed down and refused to testify in open court. It was widely known that he made a habit of intimidating his accusers by following them and parking outside their houses. He fired weapons outside their homes and threatened to place rattlesnakes in their mailboxes. In one instance, a Skidmore farmer named Romaine Henry claimed that McElroy shot him twice with a shotgun after Henry had confronted him for trespassing. McElroy was charged with assault with intent to kill. As the case dragged on without a court date, Henry claimed that McElroy had parked outside his home at least 100 times, letting his truck engine idle loudly during the small hours of the night. Friends of McElroy eventually testified that he had not been on Henry's property. This, plus the fact that McElroy had learned that Henry had hidden his own petty conviction, a fact that Henry had to admit in open court, eventually led the jury to an acquittal.

An accomplished thief and rustler, it is hard to estimate how much Ken McElroy stole over the years. He despised the wealthy farmers in the area, who he felt looked down on him and his family. He was constantly working the angles, finding out which farmer was out of town and for how long, what kind of locks they used, and making sure that he had an alibi for his whereabouts on any given night that some property or livestock might go missing. He owned numerous pistols, rifles, and even a Thompson submachine gun, and almost always kept a firearm close at hand. He also dealt in cash, lots of it. It was not uncommon for him to have wads of cash in the thousands of dollars on him that he could use to buy up stolen property which he could resell for a profit. He bribed people for information with the cash and flashed it around from time to time. In 1980 he bought a brand new Chevy Silverado, a $12,000 vehicle ($34,000 in 2014 dollars) and paid for it in cash.

Ken McElroy was also a prolific womanizer, fathering more than ten children by a string of women that he quickly abandoned. At the age of 30, while still married, he eventually found a woman that he had to have. Woman is perhaps too strong a word. Trena McCloud was 12 years old and in the eighth grade when McElroy spotted her. He pursued her for 2 years. She became pregnant by him when she was 14, dropped out of high school, and went to live with McElroy. Two weeks after Trena gave birth, she fled to the safety of her family. Although it took McElroy several months, he eventually tracked Trena down where she was staying with relatives in a nearby town. Being lonely, she began talking with him on the phone. Once he had gained her trust, he took her to her mother's home while the house was empty, shot the family dog, and burned the house to the ground. Charges of statutory rape and arson were filed. Faced with this, his next move was both outrageous and brilliant. He began threatening to burn down Trena's mother's new home if her parents did not permit him to marry her. They eventually relented and he quickly took his bride. Trena, being his new wife and the only direct witness to the arson, was protected by spousal testimony privilege and could not be forced to testify against her new husband. The statutory rape charge was dropped as well.

In 1980, one of McElroy's children got into an argument with a clerk in a local grocery store. The argument started when the clerk accused the child of stealing candy. In short order, McElroy began his familiar pattern of stalking and intimidation, focusing his attention on the store's owner, 70-year-old "Bo" Bowenkamp. He eventually confronted the elderly grocer at his store with a shotgun and shot him in the neck. Bowenkamp was severely injured but survived, and McElroy was arrested and charged with attempted murder. The subsequent trial eventually resulted in a conviction for simple assault, and it was decided by the jury that he should receive two years in prison. While the Bowenkamps wanted a lengthier sentence, the punishment afforded them a measure of justice and safety. The relief felt by the residents of Skidmore was fleeting. Immediately after his conviction, McElroy was released on bail for a three-week reprieve while his attorney filed an appeal.

McElroy figured that the conviction would likely not stand if the principal witness to the shooting, his victim, either changed his story or was unable to give further testimony. Killing or at least further intimidating Bowenkamp seemed to be his plan. First, he aimed to frighten the people of Skidmore by making them aware of his release. Four days after his conviction, McElroy came to a bar in Skidmore brandishing a rifle. He ordered a beer and began making threats towards the grocer to anyone who would care to listen. The audacity of his actions created a stir. This went on for days. Then, on July 10, 1981, the bully showed up in town apparently unarmed. While McElroy drank his beer and shot his mouth off at the local bar, the townspeople gathered to appeal to the county sheriff one last time to arrest the bully immediately. The lawman refused, but advised that the town form a neighborhood watch and implored the citizens not to directly confront McElroy. After the sheriff had left the meeting, the townspeople learned of their tormentor's whereabouts just down the street. At least 30 people walked en masse into the bar where McElroy sat. The bully surveyed the situation and decided to leave after buying a six-pack of beer for the road. He went out to his new Silverado, and got in next to his wife. His foot feathered the accelerator as he started the engine up. A moment later, at least four shots were fired into the cabin of the truck. Two of the bullets had found their mark and killed McElroy almost instantly. Trena staggered from the truck and was quickly escorted to a nearby business, shocked but uninjured. The engine roared for the next 10 minutes, his foot jammed on the gas petal, until the motor seized in a plume of pungent smoke. The interior of the truck was soaked in blood, which pooled and thickened in the hot Midwestern sun.

The response to the town's actions was swift and severe. Skidmore was soon swarming with law enforcement agents from around the state. The FBI would later open an investigation. Newspaper reporters were everywhere. The news program *60 Minutes* did a piece on it. So did *Playboy*. Some decried the act as vigilante justice; others claimed that McElroy's civil rights had been violated. One thing was certain. Ken McElroy had been murdered in cold blood in front of more than 30 eyewitnesses and no one reported seeing a thing. Trena pointed out a suspect, but no one corroborated her version of the event. The murder weapons were never recovered. In the decades since this incident, the key players have moved away or died. That's not to say that some people in the town didn't harbor any regret for what happened. Some did. David Dunbar, the former town marshal of Skidmore, said that he had one lingering regret about the shooting. "It's really a shame about the Silverado," he said. "That was a really nice truck."

'Ken McElroy's Chevy Silverado after the shooting, July 10th 1981. This event is more fully detailed in Harry MacLean's book, *In broad daylight: A murder in Skidmore Missouri.*'

This is a story with no winners or heroes, only villains and victims. At the onset, McElroy is clearly the villain. A pedophile who stalked young girls and a bully that was prone to violence and coercion is a person that earns little sympathy. But the police and officers of the court were less than valiant. Many townspeople claimed that these officials had been 'buffaloed' through a combination of the bully's strong-arm tactics and slick maneuvering on the part of his attorney. The angry mob that finally confronted and killed McElroy participated in a cover-up to conceal the truth from authorities. At least one of them was a murderer and the rest were complicit in a lie. And yet, as odd as this may sound, there is something strangely satisfying about this tragedy. It harkens back to narratives of the American West of the 1800s. It imparts a twisted moral that, in the real world, evil usually wins against good unless those on the side of right are willing to shed their values and embrace their darker impulses. The moral lesson is simple: You must fight fire with fire.[1]

This moral lesson is similar to the thinking of many of our fellow scholars in psychology. Only negative emotions, negative thoughts, and negative experiences are strong enough to sober the mind and force it to confront reality. This line of thought goes back as far as Voltaire and has some merit. A harsh talking to by a parent to a disobedient child can do wonders. A doctor giving bad news to a patient in a serious and direct manner can help the patient understand the gravity of the condition. Indeed, both the entertainment industry and academia have embraced such thought. Unforgiving celebrity judges, like Simon Cowell or Judge Judy, are revered because of their brutal honesty. Television characters like Dr. Gregory House dish out diagnoses and treatments with sarcastic wit. To their credit, academics have been a bit more restrained, but only inasmuch as they are expected to be cordial. They have probed the many "benefits" of negativity by proclaiming sentiments like "fear is your friend" (Kaiser, 2011), depressed people are "sadder but wiser" (Alloy & Abramson, 1979) and by promoting optimistic change by "getting angry" (Reynolds, 2011).

This is standard fare in how psychological research is marketed. Counterintuitive proclamations garner attention and create the requisite buzz that can potentially transform stuffy professors into media darlings. It is certainly true that approaching a topic from a new perspective can be insightful and can reveal the rigidity of traditional viewpoints. However, in scoring these kinds of intellectual points, the larger truths are often willfully overlooked. It is worth remembering what the real consequences of such negativity are for people. In most cases, fear induces panic, not clarity of thought. Depression instills pain, not wisdom. Anger encourages aggression, not hopeful optimism.

Fear

There are few experiences more terrifying than having one's life directly threatened by a person brandishing a weapon. Having a gun pointed at your face or feeling a blade close to your neck triggers some of the most primitive instincts in the human psyche. The biological response is both rapid and nuanced. Much of the initial reaction occurs in the amygdala, an almond-shaped brain structure that receives inputs from all around the body. The amygdala stimulates a response in another brain structure called the hypothalamus, which in turn, opens the floodgates of chemistry. The net result is a chain reaction of chemicals in the brain and body: 1) corticotropin-releasing hormone in the hypothalamus; 2) adrenocorticotropic hormone in the pituitary gland, which activates the adrenal glands; 3) cortisol (a stress hormone) released into the bloodstream by the adrenal glands; and 4) increased production of glucose, which serves as immediate fuel for the body and brain. Aside from this chain reaction, there is a lot going on in the body's major systems. The pulse quickens and respiration increases in an effort to move glucose and oxygen throughout the body. Muscles tense in the arms and legs as they ready themselves to be engorged with blood. Stress hormones serve to suppress the digestive tract, resulting in responses ranging from mild butterflies to significant gastric distress. The rapid movement of blood may also result in either being flushed or blanched and may increase sweating. All of this would happen within a few minutes of a life-threatening encounter (Shiota & Kalat, 2012). Next to the amygdala is the hippocampus, a brain structure shaped like a seahorse (or hippocamp) that is responsible for forming long-term memories. The proximity of the amygdala and hippocampus, and the fact that they are highly connected with each other, means that a particularly emotional event can be quickly impressed into memory.

A second set of reactions occurs in the prefrontal cortex. The frontal lobes are considered by most scientists to be the "seat of consciousness and thought." Damage to this area can create dramatic changes in a person's personality and behavior. One of the most famous cases of brain trauma in the history of psychology is the case of Phineas Gage. Phineas Gage was a railroad worker in the 1800s who had an iron rod shot through his head due to an accident that occurred while using the aforementioned rod to place explosives. The rod entered just below his left cheek bone and exited through the through the top of his head, an inch or two past his hairline, smeared with brain and blood. The railroad foreman survived this horrific accident but his personality was forever altered. In the words of those who knew him, "Gage was no longer Gage." A century later, this case was made a mainstay of psychology coursework through the writings of Antonio Damasio (1994). Damasio realized that the area that had been damaged in Gage's brain was the region of the prefrontal cortex responsible for regulating emotions. In the normal brain, effective decision-making is informed by well-regulated emotions that give value to various patterns of thought and behavior. Gage's personality changes were the result of his inability to properly regulate his emotions.

The responses of the brain and body to fear are as complex and synchronized as the medal winning routine of an Olympic gymnast. These responses are taxing, they demand much of the mind's ability to process information, and they spend a great amount of the body's energy in a brief amount of time. In striking contrast, the behavioral responses that result from these responses are typically limited to three actions: Fight, flee, or freeze. That is the paradox of negative emotions: The flurry of activity by a variety of systems produces the most minimal of outcomes. To tweak a quote from Winston Churchill "Never has so much neural activity been mustered to accomplish so little." Why?

The reason is because an individual's behavioral repertoire is typically very large. That's a fancy way of saying that most people are able to do a lot of different things. Behavioral flexibility allows for adaptation to a wide variety of situations. Without being tied to a fixed response, an individual can explore and test varying strategies to cope with an ever-changing environment. Some of these strategies will be successful, but most will not. When the circumstance is life and death, the fear response (all of those brain and body responses described previously) works to sharply curtail the range of behaviors available to those behaviors that have been the most successful in our evolutionary history. And those responses are simple: Fight, flee, or freeze. This winnowing of behavior may help us survive, but it does not improve our thought processes.

Few people make good decisions when they are in the grips of panic. Airline pilots spend hundreds of hours practicing for potential catastrophes caused by mechanical malfunctions, instrument failures, turbulence, bird strikes, and human error. Even general aviation pilots must practice stalling their aircraft in midflight and restarting it in the air. The reasoning behind such overtraining is simple: When a skill is overlearned, it becomes automatic. No thinking involved. In a panicked situation, the kind one might expect when a plane is in risk of crashing, the pilot can execute the tasks that have been drilled into her mind without having to think through her actions. Panic absorbs the critical thinking faculties of almost everyone who experiences it, sometimes making the simplest decisions almost impossible. Take skydiving for instance. One might imagine that jumping out of a plane would be much easier than flying one. In skydiving, there is really only one thing to do— PULL THE CORD. Yet, one of the most tragic and seemingly preventable accidents that can happen is the no-pull scenario. Gary Marcus (2008) found that up to 6% of skydiving deaths happen this way. A seemingly healthy skydiver with no obvious equipment malfunctions simply forgets to pull their chutes. While one cannot entirely discount suicide, the predominant thinking in the skydiving community is that some people fall prey to "horizon hypnosis," where they are so overwhelmed with fear they remain paralyzed as the ground rushes up to meet them. Hence, skydivers also spend much of their training learning various mental tricks to cope with the panic. For one thing, they are typically required to complete a number of tandem jumps with an instructor harnessed to them before they are allowed to jump solo. They are also trained to rely on their "jump watches" that tell them specifically when to open their chutes. For both pilots and skydivers, preparation does not always guarantee fearlessness.

Pilots and skydivers willingly participate in their activities and they train specifically to counteract the potential effects of fear and panic. However, fear is usually not sought out and welcomed; it is usually confronted only when necessary. Consider the case of the typical eyewitness. Eyewitnesses to crimes are usually the victims of those crimes. They are usually in close proximity to the perpetrator and often get a very good look at the criminal's face. But they are sometimes unable to remember much about that face. The reason is that when a weapon is employed in a crime, like a common mugging, the focus of the victim is fixed on the weapon. This makes sense: Focus is placed on the location of the weapon in the environment that could cause immediate injury or death. However, focus on the weapon absorbs so much of the witness' attention that processing other details becomes more difficult. Cognitive psychologists call this phenomenon weapon focus. Mitchell, Livisky, and Mather (1998) found that they could replicate this effect with third-party witnesses who observed the crime on video. They had participants in two studies watch a videotape of a staged convenience store robbery. In some conditions, participants witnessed no crime, a crime with no weapon, a crime with a non-weapon, and a crime with a weapon. The witnesses were obviously in no danger, but their attention was still drawn towards the weapon and away from other elements of the crime. This even happened when the suspect brandished an unusual non-weapon, a stalk of celery. It appears that anything perceived as a potential weapon has the ability to create results conceptually similar to the weapon focus experienced by witnesses who are in legitimate danger. Conventional wisdom would suggest that the intensity and fear of the moment should make attention and memory sharper. And it certainly does, but not in a manner that may help with a subsequent investigation and identification of the perpetrator of the crime.

Fear doesn't have to present itself in the form of mortal danger to show its effects. Many college students know this to be true every time they are faced with the burden of tough exams. The fear of failure is a major component of test anxiety and this is for good reason, especially at the college level.

Financial aid, admission into a competitive major, and scholarship decisions are often based on grades, and for students who are at the margins of a GPA cutoff, exams can be very stressful. This phenomenon has been studied by researchers in a variety of fields, including psychologists, sociologists, and researchers in education. Two meta-analyses that summarized much of the research at the time on test anxiety were conducted in 1988 and 1991, respectively. Hembree (1988) conducted a study that employed 562 studies using American students from primary school through college and found a significant negative relationship between test anxiety and academic performance. The greater the test anxiety, the lower the academic performance. Seipp (1991) conducted a smaller meta-analysis on 126 studies from European and American students and found the same thing. This is not simply a correlation, either. Many of these studies employed experimental manipulations, suggesting that test anxiety actually caused decreases in grades. More recently, Mark Chapell and his colleagues (2005) conducted a massive study using 4,000 undergraduate students and 1,400 graduate students at three universities. While the effects were a bit less pronounced for the graduate students, the results were the same as Hembree and Seipp. Lots of methods, lots of samples, and a very simple conclusion: Higher levels of test anxiety are associated with lower GPAs for students at all levels of instruction, from kindergarten through graduate school. Fear of failing didn't help these students buckle down and study—it paralyzed them and hurt their chances of success.

Controlled laboratory studies produce analogous findings using stimuli that produce the mildest levels of threat. MacLeod, Mathews, and Tata (1986) conduct an elegant study that examined how clinically anxious people processed information. Specifically, they wanted to see whether these people were intrinsically drawn to threatening information and away from other kinds of information. To do this, they gave them a deceptively simple task. Each time a dot appeared in either the top-half or bottom-half of a computer screen, they were to press a corresponding button indicating where the dot was located. The positions of the dots were manipulated relative to the position of words that also flashed on the screen. These words had been specifically selected to be threatening (Failure, Stupid, Coffin, Disease). When confronted with these words, normal people momentarily shift their gazes away from the word, which would mean that if the dot were next to the threatening word, their response to the dot would be slower. Anxious people, on the other hand, tend to shift their gazes towards the threatening items, resulting in faster responses when the dot was in the same vicinity and slower responses when the dot was elsewhere. There are two implications of such findings— one obvious and one subtle. Obviously, the threatening stimuli influenced the performance of both the control and the anxious participants, drawing their attention either towards or away from the perceived threat. More subtly, this effect was documented using the most mildly threatening situation imaginable, presenting words on a computer screen. No cord to pull. No weapon present. No test to fail. The mere presence of words shifted the attentional gazes of the participants, which hurt their performance on half the experimental trials.

Of course, these examples demonstrate the effects of situational fear. Perhaps it is true that experiencing fear 'in the moment' may compromise the mind, but perhaps in the long term, fear could manifest its true, beneficial effects. Hardly. One of the most widely accepted facts in both science and in popular culture is the corrosive effect of experiencing fear on a continual basis. Consider one of the early animal studies on the effects of fear. George Mahl (1949) employed seven dogs as his subjects. Two were described as American foxhounds while the remaining five were only described as mongrels. His main goal was to determine whether chronic stress caused ulcers in the gastro-intestinal tract of these animals. He exposed these animals to a series of random electric shocks that were strong enough to induce minor abrasions and a number of behavioral responses. At the end of the multi-month study, Mahl euthanized the animals and examined their digestive tracts. Mahl did not find increased ulceration as a result of the shocks. About half a century later, scientists (like Dr. Barry Marshall, as described earlier) would discover that most ulcers are not caused by stress, confirming what Mahl had found. But what is overlooked in this study is the wealth of effects that fear *did* have on these animals. The random shocks produced profound behavioral changes, including changes in sleep patterns, standing in rigid positions for hours on end, an increased startle response to random noises, and repetitive circling and crouching behaviors. The lack of hostility was noted as an indication that the animals were experiencing chronic fear and not anything that might approximate emotions like frustration or anger. The fear induced by the shocks also produced physiological changes that could be measured. The amount of gastric acid in the guts of the dogs went up between 4 and 13 times from the control condition to the experimental condition. The heart rates also went up by about 10 beats per minute during the experimental procedure. The animals were so scared that they were urinating and defecating almost uncontrollably. While the modern reader might look upon such research as barbaric in its treatment of animals, George Mahl should be understood in terms of the ethics of his time. He had used dogs because he understood that the use of humans for this type of experimentation was out of the question. While he may not have shared the modern sympathies of animal rights activists, he understood fear. He understood that the effects of fear were far too negative to risk potential human suffering.

Life outside of strictly regulated, modern research labs does not have the same ethical restrictions as experimental science. People diagnosed with post-traumatic stress disorder (PTSD) experience fear and suffering on a reg-ular basis. With PTSD, an initial traumatic episode can trigger a series of emo-tional and behavioral responses that can last for months and years after that episode. Essentially, the mind repeatedly and uncontrollably recreates the fear and stress of that initial experience. There is good evidence that recurrent exposure to such anxieties can literally rewire their brains associated with emotional experience and emotion regulation. When patients with PTSD are presented with reminders of traumatic episodes, two cortical events take place. First, the amygdala activity levels tend to spike with activity much higher than those of control participants. Second, the prefrontal cortex, the area responsible for keeping emotions in check, shows a corresponding reduc-tion in activity levels. This is a neurological double whammy. The area responsible for creating an emotional response goes haywire while the area responsible for dampening that response goes offline (Shiota & Kalat, 2012).

If the effects of fear do not benefit the individual in the short or the long term, perhaps fear is helpful when experienced on larger scale. Perhaps if *society* is fearful of something for a long period of time, that would force peo-ple to think clearly and make good choices. Unfortunately this is not the case either. Consider one of the ever-present dangers that have faced the western United States for the last 100 years: Forest fires. As Americans settled the great frontiers in places like Colorado, California, and Arizona, they raised animals and planted crops. A wildfire was something to be feared. It could destroy their livelihoods and decades of hard work within hours. It is not sur-prising that there was great political pressure to press emergency agencies into the task of fire suppression. As the years went by, settlers were less prone to be ranchers or farmers and more likely to be suburbanites. Still, the threat of fire could result in thousands of people being left homeless. Fire suppression was a task that was an accepted part of firefighting through much of the 20th century.

Alison Share (2012) wrote a pair of fascinating blogs at americanforests. org on the history of fire suppression in the western United States. The story was complex but the guiding principle was simple: Put out every fire, every time. But in the last few decades, the fires have become more frequent and more devastating. According to the National Interagency Fire Center in Boise, Idaho, the 10-year average between 2001 and 2011 is just over 54,000 wild-fires a year in the United States. In 2011, the Wallow Fire, which originated in Eastern Arizona, consumed 40,000 acres in just 8 hours and eventually burned an area of over 800 square miles.

The reason is simple. The knee-jerk reaction—put out <u>every fire every time</u>—one made out of fear rather than reason, led to a tremendous buildup of fuel in forests that had not experienced any natural burns for almost a century. Ecologists now recognize that periodic, natural wildfires help to burn off the underbrush, transforming it into nutrient rich ash that subsequently feeds the forest making it healthier. Stamping out every fire, every time allowed the underbrush to grow beyond its natural cycle. This underbrush sapped the strength from the larger trees and provided abundant fuel for the fires that would eventually run rampant. These fires now burn hotter than forest fires of a hundred years ago and kill many of the larger trees that provide a needed root system for the forest floor. Without this root system, the soil of the forest floor becomes unstable and can produce dramatic mudslides when saturated with enough rain. This is a disaster in two stages: The fire destroys the forest and burns down dozens of houses, then, a flood creates mudslides that further plague the survivors. The great irony is that when you consider the net costs of this worsening problem, allowing the fires to simply burn during the 20th century would have likely saved money, property, and lives. The fear of fire, one of mankind's most ancient and unwavering fears, misled everyone who considered the problem in front of them. Ranchers, farmers, suburban home-owners, politicians, firefighters, and fire experts all got it wrong. For almost a century they saw fire as the enemy. The fear of fire did not allow them to see its necessity.

'Smokey the Bear' has been the mascot of the U.S. Forest Service since 1944, advocating the simple message 'Only you can prevent forest fires.

Our point is this: Biological and psychological research both suggest that fear biases people's ability to think clearly. Its effects are immediate and powerful at the individual level and at the societal level, in the short-term and in the long-term. It affects the mind by narrowing attention, distorting memory, and clouding judgment. Fear does have evolutionary value, but rather than encouraging clear thinking, it encourages no thinking. In crisis situations, fear clears the mind of unnecessary thought because complex and reasoned thought is circumstantially maladaptive. To be sure, fear is necessary for survival and has its place as an evolutionary adaptation, but it is plainly *not* a friend of sound thought or judgment.

Depression

Depression is nearly universal in the human experience. It cuts across age, gender, class, and culture. Symptoms of depression have been documented in children as young as four and in centurions. Although women tend to express the phenomenon more prominently than men, it is by no means shackled to the X chromosome. Likewise, while depression has been observed as being somewhat more frequent among people of lower socioeconomic class, it is frequently found among even the most well-heeled of society's upper class. Depression is present in every country in the world at rates that are astoundingly resistant to cultural variation, a near constant rate between 7%–10% in any given place on the globe.

As a discipline, psychology often debates the validity of certain illness, asking the basic question "is this real?" Over the years, psychologists have considered the veracity of multiple personality disorder, repressed memory syndrome, and whether or not homosexuality is a mental illness (for those of you keeping score at home, the quick answers are: Yes, Maybe, and No). But no such existential debate exists with depression. Its reality is accepted by everyone both in stuffy academic circles and by people in the larger society. The symptoms are easily recognized and, to an extent, experienced in lesser degrees by normal people who never fall prey to the full-blown effects of mental illness. Symptoms include feelings of sadness, loss of motivation, change in sleep patterns, change in appetite, loss of energy, and loss of interest in daily activities. At some deep level, we all *know* something of what depression feels like. It hurts. The effects of depression are uniformly negative. In extreme cases, depression makes the unreasonable seem reasonable. Suicide, an act that is admonished by every major religion and by secular society as well, can become a legitimate option in the eyes of the severely depressed.

And yet, there are academic studies that bolster counterintuitive notions about depression, the idea that depression might actually help people be more in touch with reality, be more creative, and be better thinkers. One of the most provocative ideas of the last 40 years of research on depression is a phenomenon called "depressive realism." This idea suggests that depressed people are able to see the world and themselves more accurately because they lack the positive distortions associated with non-depressed people. Alloy and Abramson (1979) first identified depressive realism in what can literally be described as a "light bulb moment." Depressed and non-depressed participants in this study were given a series of trials in which they could either press a button or not and then a green light would illuminate or not. At the end of the trials, participants rated how much control their button pushing had on whether or not the bulb lit up on a scale of 0 (No Control) to 100 (Complete Control). In the first experiment, button pushing did reliably predict whether or not the bulb lit up at least some of the time (25%, 50%, or 75% of the time). The depressed and non-depressed participants both interpreted the effects of their actions correctly and their ratings on the 0 to 100 scale reflected the percentage of times the bulb was actually illuminated as a result of their actions. In the critical experiment (Experiment 2), their button pushing had no impact on whether the bulb lit up. Depressed people seemed to recognize this fact and their ratings reflected that realization. Non-depressed people, on the other hand, were still under the impression that their actions were impacting the light bulb. They were experiencing an illusion of control that the depressed people were not. Depressed people, therefore, were seeing the world more accurately than the non-depressed people.

In the next 10 years, there were dozens of published studies documenting the parameters of this phenomenon. Ten years after it was first observed, depressive realism was widely accepted in many academic circles as an essential paradox of depression. Depressed people were sadder but wiser. In a summary on the topic, Dobson and Franche (1989) concluded that depressed people appear to have a more realistic perception of their importance, reputation, and skills than those who are not depressed. One limitation of the research on depressive realism, however, was that much of it was conducted using people who were not actually depressed. That may surprise the non-academic, but the reality of data collection is that most researchers are college professors, and they tend to use the available sample—college students—for much of their data collection. Instead of using bona-fide clinically depressed people, undergraduates are surveyed with questionnaires and those that have many characteristics of depression are classified as dysphoric, a technical term that essentially means "mildly depressed" or in a "temporary state of depression." In full disclosure, we will present data collected in exactly that way later in this text (Chapter 6). Most of the time, this works just fine. Dysphorics provide data that closely approximates clinically depressed people in many cases, and such data can be collected without exploiting people who are genuinely suffering from mental illness. But this limitation would prove problematic to the concept of depressive realism.

In 1995, Keith Dobson (of the aforementioned 1989 review) published a paper with Dennis Pusch that attempted to replicate the Alloy and Abramson (1979) light bulb study. The light bulbs were replaced with a computerized simulation of a light bulb on a screen, but the concept was the same. The participants would press a button that would, in reality, have no impact on whether the light bulb lit up. However, instead of using dysphoric participants, Dobson and Pusch had three groups of participants: fifteen patients who were receiving treatment for depression, fifteen individuals who had previously experienced depression, and fifteen control participants who had never experienced depression. The study failed to replicate the effects of depressive realism. The clinically depressed participants did not see the consequences of their actions any more realistically than did the non-depressed participants. Indeed, in the summary of the methodology, it was reported that many of the participants did not understand the directions given to them. Dobson and Pusch had to add in a practice session for clarity. This should have been a clue that something was amiss. In their conclusion, they offered a cursory summation of the apparent disconnect between their results and the results of other laboratories: "... while depressive realism may be relatively easy to identify in a laboratory setting, as researchers move into domains that have greater personal relevance to [participants] the phenomenon becomes increasingly elusive" (p. 192). In the vernacular of today's youth: Oh, snap!

More recent studies have actually shown that mentally healthy people actually have fewer cognitive illusions than depressed people. For example, studies by Msetfi et al. (2005, 2007) showed that non-depressed people take into account more situational aspects than their depressed counterparts and thus have more realistic perceptions. Other researchers such as Joiner et al. (2006) and Moore and Fresco (2007) found that cognitive illusions, including illusions of control, are associated with higher levels of depression. The results of research by Fu et al. (2005), Carson, Hollon, and Shelton (2010) and Boyd-Wilson et al. (2000) reject the idea of depressive realism by showing no link between cognitive illusions and mental health, well-being, or life satisfaction. They maintain that an accurate perception of reality is compatible with happiness and mental health and incompatible with sadness and depression.

While the concept of depressive realism may be limited to academic circles, another idea has penetrated the public's consciousness: The idea that depression may actually inspire greatness. Arnold Ludwig (1995) conducted a 10-year study of 1,004 men and women who were prominent in several fields, including art, music, science, business, politics, and sports. He found that between 59 and 77% of the artists, writers, and musicians suffered mental illness, particularly mood disorders like depression, compared to just 18–29% in the less artistic professions. Indeed, he even suggests that there is more than a mere link between depression and creativity—it may even give people entree to greatness. However, it is likely that Ludwig made the classic mistake of confusing correlation with causation. Gifted individuals may have higher rates of depression, but it is far from clear whether depression boosts talent. It might be the case that increased talent levels are associated with increased levels of responsibility and stress, and that these additional burdens open the door for depression. But Ludwig's survey of success and exceptionalism falls short in another important way. It fails to fully address the cases of very talented people who were not subject to depression. The result is that depression is seen as a romanticized golden ticket to success rather than what it actually is—a debilitating illness that needs treatment rather than encouragement.

The benefits of depression, as they have been documented, are extremely limited in scope and duration. They do not come close to counterbalancing the negative effects that depression has on the mind. To say that depression makes people sadder but great is tantamount to suggesting that being in an airline crash may help people lose weight. That is technically true. During the rapid descent from a great altitude, passengers in an airplane would likely experience temporary weightlessness—then they would CRASH AND DIE. The benefit of weightlessness is real but misses the point. The same is true for depression. In some limited way, depression is probably helpful, but in almost every practical way, it hurts.

The general physiology of depression has been fairly well understood for more than four decades. At the heart of it are neurotransmitters, the chemical agents in the nervous system that allow neurons to talk with each other. Low levels of serotonin were considered to be among the chief chemical causes of depression until fairly recently. The idea was analogous to insulin in diabetics. In those individuals, low levels of insulin in the body could be boosted to normal levels with drugs. A person with low serotonin levels could boost their levels to "normal" by taking antidepressants. What may surprise many people about serotonin is what it actually does in the body. Far from being a chemical agent that simply promotes good feelings, it actually does most of its work in the lining of the gut in the digestive tract. Just about 90% of all the body's serotonin is used to regulate the movements of the intestines. From the first stages of digestion to the elimination of bodily waste, much of what serotonin actually does in the body is non-brain related. The remaining 10% does its work in the central nervous system, where it is involved in regulating the psychological experiences of appetite, sleep, and mood. This makes some sense, as these experiences are greatly informed by our gut (we tend to be more active when hungry, we tend to be content after eating, and we tend to get sleepy when full). In the course of evolution, the body learned to associate high levels of serotonin with times of plentiful food, which probably also meant relative safety and the availability of potential mates. Low levels of serotonin became linked with scarce food, increased levels of danger, and fewer opportunities for mating. Was it possible that a low serotonin level was the key to understanding depression?

Pharmaceutical companies sure thought so. Checking serotonin levels was like checking for oil in a car's engine: A quick and dirty way to explain why most people were normal and happy and some people were prone to depression. Plus, drugs that helped to regulate serotonin levels had far fewer side effects than another type of anti-depressants known as tricyclics. As a result, they churned out a number of medicines that have since become household words: Prozac, Paxil, and Zoloft (the last one even has a depressed little egg as its mascot). But that is not quite the end of the story. While these drugs are effective in treating many symptoms of depression, it is not clear that a low level of serotonin causes depression. Two meta-analyses that examined this issue showed that depressive symptoms were strongly linked to negative life events but not to genes linked to serotonin levels (Munafò, Durant, Lewis, & Flint, 2009; Risch et al., 2009). That doesn't mean that serotonin isn't playing an important role in depression; it means that it likely has company.

Two probable chemical compatriots of serotonin are norepinephrine and dopamine. Norepinephrine, is both a neurotransmitter and a hormone. In the body, it transmits sympathetic activity to target organs to work harder and, in conjunction with acetylcholine, to skeletal muscles to move faster and lift more. In the brain, it gooses the activity levels in areas responsible for attention, memory, and emotion. At moderate levels, norepinephrine creates the experience of being interested, attentive, and engaged. For depressed people, norepinephrine levels are abnormally low. This makes it harder for them to engage other people or to participate in the activities around them. Dopamine is a member of the catecholamine family, and its effects are almost exclusively in the brain (although there are some effects in blood vessels and in the kidneys). There are five kinds of brain receptors that respond to dopamine, and they all have varying roles in the experience of pleasure. In moderate doses, dopamine serves as part of an internal reward system that reinforces behaviors that are adaptive by making those behaviors pleasurable. Depressed people often have dopamine levels in the brain that are far below those that are deemed normal. There are now a variety of antidepressants, such as Stattera and Wellbutrin, which are routinely used by people to artificially boost levels of norepinephrine and dopamine.

Depression goes deeper than complex chemistry; it is actually associated with structural abnormalities in the brain itself. Neuroimaging studies of clinically depressed people show, in comparison to their non-depressed counterparts, smaller volumes of the basal ganglia (which helps regulate motor activity and helps us learn habits), the thalamus (which helps regulate alertness and the sleep cycle), the hippocampus (which regulates the formation of memories), and even the frontal lobes (which controls the conscious "self-aware" aspects of thought). It is up to some debate as to whether these brain differences cause depression or if depression causes these brain differences (or if some other factor is responsible), but the differences should not be dismissed.

The reason why is simple: Size matters when it comes to brain anatomy. Before the professional knit-pickers attack, this is not an attempt to resurrect the defunct ideas that smaller brains result in lower intelligence and bigger brains result in higher intelligence. After all, it is often claimed that Albert Einstein had a small brain: A small, intact, and proportional brain. But when particular regions of the brain like the hippocampus and the frontal lobes are marginalized, they cannot work as efficiently. It's like having one leg shorter than the other, each leg works just fine, but running is tricky. In a way, thinking is a lot like running, because the brain functions rely upon flexibility. Neural flexibility is the ability of brain areas to rewire themselves based upon experience. Neuroscientists call this rewiring process plasticity—and it is evidenced by the number and efficiency of neural connections in the brain. When the brain is very active learning a skill set, the regions of the brain associated with that skill set begin to explode in neural activity—often with corresponding increases in the size of those parts of the brain. Katherine Woollette and Eleanor McGuire (2011) studied the brains of London cab drivers to see if their experience driving a cab had served to rewire their brains. In comparison to non-taxi drivers, the posterior hippocampus, an area of the brain involved in spatial memory, was larger in the taxi drivers. Similar findings have been reported with people learning other skills, such as how to play musical instruments. So, when people are active and engaged, the involved parts of the brain tend to grow in response to experience. And guess what happens in the brains of depressed people? They tend to be smaller, particularly in the frontal regions of the brain, which are involved in higher order thought processes (Bora, Fornito, Pantelis, & Yucel, 2011).

Thus far, we have identified that depressed people have chemical imbalances for the neurotransmitters of serotonin, norepinephrine, and dopamine. Their brains show abnormalities in regions responsible for higher-level thought and mental flexibility. What is the result of all of this? It is important to remember a basic mantra coined by Marvin Minsky (1987): "The mind is what the brain does." It stands to reason that if the neural chemistry and brain physiology of depressed people differs from that of the average person, the outcome—thought—should also be different. Indeed, the effects of depression are so numerous that it is easier to think of them the way that astronomers think about the stars in the sky: In constellations. Psychologists have identified a number of cognitive distortions associated with depression that have the net result of altering their perceptions of themselves, the world, and the future. They see themselves as worthless, the world as pitiless, and the future as hopeless (Beck, 1967; Beck, Rush, Shaw, & Emery, 1979). This is what Beck termed "the cognitive triad" of depression.

The bias for negativity is the hallmark characteristic of depression. The depressed have the uncanny knack for seeing the worst of everything and everyone. This is most evident in their personal memories. Studies that have been carried out examining the autobiographical memories of clinically depressed people typically find three things. First, the recollection of specific events tends to take longer and result in fewer specific event details than the memories recalled by 'normal' people, suggesting that depression interferes with the recall task. Second, depressed people show a tendency to ruminate about their personal experiences much more than the non-depressed, suggesting an inability to fully control their thought processes. Third, these effects almost always show a bias in favor of the negative. Depressed people can recall negative events faster and with more detail than positive events and they have the tendency to think and talk about them more often (Dalgleish, JMG Williams, et al., 2007; Raes, et al., 2006).

The bias for negativity showed by these studies could be explained by the possibility that depressed people simply experience more negative events than non-depressed people. To counter this possibility, consider a laboratory study examining the recall of simple word lists. Such recall tasks have been popular with psychologists studying memory since the dawn of psychology as a discipline. Joorman, Teachman, and Gotlib (2009) conducted a study examining the impact of depression on a phenomenon called "the false memory effect." The false memory in itself is fairly straightforward. Participants are presented with a list of thematically related words (bed, nap, yawn, snooze, slumber, snore, dream, etc.) with a critical word or lure absent from the list (sleep). When asked to recall the list, a sizable number incorrectly recall the absent word as having been presented in the list. Thus, they have had a false memory for that lure. This effect is quite robust and has been demonstrated using a number of methods and samples. Joorman and her colleagues tested 25 depressed and 27 non-depressed participants with 40 such lists, which included lists with absent lures that were that were positive, negative, and neutral. For the items that were actually present, depressed people recalled fewer items than non-depressed people, a finding consistent with the research in autobiographical memory. For the positive and negative absent lures, there was no difference in the number of false memories produced by the depressed and non-depressed people. However, depressed people recalled significantly more negative absent lures than did non-depressed people.

From this, it seems clear that depression, at the individual level, creates a host of biases that result in significant distortions of reality. But is it possible that depression, at a societal level, can offer positive benefits such as creativity, innovation, and perhaps even result in a stronger economy? The conventional wisdom in the world of business is that companies that are hard-pressed during economic downturns will respond by innovating their products, their services, and their business models. But do companies really do this? If one examines the effects of economic downturns on new patents, one sign of economic creativity and innovation, the answer appears to be no.

A quick study of American history shows that economic depressions are almost always associated with anti-trust sentiments. The depression in the late 1880s led directly to the Sherman Anti-Trust Act of 1890 and a subsequent restriction in new patents. Mahal Nabar of the International Monetary Fund and Tom Nicholas of the Harvard Business School (2010) examined patterns of corporate innovation during the Great Depression. They looked at the number of patents that were submitted and patents that were pending from 142 companies during the years 1921–1938. Patents are the result of innovative thinking and the investment of capital into research and development by corporate leadership. If depression spawns creativity, then Great Depression should have spawned a flood of patents. It didn't. But Nabar and Nicholas did more than simply examine a single statistic; they examined these trends in the context of the larger economic climate. The Great Depression was not a single monolithic event. There were economic peaks and valleys that punctuated temporary recoveries and recessions. The trends for patents followed these ups and downs and showed a very consistent pattern: Patents were plentiful after a year or so of economic recovery and scarce in the wake of recession. Indeed, during the hardest years of the Great Depression, 1929–1933, patents held by these companies actually contracted. Rather than spawning innovation and creativity, hard times typically encourage people to cut their losses and go back to the basics.

Jobless workers seeking employment during the Great Depression.

Image © Everett Collection, 2014. Used under license from Shutterstock, Inc.

Consider the more contemporary topic of innovation in the fast-paced digital world of the early 21st century. Steven Johnson (2010) asked a mind-bogglingly simple and provocative question: Where do good ideas come from? He surveyed modern companies like Google and Apple as well as well as classical moments of innovation throughout human history. He concluded that really good ideas come from a variety of sources. One source is a concept that he called the Slow Hunch. When people form good ideas, they rarely have a 'eureka!' moment. Instead, they have a good idea that takes several years to fully mature into an idea that is useful. But Slow Hunches rarely turn into good ideas all by themselves. They must have the chance to blend with the ideas of other people. Historically, these ideas come together in physical spaces like the coffee houses of the Enlightenment or the Parisian salons of Modernism. These places were like innovation factories that allowed thinkers to socialize and to discuss their insights with their peers. What is interesting about Johnson's analysis is what it lacks: Harsh economic conditions were not necessary components to innovation. Quite the contrary, the Enlightenment occurred during a high water mark during the reign of the British Empire. Likewise, France was perhaps the most powerful country in the world at the birth of Modernism. Many of the most successful new companies of the late 20th century, like Apple, Microsoft, and Intel, were founded by people born after World War II, during what was the height of American economic power in the 20th century. Good ideas come from times of plenty not from times of struggle.

What happened in the world at large is analogous to what happens to the mind when faced with depression. People became more risk-aversive and less creative. In the heart of the Great Depression, business owners focused on the negative and imagined only the worst of the possibilities that lay before them. They saw their goods and services as worth less, the world as having less need for their business, and the future as having less promise. At the societal level, depression does not drive innovation—it depresses it. Yes, during times of economic hardship businesses can learn to cut costs, do more with less, and develop new ways to sell their goods and services. But we should not confuse the act of survival with real creative growth. The way that depressions work is by putting inefficient and unprofitable companies out of business. Businesses are genuinely creative during economic upswings when times are good. When profits are up, wealth is created, jobs are created, new industries and products are created, research is funded, and discoveries are made—in short, societies are built during times of economic boon and they decay during times of economic hardship.

Consider the words of Murray Moss, one of the leading design entrepreneurs in New York, while responding to the claim that the 2008 economic crisis was just what the world of design needed to make itself more creative and relevant: "Design loves a depression? I can assure you that design, along with painting, sculpture, photography, music, dance, fashion, the culinary arts, architecture, and theatre, loves a depression no more than it loves a war, a flood, or a plague" (Moss, 2009). Moss is an artist speaking about other artists, but he could have added just about any profession to that list. No one loves depression, because depression *hurts*.

Anger

The experience of anger is fundamentally different from these experiences of fear and depression. Fear narrows and heightens particular mental processes (like awareness) while eliciting particular behaviors associated with stress, withdrawal, and cowering. Depression dampens almost all cognitive processes while inhibiting a wide range of behaviors. In some respects, fear and depression share a common link in that both might be considered emotions of submission. In a state of fear the individual may retreat from a perceived threat, while in a state of depression they may just surrender to it. But not so with anger. Anger responds to a perceived threat through defiance. Anger makes snap judgments without considering their consequences. Anger activates an array of behaviors designed to engage, to confront, and *to attack*.

Anger, like fear and depression, has its origins in the physical brain and in the chemistry of the body. Experiences of anger are often short-lived and are associated with the subjective experience of losing control or of explosive outbursts. Such experiences suggest that the control centers of the brain are unable to inhibit the aggressive impulses triggered by anger. It is well known that damage to the prefrontal cortex, the seat of conscious thought, is one of the physiological bases of impulsivity (Fuster, 2008). The prefrontal cortex receives neural input from many lower brain areas and forms those inputs into a series of conscious experiences that can be evaluated and acted upon. People with damage to this area are more likely to make rash decisions without fully considering their consequences (Damasio, 1994). People with a history of anger issues, such as murderers, seem to show similar patterns of behavior as people with damage to this critical area. Although it is possible that some of these people may be truly brain damaged, the thinking is that these areas are probably malfunctioning, which compromises their ability to fully reign in their aggressive impulses. Of course, if the prefrontal cortex is filtering the impulses from more primitive cortical regions, then the impulses associated with anger have to be coming from somewhere, right?

Understanding the deeper cortical roots of anger is more challenging than with other emotions. Anger, more than other emotions, is an "embodied" emotion in the sense that the whole body is activated in its experience and expression. If you have ever seen a cat fight (the kind between felines), you may notice that the opponents seem to grow in size. This is not an optical illusion, it is a standard threat display seen in many species, and it is an example of how anger invigorates the whole body. Being angry means being active. This matters because the chief way of examining the living brain is through active brain scans, techniques that require people to remain still for long periods of time. Take fMRI as an example. The fMRI works by tracking the flow of oxygen in the brain. The reasoning behind these studies is simple: When an area of the brain is active, it will likely consume more oxygen. Hence, if a particular emotion is induced in an experiment, oxygen is likely to cluster areas of the brain associated with that emotion. In fMRI studies, people are required to remain motionless while lying on their backs, in some cases for several minutes at a time. If the experiment induces anger, participants are in a dilemma: If they get really angry, their movement ruins the study; if they remain still, they are less likely to experience true anger, which ruins the study. Research showed that participants lying on their backs still experienced anger[2], but their brains did show a reduction in the neural activity associated with anger (Harmon-Jones & Peterson, 2009).

Thankfully, the chemical origins of anger have been more clearly identified. One of the leading culprits is our old friend serotonin. Low levels of serotonin, levels that we have already identified as being associated with depression, are also associated with the experience of anger. In animal studies, rodents with low levels of serotonin have been shown to be more aggressive than animals with normal levels of serotonin (Valzelli & Bernasconi, 1979). Monkeys with low serotonin levels are more likely to instigate fights with their companions and are more likely to be the victims of such attacks. Indeed, many low-serotonin monkeys die within the first few years of life. But there may be an evolutionary payoff that is not so obvious. Surviving monkeys with low serotonin levels had a significantly higher chance of achieving 'alpha' status in the social group than their peers with normal serotonin levels (Howell et al., 2007).

These findings have been partially supported in human studies. Studies of prison inmates have found low levels of serotonin in people convicted of violent crimes such as murder and arson (Virkkunen, Nuutila, Goodwin, & Linnoila, 1987). These studies have also tracked what happens to convicted criminals with low serotonin levels after they are released from prison. They are more likely to commit subsequent violent acts and return to prison than convicts with normal serotonin levels (Kruesi et al., 1992). Perhaps more convincing evidence comes from the direct manipulation of serotonin. When researchers have used drugs to artificially lower serotonin levels, they have found that individuals prone to violence become even more violent (Van der Does, 2001). However, the effects of lowered serotonin were not exclusive to anger and aggression—people prone to depression became more depressed and people prone to drug abuse reported greater drug cravings as a result of the drop in serotonin. Moreover, drugs that boost serotonin levels are only marginally effective in treating anger and aggression disorders.

Testosterone is also one of the chemical agents associated with anger and aggression. Testosterone is a steroid hormone linked to the development of typical masculine characteristics such as increased muscle mass, increased bone density, and increased growth of body hair. On average, a man has about seven times the amount of testosterone as a woman. In animals, high levels of testosterone have been linked with aggressive behavior such as pronounced territoriality and sparring behaviors. The term "alpha male" has its origins in the social order that forms naturally in wolf packs. The alpha male is the strongest and most skilled hunter in a pack, and he is afforded the luxuries of leadership: First to eat after a kill, and the only one allowed to mate. The alpha male has higher levels of testosterone than the other males, and his presence may inhibit testosterone production among other male members of the pack. Of course, the alpha male does not have it easy; he must be wary of threats to his authority that can come from within the pack as well as without. A similar dynamic can be seen in prides of lions. The strongest male fights for mating rights and enjoys a life of ease, allowing the females to hunt for food and raise the young. The only real responsibility of the male lion is to offer protection from outside threats, usually rogue males who seek to usurp the male's authority. Like the alpha males found in wolf packs, dominant male lions are typically coursing with testosterone.

In humans, testosterone is associated with a person's sex drive, male pattern baldness, and the tendency for aggressive outbursts. Men are more aggressive than women, especially between the ages of 15 and 30, when testosterone levels are at their highest in males. These are ages when men are the most likely to commit violent offenses such as assault, rape, and murder. As men age, they lose their aggressive tendencies. But here is where things get tricky. The relationship between testosterone and aggression is not as clear-cut as it is in the rest of the animal kingdom. Only about half of the studies examining the relationship between testosterone and aggression in humans find this relationship. It is also the case that only a fraction of the studies that link the two actually show a causal relationship. So, it is unclear that higher testosterone actually causes aggression in humans. What is clear is that testosterone triggers growth in attributes of physical strength and endurance, attributes that certainly make it easier for an aggressive tendency to be acted upon. And the data that is available is tantalizing. For instance, Beaver, Vaughn, Delisi, and Wright (2008) conducted a study on a representative sample of young males in the United States that found a link between using anabolic steroids, the chemicals that athletes take to gain strength rapidly, and violent behavior. Compared with their peers who did not use steroids, steroid users reported greater involvement in violence even after controlling for the effects of socioeconomic factors and previous violent behavior. This suggests that the steroids did not simply exacerbate violent tendencies but may have caused them.

The effects of anger on the mind are often as dramatic as they are short-lived. One effect is known as the hostile attribution bias, the tendency to see ambiguous actions as being hostile. For instance, if a person bumps into you when you are angry, a hostile aggression bias would be to infer that they hurt you on purpose. This bias is so pervasive that it often manifests itself in situations that are clearly illogical. In the previous bumping example, for instance, it is entirely possible that the other person did bump you on purpose. But many people have found themselves getting angry at inanimate objects. Video game players have been known to smash computer screens. Vending machines have been enthusiastically smacked after stealing paying customers' bills and coins. Phones have been smashed when calls get cut off. The first author of this text (RW) even found himself gleefully smashing apart a piece of home-assembled furniture after hours of frustrating labor with little to no progress (the name of the brand will not be revealed, but it does rhyme with Ikea). Of course, there is no possible way that an object can intend hostility. That's the hostile attribution bias at work. The consequences (lost video game, stolen money, dropped call) all seem to the result of an intentional act of hostility against us. And the effects of this bias are widespread. A meta-analysis of 6,000 participants in 41 different studies showed a strong relationship between hostile attributions and aggressive behavior (Orobio de Castro, Veerman, Koops, Bosch, & Monshouwer, 2002). Bottom line, if people think they have been intentionally hurt or slighted by someone, they often feel compelled to hurt them back.

Anger also allows negative stereotypes to be activated and used to judge others. In a 1994 study, Bodenhausen, Sheppard, and Kramer induced a mildly angry mood in a group of participants, and a mildly sad mood and a neutral mood in two other groups of people. Next, participants were asked to read two alleged cases of student misconduct. The first case was an assault and the second case was a cheating incident. Each case was described in a short paragraph. For half of the assault cases, the student defendant was given an obviously Hispanic name 'Juan Garcia' while the remaining cases described the defendant with the name 'John Garner.' The Hispanic name was used to activate the racial stereotypes associated with Hispanics. Anger had a very specific effect on perceptions of guilt: The angry participants were more likely to see 'Juan' as being guilty than they did 'John.' This was not the case in either the sad or neutral conditions, where there was no difference in judgments of guilt. For half of the cheating cases, the student's name was followed with a sentence describing him as "a well-known campus athlete," while in the remaining cases, this description was omitted. This tidbit of information was used to activate the common stereotype of the dumb athlete who might be more prone to cheating. Again, anger had a very specific effect on perceived guilt: The angry participants were more likely to see the athlete as guilty than the non-athlete. This difference was not found in the sad or neutral conditions.

Anger at the level of the individual can distort thought, but what about at a societal level? Few events have shaken a civilization like the events of September 11, 2001. The emotions expressed by the leaders of the world and ordinary citizens seemed to be universal. Horror. Shock. Disbelief. These were the emotions that were expressed in the weeks after the attacks. As the horror began to fade, the emotional disposition of the nation changed to anger. Al Queda was identified as the group responsible for the attacks, and Osama Bin Laden quickly became America's most wanted. Even people who would typically describe themselves as peaceful found it difficult to express anything but fury. Dr. Howard Barnes, a professor of history at Winston-State University, exemplified this feeling. A lifelong liberal peacenik, he found himself being interviewed by a local media outlet in late 2001 about the historical implications of the new war in Afghanistan. When asked about what should happen to Bin Laden if the terrorist was ever captured, his reply was quick and curt: "They should shoot the son-of-a-bitch." He paused and then added sheepishly, "You probably shouldn't print that last one."[3]

Howard's sentiment reflected more than the mood of the country. He found his thoughts and beliefs awash in the powerful currents of the forces around him. Television and newspapers stoked emotions that had long abated since the end of the Cold War in the early 1990s. Every conversation seemed to find its way back to the events of that tragic morning and the newfound enemy, Islamic terrorism, that was seemingly already at the gates. New fears and anxieties flooded the culture in a way that they had not since the bombing of Pearl Harbor. Howard's lifelong beliefs could not withstand the anger they confronted. Everyone was mad as hell.

The invasion of Afghanistan and the subsequent invasion of Iraq were both met with widespread support by the American public. While there were many voices of dissent, particularly for the latter war which was seen more of a "war of choice" than the former, the fact is that the U.S. went to war with anger in its heart and vengeance on its mind. In the year after 9/11, Cheung-Blunden and Blunden (2008) surveyed 588 participants about a variety of things related to the attacks and their impressions of blame, anger, and desire for military action. In one part of the study, they measured participants' anger responses to pictures of the 9/11 attack. They entered all of this data into an analysis called a structural equation model. This analytic tool allows the investigators to explore the various relationships between what are essentially outcome variables (stuff that happens) and predictor variables (stuff that makes other stuff happen). The practical upshot is that the results of this analysis can produce an empirically validated flowchart of how factors are interrelated. To make a long story short: Reminders of 9/11 → Anger → Support for War. While the images of 9/11 did not always produce anger in participants, when they did, all signs pointed to war. Angry people were more likely to blame Islamists, Islam, Bin Laden, and more likely to support military action over more nuanced, diplomatic alternatives. Cheung-Blunden and Blunden concluded that these results generalized to Iraq, where anger stoked hate to the flashpoint. Anger was the deciding factor over everything else. It narrowed the decision frame from a field of options to a singular choice: Attack.

The major combat operations in Operation Iraqi Freedom lasted just 21 days. According to U.S. President George W. Bush and British Prime Minister Tony Blair, the primary mission was to disarm Iraq of weapons of mass destruction, to end Saddam Hussein's support for terrorism, and to free the Iraqi people. The invasion initially enjoyed support from two-thirds of the American people. The troops were seen as liberators, and the Iraqi people were free from the rule of a tyrant. Indeed, the honeymoon period lasted just long enough to get Bush re-elected in 2004. Then the bottom dropped out. Many of the concerns voiced by the war's detractors seemed to spring to life: The weapons of mass destruction that were widely touted as a chief reason for attack never existed; there were ethnic differences within Iraq that were not considered; the invasion allowed terrorist organizations to gain a foothold in Iraq that they probably would not have gotten under Hussein; the list is lengthy and is best reserved for a more informed debate by political scientists and historians. The point is that the short sightedness of anger had led America into a war that would cost more in blood and heartache than most everyone imagined. Anger did not clarify a nation's thinking, it blindsided it.

Bullies in the Seat of Consciousness

This chapter began with a graphic account of a town bully named Ken McElroy who was shot and killed by unknown assailants in the town that he terrorized for more than a decade. The summary really didn't capture the totality of what happened in that small town. More than 30 years after his death, people still shudder at the mere mention of McElroy. Some of the details are almost beyond belief (e.g., he once threatened the town minister with a machine gun!). But in the end, the story of Skidmore's least favorite son was really a story about fear, depression, and anger. The people of Skidmore undoubtedly feared McElroy because of his hot temper and unpredictable nature. The women in McElroy's life, most notably Trena, were most likely victims of battery and sexual predation, and they lapsed into the depressed state of submission so common among victims of abuse. And the angry crowd that had hastily assembled to confront McElroy was in no mood for a calm, rational discussion. Fear was hardly anyone's friend in that small Missouri town. Depression did not give Trena the wisdom to leave her abuser. And anger did not provide any optimistic solutions to a crowd of people who felt betrayed by the justice system—it only gave someone a pretext for murder.

This chapter emphasized that feelings of fear, depression, and anger have their origins in the anatomy and chemistry of the brain. These primordial emotions arise from primitive parts of the brain and are associated with imbalances of neurochemicals that ultimately serve to influence the frontal lobes, the seat of human consciousness. Perhaps in small, measured doses, they might instill clarity of thought, sound judgment, and optimistic yet realistic problem solving. But in larger doses, these emotions bully the mind by forcing it to retreat and cower in fear, to surrender in a state of depression, or to blindly attack in a fit of anger. This happens at the level of the individual who experiences these emotions by systematically distorting reality and preventing that person from thinking rationally. This happens at the societal level where they sap entire nations from the ability to make sound policy choices based upon evidence instead of rumor. Fear, depression, and anger are not just discrete emotions experienced in the minds of individuals, they are cultural forces that can shape the destinies of civilizations. And they do so in ways that are remarkably analogous to the ways they shape the choices made by individual minds, by twisting the truth and robbing the human condition of its higher aspirations.

What is most astounding about the effects of negative emotions on the mind is not how corrosive they can be to logic and reasoned thought; it is the ability of the human mind to persevere despite these effects. Fear, depression, and anger do hurt the ability of the mind to think clearly, but the effects of these emotions are not everlasting. The mind is able to recover from negative emotions more quickly than most people imagine. It is in the recovery from these emotions, not in the emotions themselves, that people show their true wisdom, courage, and clarity of thought. People are resilient. They can cope. They can heal. And they can move on.

CHAPTER 4

Forward, Together, Forward

At 3:05 p.m. on February 14, 2008, a 27-year-old former student in sociology entered Auditorium 1 in Cole Hall on the campus of Northern Illinois University (NIU) armed with a shotgun, three handguns, and at least eight loaded magazines. He wore a black t-shirt with the word "terrorist" written across it. The lecture hall was filled with approximately 120 students in an oceanography class. The instructor, a graduate student named Joseph Peterson, was reviewing a recent exam. In the course of 6 minutes, over 50 rounds of ammunition were expelled, 25 people were injured, and 5 students died (Gayle Dubowski, age 20; Catalina Garcia, age 20; Julianna Gehant, age 32; Ryanne Mace, age 19; Daniel Parmenter, age 20). The shooter committed suicide as well.

Society has become largely numbed to these kinds of events. The mass shooting at Columbine a decade earlier remains the archetypal mass-shooting event. Although not the first mass shooting in the United States, Columbine was notable because it seemed to have all of the elements essential for a dramatic narrative: The sheer scope of the carnage (33 people were shot, and 13 victims were killed over a period of 45 minutes), the youth of the perpetrators and victims (as young as 14), and the detailed preparation that went into the act (as long as a year of planning). The massacre at Virginia Tech in April of 2007 came close to rivaling Columbine in that the death toll was much higher (32 victims) and the perpetrator had sent a macabre videotape to NBC news to foretell his attack. The horror of Sandy Hook was heartbreaking. In comparison, the scope of the NIU shooting, while tragic, was somewhat smaller. And so the national attention paid to it was brief.

The media approached the episode with the all-too-familiar tropes of questions and commentary. Did university police respond appropriately and quickly enough? Were there warning signs given off by the shooter in the days leading up the shooting? What more could have been done? And of course, why did this have to happen? Pan to footage of glassy-eyed students looking to the ground, the sky, or at some undetermined point on the horizon. Quote the subdued words of a community leader trying to delicately walk the line of expressing both sadness and courage in the face of hardship. Invite pundits to consider the event in the context of larger societal issues such as mental health, law enforcement, and the effects of violent media. End the segment in somber reflection on the pain and suffering that the people of this community will keep in their hearts for a long time, perhaps forever.

The implication of such commentary is clear. Tragic events like these elicit strong emotions that are long lasting and nearly impossible to deal with. But there is rarely a follow-up that examines how people actually cope with such events. Make no mistake, the event that took place in Cole Hall on that February afternoon was every bit as tragic and as impactful as any event that might seem more dramatic or more devastating in the eyes of onlookers. The university locked down the campus, cancelled classes for a week, and gave a wide berth to first responders and the requisite investigations that would follow. Two decisions seemed obvious to the outsider: 1) Cole Hall would be closed for the foreseeable future, and 2) the class in which the shooting had taken place, Introduction to Oceanography, would be cancelled.

Well... yes and no. The university closed Cole Hall for nearly 4 years and spent 9.5 million dollars refurbishing it. Auditorium 1 will never house classes again. Introduction to Oceanography was moved to another location on campus, but it was not cancelled. Students were allowed to drop or even withdraw from the university, but by and large, they didn't. In fact, only 10 students that were enrolled dropped the class, a number that was about on par with other courses of that size. The instructor, *who had been shot in the attack*, continued to teach the class with only one significant change to the course: No more unannounced quizzes. No materials were cut and no exams eliminated; the course continued pretty much as scheduled after a 10-day respite.

To be clear, NIU made many accommodations to meet the needs of those who were traumatized by the episode. Indeed, the university has rightfully been commended for its response both in the immediate aftermath and in the long-term. Commendations notwithstanding, the real focus here is on the actual survivors of the attack, the ones in the auditorium who witnessed the violence firsthand. No one would have criticized any of the students if they had decided that they couldn't handle the emotional burden of going to the very same class in which they had seen their peers murdered. No one would have thought less of the instructor, a graduate student teaching one of his first courses, if he would have opted out of teaching for the rest of the semester. Certainly, others have quit with far less cause. And yet, the instructor and the vast majority of the students chose to finish the course despite having every reason to quit. They behaved like survivors, not victims. They demonstrated a phenomenon that occurs far more common than it is often considered— resilience.

A memorial was built as a testament to events of that terrible day. Fittingly titled 'Remembered,' the memorial includes five red granite walls representing the five victims, inscribed with the words 'Forward Together Forward Together Forward' a variation on the school's Husky Fight Song.

$\mathcal{S}$cientific discoveries can often be attributed to serendipity, accidents, or mistakes that lead to unexpected and insightful results. For instance, Ivan Pavlov (1927) was a Russian physiologist who was primarily interested in the process of digestion. His research involved studying the changes that occurred in the digestive juices of dogs while they ate. He noticed that after a period of time, the dogs became familiar with the feeding routine, and often began salivating in anticipation of the food. This anticipatory drool interested him because this response had previously been observed only when eating the food, not before. Of course, what Pavlov had observed would become known as classical conditioning, a phenomenon understood by animal trainers for centuries. But this accidental discovery would transform Pavolv's research and would serve as the foundation for a scientifically rigorous approach to psychology known as Behaviorism. Popular culture would incorrectly remember the physiologist as a psychologist.

At the heart of this book is a case of serendipity. Not as profound or as transformative as the insight made by Pavlov, but it was a genuine case of a happy accident that led to the discovery of a phenomenon. In fact, this case of serendipity happened during the most tedious of tasks for researchers in any discipline: Cataloging old data. Charles "Chuck" Thompson was a researcher at Kansas State University who specialized in autobiographical memory, the memory for events from our own lives. Over the years, he conducted numerous diary studies like the ones mention in Chapter 1. Most of his studies focused on how people remembered the temporal aspect of an event (when the event happened). Being the newest member of the research team under Charles "Chuck" Thompson, the first author of this text (Rich Walker, RW) was given this task.

Time, Memory, and Perspective

Think back to a major life event other than a birthday or anniversary (events that you would likely know the exact date). When did that event happen? One of the reasons why this question is so hard to answer is that memory for life events usually focuses on details such as what happened, why it happened, and who was there. These are the core details of most life events. When events happen is usually less important. Thus, what most people tend to do is make informed guesses about when they think the event happened. These judgments are affected by many things, like how important the event is to a person's current state of mind. If an event is highly relevant to what a person is doing and thinking about at a particular point in time, the event will often be judged to be more recent than it actually is. This phenomenon is called telescoping, the idea being that a temporally distant event is brought nearer to someone much in the same way that a telescope seems to make distant objects appear closer. Ask anyone in the midst of reminiscing about high school how long ago the events feel and their subjective experience is often "not that long." Likewise, if you ask someone focused on the here and now about the perceived age of the same events, they might judge the events to be older than they actually are. This "opposite effect" of mental time travel has been given the clumsy moniker of "reverse telescoping." Both of these phenomena, however, underscore the same general idea: We judge the age of autobiographical events relative to how we think about ourselves in the present moment. The more similar the event feels to our current self, the more recent we judge that event to be. The more dissimilar the event feels to our current self, the older we judge that event to be. That is why reminiscing can sometimes make us feel young and refreshed and other times make us feel old and tired. As Indiana Jones once said, "It's not the years, it's the mileage." Indeed.

Chuck Thompson's studies typically involved people keeping diaries of daily life events and then being tested on the contents of their diaries at some point later in time. Each participant typically provided between 20 and 30 pages worth of data, and each study included from 20 to 50 participants. Each line of data was carefully coded, recorded, and filed. An individual participant would have enough data to fill an afternoon. RW began this task in the spring of 1994, working several hours a week. In the fall of 1994, a half-empty file was discovered. The participant had kept a diary for nine months but had never been tested. RW discovered that the diary belonged to a fellow graduate student that was still in the graduate program at Kansas State. It was quickly decided that this participant would be tested, four-and-a-half years after he had stopped recording events in the diary.

The testing protocol was straightforward. The student had recorded about 270 events in the diary that included a mix of positive and negative events, each described in about 6–10 sentences each. Along with each diary entry, the student had also rated the event along several dimensions. Most relevant was a rating of event pleasantness, or how pleasant or unpleasant the event was at the time of the event. This rating was made on a 7-point scale ranging from –3 (Extremely Unpleasant) to +3 (Extremely Pleasant) with 0 being Neutral. During the testing phase, the student would be read each event in a random order and asked to rate how pleasant or unpleasant the remembered event was now at the time of test, using the same −3 to +3 scale described previously. By comparing the initial pleasantness rating to the current rating, any perceived change in the emotional content of the memory could be assessed.

The absentee participant was surprised with the discovery of the recovered diary entries and with the plans to conduct a memory test. Over the next three days, the student dutifully went through the testing protocols that were set up in three 2-hour blocks. The data was carefully recorded and then coded into a format that could be readily analyzed. And then it happened. A finding that was not expected. Serendipity.

RW plotted the Initial Pleasantness ratings for positive and negative events and then placed them beside the Current Pleasantness ratings for positive and negative events. The pleasantness ratings in this study were a proxy for how strongly people had experienced the positive and negative emotions associated with the events. Initial ratings reflected their emotions when the events had occurred while current ratings reflected their emotions at the time of test. Psychologists sometimes use the term *affect* when describing emotions (positive affect = positive emotion, negative affect = negative emotion). The first thing that RW observed in the graphs was the ratings of Initial Pleasantness were larger than the ratings of Current Pleasantness. This was not too surprising. Over time memories tend to fade and it seemed no great leap to intuit that something similar would probably happen with emotions. The second thing RW noticed was that this fading seemed to be more dramatic for negative events than for positive events. This seemed interesting but was not really relevant to Chuck's main line of research, so RW put together the data graphs and told the research group about what the research had found. They were under-whelmed by the pleasantness finding, but Chuck seemed to sense a growing interest on RW's part, so he suggested that he search back into some data that he had collected several years ago that used similar methodologies. He vaguely remembered collecting event pleasantness data in a few other studies.

RW began digging through data files, in filing cabinets, old boxes, and scanning dozens of 5 ¼ inch floppy disks (for those under 30, imagine flash drives that were 10 times larger but paper-thin, held 100 times less data, and were very fragile). Two more studies were found: The first was a diary study with 43 participants in which they kept diaries for 3.5 months; the second was a diary study with six participants in which they had kept diaries for a full year. Both studies had included ratings of event pleasantness at the time the event had been recorded and at the time of test. The data was plotted for each study and the same pattern emerged in the numbers. Table 4.1 presents the mean initial and final pleasantness ratings for positive and negative events for

EVENT EMOTION						
	Pleasant			Unpleasant		
Retention Interval	Initial Rating	Final Rating	Absolute Change	Initial Rating	Final Rating	Absolute Change
3.5 Months	2.17	2.12	0.05	−1.48	−1.32	0.16
1 Year	1.39	0.93	0.46	−1.48	−0.68	0.80
4.5 Years	1.59	0.47	1.12	−1.62	−0.16	1.46

TABLE 4.1   Mean initial and final pleasantness ratings and mean change between initial and final pleasantness ratings presented separately for 3-month (43 participants), 1-year (6 participants), and 4.5-year (1 participant) retention intervals (adapted from Walker, et al., 1997).

the 3.5-month study, the 1-year study, and 4.5-year study. The table also includes the mean drop in pleasantness ratings for positive and negative events for each of the 3 studies (Walker, Vogl, & Thompson, 1997).

Two things should become clear when examining this table. First, longer retention intervals are associated with greater drops in emotional intensity. The older the event, the more the emotion has faded. Second, the drop in emotional intensity is always greater for negative events than for positive events. On the face of it, this finding suggested that a healthy coping process was operating in the positive and negative memories of the participants in these studies. A few years later, this finding would be described as the *Fading Affect Bias*, the tendency for negatives emotions associated with events to fade more than positive emotions associated with events (Walker, Skowronski, & Thompson, 2003). The data in the change columns in Table 4.1 were transformed into a data graph that quickly captures the effect. Figure 4.1 presents the mean drop in emotional intensity for positive and negative events for the 3.5 month, 1-year, and 4.5-year studies. *Please note that the scores for the negative events have been reversed so that the change scores align with the positive events. Higher bars indicate more emotional fading.* Again, two things should become clear. First, older events showed more fading than recent events. Second, negative emotions always faded more than positive emotions. That consistent gap between the grey bars and the white bars is what all the fuss is about: The Fading Affect Bias.

The Fading Affect Bias, this differential fading of positive and negative emotion, was something that had been observed by psychologists more than 50 years before it had been rediscovered. Cason (1932) asked participants to describe personal events from the week prior and to rate how they felt about each event at the time the event happened and at the time they described using a scale similar to the −3 to +3 scale described previously. Three weeks later

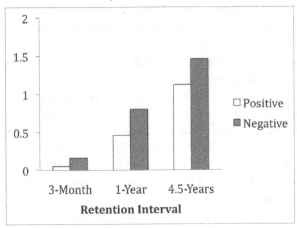

FIGURE 4.1   The mean drop in emotional intensity for positive and negative events for 3 retention intervals: 3 months, 1 year, and 4.5 years (adapted from Walker, et al., 1997).

the same participants were asked to make another judgment about the feelings associated with the events using the same scale. He found that the feelings associated with the events became weaker over time and that this trend was stronger for negative events. This finding was nearly identical to the one found in 1997 with one important limitation, it relied only on retrospective reports of emotion. People might have been distorting the initial emotions associated with their memories, which would render any perceived changes in those emotions meaningless. The 1997 diary study accounted for that issue and still found that negative emotions had faded more than positive emotions.

David Holmes (1970) continued the work started by Cason. Holmes hypothesized that the differential was likely due to differences in how well people remembered positive and negative events. Perhaps people simply remembered the positive events better than the negative events. He had participants record positive and negative events for a 1-week period. They rated the emotion associated with the events at the time they had occurred and after a 1-week interval. He found two things: First, the emotion associated with negative events had faded more than the emotion associated with positive events, thus replicating Cason's findings. Second, there was no substantial difference in how well people remembered positive and negative events. One of the weaknesses of Holmes' study was that it relied upon a handful of events for each participant. Perhaps people were 'cherry-picking' the events in their diaries and it was that self-selection of events that was driving the effect. Almost 30 years later, Walker and his colleagues (1997) replicated these results, but these participants had sampled at least three-months worth of daily events. The finding was the same: People remembered negative events about as well as they remembered positive events, suggesting that the emotion was fading, not the memory itself.

Diary studies do not just provide disembodied ratings for things like emotions. They come alive with detailed descriptions of the events in people's lives. These descriptions provide some insight into what kinds of events are showing evidence of fading emotion. It is easy to imagine that college students would provide garden-variety negative events, including breakups, failed tests, and fights with roommates. In other words, college students would likely record events that were prone to emotional fading. Negative, to be sure, but the kind of events that have limited emotional impact. This is not the case at all. One surprising aspect of this research is that participants routinely record deeply personal and sometimes disturbing events in these studies. People have reported being attacked and robbed, using illegal drugs, getting fired from their jobs, contracting sexually transmitted diseases, suffering significant injuries, getting arrested, and coping with the deaths of loved ones. While these events are in the minority, the fact that participants are reporting them with some frequency suggests that their emotional lives are quite diverse and that the phenomenon of fading emotion extends to a wide variety of life events.

Simply put, evidence of the Fading Affect Bias suggested that people are able to overcome the negativity associated with all kinds of life events. Therefore, negative emotions were not all powerful and everlasting. People could experience disappointment, grief, fear, or anger...and then they could move on. Your grandmother might have considered these findings and offered this tidbit of folk wisdom: "Time heals all wounds." But as it turns out, your grandmother probably didn't know much Freudian psychology, which is almost certainly for the best.

Sigmund Freud (1915, 1937) proposed denial and repression as the cornerstones of his psychoanalytic theory. They are the primary defense mechanisms of the human psyche. When faced with pain or hardship, these twin ramparts are swiftly employed as the ultimate protection the mind has against the harshness of reality. One distorts perception while the other distorts memory.

Let's consider denial first. Denial occurs when people refuse to accept as fact a facet of reality that they are uncomfortable with or that they find inconsistent with their worldview. In Douglas Adams' (1980) classic science fiction spoof *The Restaurant at the End of the Universe*, people could buy a pair of Joo Janta 200 Super-Chromatic Peril Sensitive Sunglasses. These shades were especially designed to help people develop a relaxed attitude towards danger. They worked by turning completely black at the first hint of danger, thus preventing the person from seeing anything that might upset them. In much the same way, denial works by allowing people to ignore any facts that might disturb their sense of well-being. A person might choose to deny the fact outright. Although this kind of denial is rarely captured for all to see, election night 2012 presented a very clear example of this kind of denial. Karl Rove, a conservative commentator and George W. Bush's political consultant, was on Fox News helping to interpret the election results. The focus was on the swing state of Ohio and without its electoral votes, a victory for Romney would be impossible. To his credit, Rove had a keen understanding of voting patterns in the many precincts of the Buckeye state. He knew local Republican leaders, and he had a substantial network of individuals who were feeding him inside information throughout much of the day. The state's trend favoring Barack Obama became clear just after 11:00 p.m., and soon after media outlets began declaring that the President would be re-elected. Fox News did so just after 11:00 p.m. EST. But then Karl Rove broke in on the panel discussion of the results and admonished his colleagues for declaring a winner prematurely. For the next 40 minutes, the conservative outlet found itself in a quandary. The election results were clear to just about everyone except to one of their most valued commentators, who was wholly denying the obvious fact that Obama had been re-elected. Karl Rove was refusing to acknowledge reality partly because he disliked it but mostly because his mental blinders wouldn't allow him to see it. Of course, outright denial cannot be maintained for very long in the face of overwhelming evidence. In the end, even Karl Rove had to admit defeat.

Repression, however, is slipperier, and as it happens, much more relevant to the phenomenon of the Fading Affect Bias. Repression occurs when people fail to remember unpleasant experiences that might upset their generally positive view of themselves. If a person was molested as a child by someone close to them, the memory of that event might challenge their self-image and how they thought about the people they trusted. One could avoid any threats to the self by repressing the memory into the unconscious mind so that it could be dealt with later. The problem with repression, however, is that while the memory may be temporarily unavailable, the negative emotions associated with the memory continue to plague the mind. These unresolved emotions might manifest themselves in mood swings, unexplained anxieties, or more serious psychological problems. Repression is much trickier to spot than denial because evidence for or against it relies solely on events buried in an individual's memory and not events that can be observed in the here and now.

A mobster might lament that "the trouble with buried bodies is that they don't always stay buried." Likewise, the trouble with repressed memories is that they don't always stay repressed. They can resurface unexpectedly and wreak havoc in a person's life. Trained therapists can help potential victims of abuse recover their repressed memories in a controlled fashion so that the memories and emotions can be properly dealt with. At least that's how it's supposed to work. In the 1990s, cognitive psychologist Elizabeth Loftus challenged the reality of repression by questioning the validity of memories that had been recovered in some therapeutic settings. In the late 1980s and early 1990s, there was a rash of people recovering child memories of abuse, some of which that seemed outlandish (e.g., childhood sexual abuse committed by devil worshippers). Some of the techniques used to help recover these repressed memories, like hypnosis, had also been shown to distort memory. Loftus, an expert in eyewitness memory, knew that people's memories were far more malleable than most people realize. She had demonstrated in numerous studies that even minor changes in question phrasing could have dramatic effects on memory. She argued that many of the memories being recovered using dubious methods were actually false memories, created as a byproduct of an interaction between a client in genuine psychological distress and an overzealous therapist looking for (and suggesting) a history of childhood abuse that never actually happened. The attack that Loftus launched against repressed memories was withering and made Loftus a very controversial figure in psychology.

Loftus provided a near fatal blow to the concept of recovered repressed memories in a study that has been dubbed "the lost in the mall" study (Loftus & Pickrell, 1995). In her study, 24 participants were given four short stories describing childhood events that were supposedly provided by family members. Participants were instructed to read the narratives and to try to remember as much as they could about each memory. Three of the event narratives had been provided by a family member while the fourth story was false. It described an event that took place when the participant was about fice years old and had gotten lost for a few hours at a local shopping mall or department store. The interview sessions were friendly and upbeat, but the researcher did press the participants to recall as much as they could. Of the 72 true events, participants remembered 49 or just over two-thirds of them. Of the 24 false stories, 7 people remembered the false event as having actually happened. Although they were not able to describe the event with the same clarity as the real events, Loftus had made her point. A genuinely false memory could be implanted into the mind of an unsuspecting person with very little difficulty. Critics rightfully pointed out that her research, while establishing the reality of false memories, did not automatically eliminate the possibility of repression. It could still be likely that repressed memories were very real and quite common.

The Fading Affect Bias, first documented by Cason (1932) and Holmes (1970), added another stake in the heart of repression, one that might not be obvious on the surface. Essential to the concept of repression is not only that the memory itself be buried in the unconscious mind, but also that the negative emotions associated be retained so that they could torment the conscious mind. Indeed, that is the whole point behind repression; unresolved negative emotions flare up but cannot be directly linked to specific events because the memory for those events has gone missing. The Fading Affect Bias showed that the exact opposite was happening most of the time: Emotions faded while the memories remained. Again, while not entirely disproving the concept of repression, findings like the Fading Affect Bias implied that there was another process operating in memory altogether, a process that can, unlike repression, be readily documented and that shows most people fully capable of coping with life's setbacks.

Documenting a phenomenon in science is hard. A researcher must identify and eliminate alternative explanations for that phenomenon before it can be accepted as factual. This is the healthy skepticism proffered by folks like James Randi and Michael Shermer and is the reason why most of the new scientific discoveries trumpeted in the media and on the Internet rarely go anywhere beyond the first press release. The Fading Affect Bias could well have been such a phenomenon: Interesting at first blush but readily explained by more pedestrian means. That's the way science really works; it doesn't march confidently from one study to the next under the banners of hypotheses and theories. Science meanders a bit, cautiously testing its footsteps before moving ahead. This happens more so with the 'soft sciences' like psychology, which tries to understand the unseen nuances of the mind. Before continuing with the argument that the Fading Affect Bias is evidence of healthy emotional coping, let's first consider four alternative explanations that would render it a mere quirk of data, an illusion with no foundation in reality.

1. The Fading Affect Bias Might Be the Result of How It Is Measured

A broken bathroom scale can alter your perception of how well or how poorly your diet is going. Likewise, the rating scales employed in psychological studies can sometimes inadvertently skew the results of the studies that use them. The change in emotion that constitutes the Fading Affect Bias is dependent upon two such rating scales. The initial pleasantness rating, or how participants felt about the event when it happened; and the current pleasantness rating, or how they felt about the event now. Both were made on the same 7-point scale (−3 Very Unpleasant to +3 Very Pleasant). In one study (Walker, Skowronski, Gibbons, et al., 2003), participants did not make such ratings. Participants were instructed to recall positive and negative memories and then verbally describe the emotion they associated with each event at the time that it occurred and at the time they were recalling it. Participants used almost 90 different words to describe their various emotional states. Those words were then rated in terms of their emotional intensity by other participants in another, unrelated study. Those ratings were then used as data for the event memories recalled by the participants in the earlier study. The results were clear. First, the emotions were initially stronger when the events occurred than when the events were later recalled, suggesting that the emotions had faded. Second, this effect was always stronger for negative events than for positive events. The Fading Affect Bias was not the result of biased rating scales.

2. The Fading Affect Bias Might Be the Result of Regression to the Mean
Regression to the mean is a statistical phenomenon that occurs when a particular measure is taken at two points in time resulting in two different sample means (Nesselroade, Stigler, & Baltes, 1980). The movement in the scores from Time 1 to Time 2 might indicate a real change or it might represent nothing. How is that possible? In any given distribution of scores, most of the scores are congregated around the mean. The more times a researcher samples that distribution of scores, the more likely the sample will come from a place close to the mean. So, if the sample taken at Time 1 is far from the mean, chances are pretty good that the sample taken at Time 2 will be closer to the mean, which makes it look like there is a shift from Time 1 to Time 2, when in reality all that is happening is "regression to the mean." Sports fans may know about this effect by another name, "the *Sports Illustrated* Jinx." A player or team is highlighted on the cover of the magazine because of a standout performance. In the next few weeks, the player or team has a disappointing game that seems to erase the previous accolades. Being on the cover appears to have cursed them. In reality, what has happened was deceptively simple. Athletes on the cover of such magazines are at the top of their game, which means that they are very talented and that they have probably benefited from some luck. Since there is only one way to go from the top (down), a lackluster performance is to be expected after reaching a sport's zenith. The talent remains, but the law of averages dictates that luck runs out. The change in performance is not the result of being cursed, just the consequence of probability.

Since the Fading Affect Bias relies upon two samples of emotion, initial (Time 1) and current (Time 2), it is possible that the change in these scores simply reflects a systematic statistical aberration. Perhaps the first rating that participants make is always more intense than the second rating that they make and this difference creates the appearance of change. To test this possibility, Landau and Gunter (2009) conducted a simple study in which the order of the ratings was reversed for half of the events that participants recalled. Rather than making the initial rating FOLLOWED BY the current rating, the order was simply reversed. If the sequence manipulation reduced, eliminated, or reversed the Fading Affect Bias, regression to the mean would be the most likely explanation. The manipulation did not have any effect, suggesting that regression to the mean is not a tenable explanation for the Fading Affect Bias.

3. The Fading Affect Bias Might Be the Result of Wishful Thinking

Chapter 2 already described the various biases that result in most people holding the belief that negative events and emotions are more frequent and more powerful than positive events and emotions. However, it is still possible that participants' beliefs about how emotions change over time might influence how they perceive emotional changes in their own memories. Put more simply, if people believe that negative emotions fade more than positive emotions, that belief might create the illusion of the Fading Affect Bias. Tim Ritchie and others (2009) tested this possibility by examining people's theories about emotional change and whether they predicted actual changes in emotion. If they did, it would suggest that Fading Affect Bias was a kind of emotional placebo effect. One thing should be pointed out is that most people do not hold beliefs consistent with fading emotion. Much like was argued in Chapter 2, many people tend to believe that emotions last much longer than they actually do, particularly negative emotions. The results suggested that perceived changes in emotionality were not informed by participants' theories of emotion. No matter what they believed, the emotions ascribed to their events faded in a fashion consistent with the Fading Affect Bias.

4. The Fading Affect Bias Might Be the Result of a Biased Sample

The initial data supporting the Fading Affect Bias came from the stereotypical participant found in most psychology studies: White middle-class college students between the ages of 18 and 25. That is a rather narrow slice of humanity. To their credit, these participants provided a wealth of data that included a diverse set of event memories. But if a phenomenon is ever going to have any "street cred," it has to be documented in lots of different kinds of people. To that end, Tim Ritchie and a host of his colleagues around the world (2014) documented the Fading Affect Bias in a variety of samples, including African Americans, Ghanaians, Caucasian Americans, Native Americans, Germans, New Zealanders of European Descent, New Zealanders of Maori and Pasifika descent, Caucasian British, Irish, and Black British. Table 4.2 includes the absolute values of the means for initial affect and current affect ratings, and the mean affect fading score for pleasant and unpleasant events. Ritchie and The Fading Affect Bias can be clearly observed in each of these samples: Stronger in some, weaker in others, but never absent. Ritchie and his colleagues also conceptually replicated the Fading Affect Bias in a sample from Puerto Rico (for a complete summary, see Schrauf & Hoffman, 2007). Clearly, this is a robust effect that has been documented in a variety of samples on three continents and two island nations.

	NEGATIVE AFFECT		POSITIVE AFFECT		FADED AFFECT	
Sample	Initial	Current	Initial	Current	Negative	Positive
African-American	2.25	0.98	2.51	1.81	1.27	0.70
Ghanaian	2.58	1.02	2.68	2.04	1.56	0.64
Caucasian American	2.32	1.00	2.37	2.00	1.32	0.37
Native American	1.93	0.78	2.23	2.16	1.15	0.07
German	2.28	1.10	2.48	1.97	1.18	0.50
Caucasian New Zealander	2.42	1.47	2.41	2.01	0.96	0.40
Maori & Pasifica	2.15	1.43	2.36	1.99	0.73	0.37
Caucasian British	5.09	3.54	5.34	4.82	1.56	0.52
Irish	5.14	3.02	5.28	4.73	2.12	0.56
Black British	5.00	3.15	5.42	4.58	1.85	0.84

TABLE 4.2   Mean ratings of Initial Affect Intensity, Current Affect Intensity, and Faded Affect for positive and negative events per sample (adapted from Ritchie, Batteson, et al., in press).

To describe the Fading Affect Bias purely in terms of emotional fading is incomplete. The emotions associated with event memories do more than simply fade away with the passage of time. Some emotions are rigidly fixed to memories people have of the past while others go through remarkable transformations over time. Still others recede in memory, only to come roaring back to life in an instant. Tim Ritchie et al. (2009) analyzed the responses to 1,200 autobiographical events and identified four ways in which emotions might change over time. Fixed Affect referred to those instances in which the emotions did not change at all. Fading Affect referred to the emotions that showed fading. Flourishing Affect referred to those emotions that became stronger with the passage of time. Finally, Flexible Affect was used to describe events that were initially rated as being positive or negative, but when recalled later had switched to the opposite emotion (e.g., a negative event that was later recalled as being positive). The results of the analyses showed that Fading Affect (47% of all events) was the most common type of emotional change. Fixed Affect (37% of all events) was the next most common experience, followed by Flourishing Affect (12%), and Flexible Affect (4%).

Ritchie et al.'s (2009) results get even more interesting when it is broken down by whether the events are positive or negative. When an event was positive, most events retained their emotionality (49% Fixed Affect) or showed evidence of emotional fading (37% Fading Affect). Less common were cases in which the emotions surged (10% Flourish Affect) or switched from being initially positive to being remembered negatively (1% Flexible Affect). When an event was negative, emotional fading was the most common experience (51% Fading Affect), followed by static emotions (38% Fixed Affect). Interestingly, negative events were much more likely to demonstrate emotional flexibility than positive events (6% Flexible Affect). While the percentages change a bit from study to study, the overall trends that Ritchie and his colleagues documented are stable.

What these statistics tell us is straightforward. Most emotions tend to do one of two things: They fade or they stay put. If the emotion is negative, it is more likely to fade than do anything else. If the emotion is positive, it is more likely to stay put than do anything else. Relatively few positive or negative emotions become stronger with the passage of time or switch from one polar extreme to the other. The overall pattern, however, is that most emotions move from sharp intensity to blunted neutrality. This probably happens because maintaining strong emotions for any length of time takes considerable time and effort. This is particularly true for negative emotions, which tend to sap a person's energy more dramatically than positive emotions. This is mental energy that could be better spent on other things, like dealing with the daily chores of living in the present. Over time, those emotions simply become less and less relevant to what is happening now.

But how long does it take for the emotions to start fading? Weeks? Days? Research suggests that differential fading begins less than 24 hours after an incident occurs. Gibbons, Lee, and Walker (2010) conducted a fine-grained analysis of events over a retention interval of just over three months. They found that negative emotions showed greater fading than positive emotions only one day after the event had occurred. Figure 4.2 presents the mean drop in emotional intensity for positive and negative events across a 90-day retention interval. The data is messy, and to be sure, does not always show a consistent Fading Affect Bias. This is probably because a day-to-day analysis is more likely to reveal the influence of the different kinds of emotional change (Fixed, Fading, Flourishing, Flexible) than an analysis that summarizes the effects of lengthy time periods. But the overall trend is clear, negative emotions showed consistently more fading than positive emotions almost immediately after they occurred. Apparently, Lenny Kravitz was right, *Yesterday is gone*. The emotional impact of most life events is extremely short, and the Fading Affect Bias begins to show itself as little as 24 hours later.

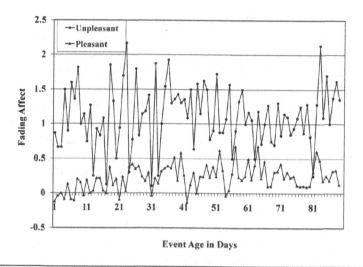

FIGURE 4.2   The mean drop in emotional intensity for positive and negative events across a 90-day retention interval (adapted from Gibbons, et al. 2010).

Emotional fading within 24 hours? To be sure, a lot can happen in that span of time, but is it really possible that people begin picking up the pieces that quickly? You bet. Joachim Stoeber and Dirk Janssen (2011) enlisted 149 participants to complete daily diary reports for 3 to 14 days, reporting the most upsetting failure they experienced each day, how they dealt with the failure, and how satisfied they felt at the end of the day. Most failures occurred at work (38%), followed by failures in their social lives (15%), personal chores (12%), health (9%), household (8%), money (7%), and family/companions (6%). By the end of the day, many of these failures were already starting to show evidence of being reconciled. Three of the most effective strategies for coping with daily failures were to 1) engage in positive reframing; 2) use humor to diminish the impact of the disappointment; and 3) simply accept the failure and to move on. Indeed, a prominent social psychologist had already proposed a mechanism that complemented results like the Fading Affect Bias.

Shelly Taylor's Mobilization-Minimization Hypothesis (1991) helps to explain these findings. This hypothesis posits that all emotions instigate two sets of responses that occur across a wide range of psychological and physiological domains. The first response is the mobilization of resources to cope with the immediate consequences of a negative event. The second response occurs in a more delayed fashion, perhaps over the next several minutes or hours to try to return a person's emotions, cognitive functions, and body to a state of normalcy. Consider what might happen when a person is unexpectedly punched in the face. The person would experience pain and surprise, muscles would be engorged with blood as the body starts preparing to fight or flee, the attention would focus on the attacker to ascertain the potential causes for the punch and what their immediate intentions are likely to be, and the mind would try to quickly fashion an appropriate response. All of this would happen in a few seconds while a person is reeling in surprise. It is the process of minimization, and its goal is to reduce the impact of the event that is most relevant to fading emotion. Once the attack has been adequately resolved, whether through fight or flight or some other alternative, the body releases endorphins to help numb the pain from any injury that was sustained, the attention becomes diffused, and the mind begins to relax. These reactions occur across a wide range of mental and physical systems with two overarching goals: Deal with the immediate situation and then move past it.

Let's look at this theory another way. Strong emotions demand a lot of our mental and physical resources when they occur. The mobilization of resources that Taylor writes about is a system-wide set of processes. Chemicals are being dumped into the bloodstream, muscles are engorged with blood as they ready for action, and the gastrointestinal tract flutters and contracts. Gut-wrenching situations are literally gut wrenching. All of this can make us tire quickly. Ask any boxer or football player. Being "full-on" for just a few minutes is exhausting. The emotional high that can spark tremendous feats of performance is fleeting and is often followed by the need for a respite. Emotions marshal the combined forces of the mind and body for a limited time and then demand repose.

The theory further posits that the state of normalcy for the human condition is to be in a state of slight positivity, not neutrality. Think of positive and negative emotions as being like a teeter-totter on a playground. A balanced teeter-totter responds to weight on either side in the same way. But if one side is shorter than the other, it means that more pressure will have to be exerted on that side to create balance. In these terms, negative emotions are short-sided in Taylor's theory, meaning that the dampening effects tend to be stronger for negative emotions than for positive emotions. The practical upshot is that without much direct effort or intervention, the mind naturally moves towards a state of positivity by selectively dampening negative emotions more vigorously over time. Coping and resiliency may be hard-wired into the human emotional system as a kind of default setting to help people return to a state of normalcy. Positivity is normalcy, the emotional condition in which the mind operates at its best, capable of perceiving reality and optimistic enough to act upon those perceptions.

Back in 2008 on the campus of Northern Illinois University, thoughts of coping and resiliency were the last thing on anyone's mind. The students and faculty were reeling and many thought that the campus community wouldn't recover for months. But then something paradoxically quite mundane and mind-bogglingly extraordinary happened: Life went on. Classes resumed replete with daily quizzes, term papers, and boring lectures. And in the psychology department, data collection continued on a project examining people's perceptions of emotions and resiliency. Hartnett and Skowronski (2010) had started collecting data before the campus shooting with a rather modest goal, to better understand a phenomenon called affective forecasting. Affective forecasting is a lot like weather forecasting. In weather forecasting, one might wonder "how long do you think this cold spell we're in is going to last?" while in affective forecasting, one might ask "how long do you think the emotion you experience as the result of a life event is going to last?" People are notoriously bad at making these predictions, often imagining that their emotions will be felt much more strongly and last for much longer than they actually do. This finding had been documented in many studies of everyday emotions and events (missing the morning train, not making tenure, the end of a romantic relationship, receiving a surprise gift, having your favorite team win or lose the big game, etc.). The Valentine's Day shooting offered a painful opportunity to study this phenomenon with emotional reactions following a real and severe emotional event. Hartnett and Skowronski wondered whether people would be able to accurately predict how long the feelings of shock and sorrow would last. How would the students of Northern Illinois University cope with this tragedy? Would they experience the affective forecasting error, or are the feelings associated with a mass-shooting situation so strong as to defy explanations provided by the affective forecasting literature?

In the fall 2007 semester, 307 participants completed the Profiles of Mood States questionnaire as part of data collection for one of the author's dissertation projects. The Profiles of Mood States is a 36-item scale that asks participants to rate the extent to which they are experiencing six emotional states: depression, tension, anger, fatigue, confusion, and vigor.

Essentially, it is an emotional snapshot of what a person is feeling at that time. An additional 63 participants completed the same survey between February 27 and March 3, 2008, just three weeks after the shooting. Using the fall 2007 data as the baseline for normality, what kinds of emotions would the post-Valentine's Day data show? One could imagine increased levels of depression, tension, anger, fatigue, and confusion (and corresponding lower levels of vigor) as the students were deluged with reminders of the tragedy. For five of the six emotional measures, there was no significant difference between the baseline period before the shooting and the period immediately following the shooting. The students reported that they were no more depressed, stressed, confused, or fatigued than the students assessed before the shooting. The only emotion that showed a noticeable change was that students were angrier after the shooting than before (it should be pointed out that even post-shooting, the average level of anger did not rise above the midpoint of the scale).

But that is not what you would imagine happening, is it? Indeed, in the fall 2009 semester, Hartnett and Skowronski (2010) studied this by collecting POMs data from first-year NIU students who were not on campus the previous year. Fifty-five students completed the Profiles of Mood States and then they were asked to think about the Valentine's Day tragedy as if they had been on campus at the time of the shooting. Specifically, they were asked to *imagine* how they thought they would have felt two to three weeks after the shooting (again, had they been students at NIU and on campus at the time of the shooting). They then completed the Profiles of Mood States again. By comparing their baseline emotions to their imagined emotions, Hartnett and Skowronski (2010) were really capturing the emotional forecasts of these students in a way that would be comparable to the students they had assessed the previous semester. The results could not have been more different. When participants imagined their emotional responses to the shooting, they reported significantly higher levels of depression, anger, fatigue, tension, and confusion as well as significantly lower levels of vigor. In contrasting the students who were on campus during the time of the tragedy to students who imagined being on campus at the time of the tragedy, the results are clear. The students who were at NIU during that difficult period had demonstrated remarkable resilience while the students who were not on campus had imagined themselves as being much more emotionally affected by the tragedy. This led Hartnett and Skowronski to conclude that the capacity to cope with even the most horrific of circumstances is an ability that largely goes unnoticed. People are resilient, but they often don't know it.

The findings of Hartnett and Skowronski are consistent with the work of George Bonanno. George Bonanno (2004) has argued that psychology has significantly underestimated people's ability to thrive after tragic events. Bonanno has studied grief and coping in traditional situations like after the loss of a loved one and in the face of national crises, such as 9/11 and the SARS outbreak (Bonanno, Ho, et al., 2008; Bonanno & Mancini, 2008; Bonanno, Rennicke, & Dekel, 2005; Bonanno, Wortman, et al., 2002). He has identified four basic paths that people follow after experiencing a significant loss or tragedy: resilience, recovery, chronic dysfunction, and delayed trauma. He coined the term "coping ugly" to characterize the last two paths. These are the paths associated with prolonged depression and post-traumatic stress disorder. But these paths are the ones that are taken least often by most people, even in the direst of circumstances. Consider the results of a population-based survey taken a month after the attacks of 9/11, the results of which suggested that about 7% of the population of Manhattan would be classified as having PTSD-related disorders; however within six months, the same survey indicated that the number had dropped to just over 1% (Galea, Ahern, et al., 2003; Galea, Vlahov, et al., 2003). Those who were psychologically traumatized in the immediate wake of the attacks were in the minority. Those who were still traumatized months later were in the extreme minority. Such findings indicate that resilience and recovery make up the most common responses people show in the face of tragedy. Resilience and recovery are two different animals, behaving quite differently. Resilience is steady and stable resistance throughout the entire course of an episode, not merely the absence of psychopathology. Recovery occurs when the individual is initially put off-balance by the upsetting event—recoiling, faltering, and perhaps event breaking down for a period—but then they move back to a state of being functional and productive. This is what happens most of the time for most people, be it in the midst of tragedy or further down the line.

The NIU Tragedy: A Personal Memory by Jessica Hartnett

My article, Hartnett & Skowronski, 2010, tells the story of hope for communities recovering from tragedies and demonstrated that the affective forecasting error appears to apply to even large-scale tragedies. The reason I was able to co-author this study is because I was attending graduate school at NIU and on campus at the time of the shooting. To be clear, I didn't know any of the victims personally, but NIU and DeKalb, IL were my home for six years. It is where I started my career, met my husband, and made lifelong friends. And the shooting broke my heart, but many of my memories surrounding the shooting actually reinforce the fact that love and goodness can still be found even after something awful. And I think that feeling is at the core of this book: There is awfulness. We aren't denying that. But we get through the awful. And even in the midst of the awful, there are still good things. Here is a bit of my story.

The time right after the shooting is a blur. I remember being in lock down with my friend Kristina after we left our weight training class in a building across a common area from Cole Hall, the location of the shooting. I remember watching live feed of my university being captured by the news helicopters circling campus. I remember seeing rows and rows of ambulances from around the NIU area, eager to provide help to the injured. I went to work on campus the next day because routine is good and my graduate advisor, John Skowronski, and fellow graduate students were a source of comfort and normality. There were black and red and white ribbons tied around trees all over town. I cried frequently and randomly. I spent a lot of time with my dearest friends, watching lots of CNN and local news, hungry for information about the shooting. Classes were canceled for a week. There was a big memorial. Then, it was time for classes to resume. In the time-honored tradition of feeding the grieving, the psychology department decided to put out a table of food and treats in the lobby. I made a lot of cupcakes. Then Monday morning came and classes started back up. I was teaching an 8:00 a.m. section of Social Psychology that Monday.

I am not a counseling or clinical psychologist. Helping strangers with deep emotional problems is not my calling. I was worried about how I was to handle the feelings that my 60 students were experiencing after the shooting. I knew that my class would be the first post-shooting class for my students, and I didn't want to further hurt them with perceived insensitivity. During grief counseling provided to my department, we were told that however we would handle the first day back would be the right way for us to handle the first day back. So, I spoke briefly and uncomfortably about the shooting. I introduced the counselor in the classroom. It was amazing…hundreds of mental health professionals from around the country descended on DeKalb so that there would be a mental health professional in every single classroom on the first two days back to class. NIU has about 20,000 students, so this isn't a small feat. Then I lectured for 30 minutes before dismissing the class. I was relieved to have that experience over with but wasn't completely happy with how it turned out.

Then I got an email from my friend and fellow graduate student, Lisa. She is one of the lifelong friends I watched too much CNN with. She is also one of those psychologists that deal with feelings. (She is a school psychologist, one of the warriors who advocates for our children.) Lisa had volunteered to assist with mental health services on campus after the shooting. She was helping coordinate all of the counselors temporarily on campus, including the one who had been present in my classroom. And Lisa was swamped. Her headquarters was the Women's Resource Center on campus, a beautiful old house that is across the street from the psychology building. She was doing her best to keep the counselors informed, fed, warm, on time to the classes they had been assigned to, and filled with coffee. Just Lisa. So a number of Lisa's friends, myself included, went over to help.

In lieu of knowing what I was supposed to do in such a situation (a feeling I was having a lot that day), I looked for chores. I chipped away at the ice on the stairway of the building. I put down salt. I emptied overflowing garbage cans and cleared dining tables. I wasn't mending hearts. But I was taking care of the people who were. That day I learned that everyone has something to offer and you shouldn't have any assumptions about what the thing you have to offer is going to be. I felt like I wasn't

> helping my students sufficiently because I am not a human who can sit and mourn and be vulnerable in a large group. But I could make cupcakes. I could help the helpers. Even then, when we were all so sad, there was hope and abundant goodness in the hearts of the people around me. My brave students coming back to class. My friends comforting me and then knowing they could seek me out for help. All of the counselors who were drawn to our town to provide help.
>
> In spite of the tremendous loss NIU experienced, I remember all of the goodness.

This is not to dismiss the genuine pain and suffering that people experience in these kinds of situations. These are authentic experiences that demand real empathy and sympathy. But the emotions don't last forever largely because they can't. Most people are not wired that way. It is in the nature of humans to move forward. This was the case at Northern Illinois University after that dark day in February. People mourned and then they moved on. Classes resumed, even the class that was directly affected by the shooting continued, taught by the same instructor who had been shot in the attack.

In a way, the enormity of the circumstance seemed to strengthen their resolve to continue. Time and perspective afforded them the emotional space in which they could come to terms with the reality of what happened to them. They gained strength from their social networks, from their religious faith, and from the kind words and actions of the larger Northern Illinois University family. But mostly, they benefitted from the natural coping systems embedded in their minds that moved their emotional experience towards recovery and hope. This sentiment was echoed in an email exchange with Dr. Joseph Peterson[1], now a professor at the University of Wisconsin-Oshkosh. When asked about his decision to continue teaching the course, Joe Peterson was quite transparent. "I did finish the course. I wasn't sure if the class would want me to at first. A few days before we resumed, I emailed the entire class and asked them if they would be alright with me continuing the class with them. I was worried that it might trigger bad memories and responses. The response was overwhelming; they said they didn't want anyone else. It was good for me too; I got to work through my emotions with ~145 people who were going through the same thing I was. It was definitely the most surreal course I have ever taught, but that is to be expected considering everything. I guess the decision was based on a lot of things; the students' needs, my needs, and a duty to finish what we had started together."

Forward, Together, Forward.

CHAPTER 5

Thinking, Telling, and Praying

If the name Chris Pritchard does not mean anything to you, try Googling "Dungeons and Dragons murder," and that will change. The particulars of how he masterminded his stepfather's murder have been detailed by many news outlets, commented on by cultural critics, inspired not one but two made-for-television movies. *Honor Thy Mother* (Greene, 1992) and *Cruel Doubt* (Simoneaux, 1992) as well as the book *Cruel Doubt* by Joe McInnis (1992). The story is filled with lurid details: drugs, alcohol, murder, a two million dollar inheritance, and perhaps the most unusual element, an unhealthy obsession with the fantasy role-playing game Dungeons and Dragons. Here is the short version of the story: Pritchard was convicted in 1990 for planning the murder of his stepfather, Lieth Von Stein, and the attempted murder of his mother, Bonnie Von Stein. Although he wielded no weapon and did not participate in the physical attacks, he plotted with the attackers and even drew a map that guided them to their prey. He spent seventeen years in prison paying his debt to society and was paroled in the summer of 2007. But his story doesn't end there. Pritchard used his time in prison, by all appearances, to actually reform his character.

Pritchard reconciled with his mother, who still carries a scar from her attack, before he was convicted. In prison, he began the nearly two-decade-long process of redeeming his character. He renounced drugs and alcohol, a task that is not as easy as one might imagine while incarcerated. He voluntarily spent much of his time alone, contemplating the path that had led him so far astray. He stopped blaming others for his own actions. He accepted his guilt and his responsibility for the death of his stepfather. When he was released from prison, he was a free man, rehabilitated from his chemical addictions, but he still carried the overwhelming burden of his actions. His next step was truly transformative. He sought mercy and salvation in the eyes of the Lord. But this was not the jailhouse conversion that one might expect from a man convicted of murder. This was no ploy for early parole: His religious conversion happened after he left prison. He is now an active church member living in the central piedmont of North Carolina. He speaks openly and plainly about his sins and he speaks passionately and joyfully about his devotion to God. Not surprisingly, one of his favorite stories from the Bible is the parable of the prodigal son. After turning away from and sinning against his father and God, the prodigal son sincerely cries out for mercy and he receives it. His father accepts him back into the fold after all of his misdeeds and even celebrates his return with a feast. At the heart of the story are the concepts of contrition and forgiveness, topics central to Pritchard's journey.

The story of crime and punishment is a familiar one in the justice system, but such experiences typically end with recidivism, not redemption. Indeed, Pritchard understands that, "When you do wrong, you're supposed to be punished. That's the bottom line. That's how it works."

The sad truth is that it usually doesn't work for many convicted criminals.

Recidivism rates within five years of release from prison hover near 50% (*Pew Trust Report*, April, 2011). The numbers vary by state, by gender and race, and by crime, but the 50% mark is a useful benchmark for thinking about how the American justice usually works. Parolees often have little or no work history, possess few professional or trade skills, have drug and alcohol dependency issues, and often have few connections to people who are genuinely interested in helping them stay out of prison. Society often continues to punish ex-convicts long after their time has been served through formal restrictions and informal stigma. Some of this is common sense. Why hire a person with a criminal record when you could hire someone without one? But much has to do with the way society perceives convicted felons. They become personifications of their crimes in the eyes of other people and are seen only in that light. This marginalization is likely a major factor in why the recidivism rates are so stubbornly high. Seeing no opportunity for honest work or avenues for real growth and change, crime might serve as a tangible meal ticket for some or as a way to vent their frustrations back on to society for others. However, the downward spiral that ex-convicts may find themselves in is not entirely society's fault. Many convicts, both in and out of prison, refuse to accept responsibility for their crimes, and such strident refusal to do so helps to reinforce the distrust society has for them. They do not seem sorry for the crime they committed, only sorry that they got caught. They often turn away from the few genuine opportunities offered to them for real, substantive reform. As with many debates, this could quickly transform into another manifestation of the omnipresent culture of war that seems to be consuming our collective consciousness; in this instance, a contest between the merits of individual accountability espoused by conservatives and the virtues of social responsibility championed by liberals.

And yet, what seems like an insoluble conflict between implacable adversaries can be resolved, if only a few lessons are taken from cases like Pritchard's. First, his story underlines the fact that emotional and spiritual transformations are possible even in the most extraordinary of circumstances. As noted in Chapter 2, this reality goes against the beliefs of most people, the belief that negativity, in all its forms, seems to be more powerful and long lasting. But it isn't. Negative emotions fade, positive emotions survive, and sins can be forgiven.

Second, the story highlights the role of time and patience in such a transformation. The spiritual and emotional changes did not occur overnight, or even over several months. It took almost twenty years. To quote Pritchard himself, "It took me years to get my head screwed on straight." His observation is spot on. When Pritchard went to prison, he was a young man in his early twenties who did not consider what might happen after he was finally set free. Prison was the only future he considered at that time. While it is true that everyday emotions can begin to fade fairly quickly, sorting out the long-term ramifications of the behavior like Pritchard's take much longer. The passage of time affords a person the benefits of emotional distance, maturity, and clarity of thought.

Finally, the story calls attention to the role of rehearsal and disclosure in the journey towards absolution. Rehearsal is a key process in memory consolidation; in other words, how people form fixed and stable long-term memories. In many ways, it is the same process used by actors to learn their lines, except that rather than learning dialogue people use rehearsal to mentally replay their own experiences in order to better understand them. Some of this rehearsal is private, occurring solely in the mind. This is the realm of thought. Some of this rehearsal is social, occurring in the conversations between friends, colleagues, and even total strangers. This is the realm of storytelling. And finally, a third kind of rehearsal occurs in the private conversations one can have during the ritual of prayer. Prayer exists in the space between private thought and social conversation. The mix of privacy and intimate disclosure afforded in prayer allows for deep reflection and self-discovery.

Thinking. Talking. Praying. Pritchard had the time to do all three. He mentally replayed the sequence of events as the mental fog induced by habitual drug use slowly lifted away. He has spoken about what happened numerous times to people in large public settings and in much more intimate situations. And he has prayed and continues to pray every day for God's love, wisdom, and mercy. In this chapter, three mechanisms of emotional change will be considered: Thinking, talking, and praying. These mechanisms can be observed and, in some cases, manipulated in psychological research. These mechanisms have consequences for the emotions associated with life events that are demonstrable and distinguishable. Thinking, talking, and praying can transform the way in which a person experiences everyday life events and ultimately how a person gives meaning to the entirety of life itself.

Thinking

We have millions of memories. From time to time, these memories, tucked away in our neurons, surface for a variety of reasons. We all have the experience of unintended memory prompts (e.g., your co-worker mentions that her daughter has an ear infection and you have a strong memory of a sleepless night with your own child), memories prompted by real-time decisions (e.g., you almost go out to a restaurant until you remember the terrible service you had last time you visited), or memories that haunt us (e.g., where you were on 9/11/01).

But why do we constantly refer back to the past so often? To quote another psychologist: "Thinking is for doing" (Fiske, 1992). That is to say, our minds are the result of millions of years of evolution. And evolution gets rid of the waste (sorry, Cro-Magnons!). And evolution has created and maintained complicated brain structures to help us retain and retrieve memories. Thus, it is reasonable to assume that access to and use of our memories helps us survive. But how?

Certainly, much has been written about the negative effects of revisiting old memories upon well-being. Great literature has often warned against it, in the form of Jay Gatsby (don't be obsessed with memories of your former flame; Fitzgerald, 1925), Ms. Havisham (don't be obsessed with memories of being left at the altar; Dickens, 1860), or Franny and Zooey (don't be obsessed with memories of past accomplishments; Salinger, 1961). And, of course, the story of Pritchard echoes the Dostoyevsky's 1866 classic *Crime and Punishment*—with the significant difference that the novel described how being obsessed with guilt following a murder slowly destroyed the novel's protagonist, while Pritchard found redemption.

Moving away from literature, modern psychology considers "recurrent and intrusive distressing recollections of the event, including images, thoughts, or perceptions" to be criteria for a diagnosis of post-traumatic stress disorder (American Psychiatric Association, 2013). A feature of dementia is a mix-up of the present with time periods from the past. One of the author's grandfathers (who died from Alzheimer's disease), frequently thought he was 18 and attending basic training camp in preparation of serving during World War II...in 2008.

Well, then, why do we have complex brain structures for the storage and retrieval of memories if popular belief is that they exist to foil us? Is thinking about the past always bad? We will explore four bodies of research literature that provide evidence that thinking about our memories can increase well-being and help us understand who we are. First, research on thinking about the past (here, called nostalgia) has found that revisiting the past can actually increase feelings of positive regard and even social bonding. We will then consider two separate lines of research looking at how writing about the past affects us. They come from seemingly disparate fields: Applied positive psychology and the psychology of writing about trauma. They both have come to the same conclusion: Writing about the past makes us feel better and can even make us healthier. Finally, we will circle back to research linking thought to the experience of fading emotion.

Nostalgia

One way in which we revisit the past is via nostalgia. On the surface, this seems to tap into the popular psychology notion that thinking about the past is bad for us. Thinking back, with great feeling, upon times in our past that can never be again should only cause us pain. Such daydreaming seems, at best, a waste of time and, at worst, a possible trigger for undesirable pain and yearning. However, while romantic notions of yearning for a lost love may dominate our thinking about nostalgia, such memories represent only a small fraction of our autobiographical memory. Costantine Sedikides and Timothy Wildschut (along with several co-authors) have performed extensive research in this area, and he has found evidence of just this. Their data suggests that nostalgia is a coping mechanism we employ when we are in bad moods, and that nostalgia makes us feel closer to our friends, better about ourselves, and happier (Wildschut, Sedikides, Arndt, & Routledge, 2006). One of the 2006 studies started by putting people into either a positive, negative, or neutral mood by reading a positive, negative, or neutral news story. Participants then completed mood scales (indeed, their mood matched the story they read) as well as a nostalgia scale. The nostalgia scores were highest among the individuals in the bad mood condition, taken as evidence that nostalgia is used to cope with a bad mood. However, arguing that nostalgia is a coping mechanism (and not a negative side effect) is conjecture. As such, in a subsequent study, participants were either asked to recall a nostalgic event in their life or any event that happened in the last week of their life. Participants then completed surveys of social bonding, positive self-regard, and positive affect, and the nostalgia participants scored higher on all three scales than did their non-nostalgia counterparts.

But the role of nostalgia goes beyond just feeling good. Some evidence suggests that nostalgia bolsters the very meaningfulness of our lives (Routledge, Arndt, Wildschut, Sedikides, Hart, Juhl, Vingerhoets, & Schlotz, 2011). In this study, each participant was put into a nostalgic mood. The method for doing so is very clever: At an earlier time, participants listed songs that were deeply meaningful and nostalgic for them. At the time of the experiment, participants are presented with the lyrics of their previously nominated, nostalgic song. The control group for this experiment consisted of individuals who read the lyrics of someone else's nostalgic song. The results found that reading the meaningful lyrics made a person feel more nostalgic when compared to the control group (which just demonstrates that the manipulation worked) AND that the nostalgic song group also reported finding life more meaningful.

However, the usefulness of nostalgia in order to increase positive self-regard and a sense of social bonding may be mediated by something known as "attachment-related avoidance" (Wildschut, Sedikides, Routledge, Arndy, & Cordaro, 2010). Attachment-related avoidance is a tendency to not find comfort in bonding with other people during tough times. It is thought to be the result of having a childhood in which caregivers didn't provide consistent support and comfort. Across five studies, Wildschut and his colleagues found that people who were high in avoidance do not seek out nostalgia as a way of coping with loneliness (while non-avoidant people use nostalgia as a coping mechanism for lonely situations). Oddly, it appears that we use nostalgia in place of calling or visiting someone we love if we have healthy attachments, while people who are less capable of social connectedness tend to avoid the use of old memories for such purposes.

To this point, we've provided evidence to suggest that revisiting old memories can help us make peace with unpleasant old memories, can increase positive affect, and can even be used as a coping mechanism for dealing with feelings of loneliness. Next, we will discuss two bodies of literature that explicitly studied the impact of past memories, good and bad, on well-being.

Purposeful Reflection on the Good and the Sad

More evidence for positive side effects of thinking about the near-past is an intervention from Positive Psychology known as the Three Good Things intervention. Positive psychologists, in addition to studying subjective well-being, positive emotion, and character virtues (Seligman & Csikszentmi-halyi, 2000) have created practical interventions that individuals can employ to increase well-being. One such intervention is the aptly titled the "Three Good Things" exercise, which consists of writing down three good things that have happened over the course of the day and a brief description of why those good things happened ("I dropped my son off at daycare and I watched him scamper off to play with his friends, because my son is friendly and the day-care staff encourage such behaviors"). The three good things are typically recorded at the very end of the day, the exercise is maintained over the course of several days or weeks, and the short-term reminiscing is limited to the last twenty-four hours. Follow-up efficacy research has demonstrated that this exercise seems to increase well-being for weeks after the initial experiment (Seligman, Steen, Park, & Peterson, 2006). Compared to a control group, happiness levels are higher in the experimental group a full *six months* after the completion of the Three Good Things task.

While the long-term effectiveness of the Three Good Things Intervention may be surprising, it really isn't that surprising to learn that writing about the pleasant things in our lives makes us happy. So does watching an uplifting movie or eating a really good cupcake. But the positive gains made by reflecting on the past are not limited to positive reminiscing. Indeed, research has found that writing about traumatic events, like one's own battle with cancer, can make people happier. Since the 1980s, social psychologist James Pennebaker has been asking research participants to write about their own unpleasant memories. While this seems to be the opposite of the Three Good Things exercise, the outcomes of the exercises are similar in the ability to increase well-being.

In one of his earlier studies (Pennebaker, Kiecolt-Galser, & Glaser, 1988), undergraduates were asked to write (four times on four consecutive days) about either "their most traumatic thoughts and feelings" or about the mundane details of daily life. Blood samples were collected from all participants at the very beginning of the study, at the conclusion of the study, and six weeks after the end of the study. The blood work was then tested for immune system functioning and found gains in functioning for the trauma group (and especially strong gains for individuals who indicated that they were writing about traumas that they had never shared with anyone else).

A second study used a group of medical students and studied immune system functioning following a Hepatitis B vaccine (Petrie, Booth, Pennebaker, Davison, & Thomas, 1995). This group was used since vaccination taxes the immune system. Previous work found the effectiveness of the vaccine is hampered by stress (hence, an intervention to lower stress may increase the effectiveness of the vaccination). This study was very similar to the 1988 study: Again, a control group that wrote about time management in their daily lives and an experimental group assigned to write about personal traumatic events once a day for four days. And not just any trauma, but the worst and most traumatic experiences from the individual's past. The medical students then received their vaccination. Over the course of the experiment, blood was drawn to monitor the students' responses to the vaccination. Researchers found that the students in the trauma writing condition, who were asked to think about awful stuff from their past, actually had a healthier immune response than their non-trauma peers.

Together, these two studies imply that thinking about past trauma is beneficial. Writing about it appears to increase subjective well-being and improve immune system functioning.

Thinking and the Fading Affect Bias

Given the wealth of research showing that thinking (and writing) about our pasts can help create positive moods and help people cope with life's hardships, it should come as little surprise that researchers have tried to examine the link between such retrospective thinking and the Fading Affect Bias. Of course, being psychologists, they adopted a slightly different term for such thinking: rehearsal (Ritchie, Skowronski, Wood, Walker, Vogl, & Gibbons, 2006). Here, rehearsal refers to simply thinking about the memory and reliving it mentally. There are two main classes of rehearsal: private and social. Private refers to simply thinking about the memory while social rehearsal refers to instances when we share memories with other people. This was examined in one research study by asking participants how often they 1) rehearse for no apparent reason; 2) rehearse in response to one's own good or bad mood; 3) rehearse when reminded by environmental cues; 4) rehearse to reflect on the meaning of an event or to better understand it; 5) rehearse the event so it is not forgotten; and 6) rehearse the event to make myself think or feel about myself in a certain way. The researchers found that when people engage in "revisiting a memory to better understand" or "savor the memory," people tend to speed up the Fading Affect Bias.

Walker, Skowronski, Gibbons, Vogl, and Ritchie (2009) followed this research up by having 337 participants retrieve a number of positive and negative memories and then asking them to consider how often they had thought or talked about the events since they had happened. Specifically, they asked how often 1) the memory had unexpectedly popped into their minds (involuntary rehearsal), 2) the memory had been thought about to help maintain the memory's accuracy (maintenance rehearsal), 3) the memory had been thought about to re-experience its emotional content (re-experience emotion rehearsal), and 4) the memory had been thought about to help understand the event (understanding rehearsal). Negative memories were a bit more likely to be involuntarily rehearsed than positive memories. Positive memories were more likely than negative memories to be rehearsed for all of the other reasons (maintenance, re-experience emotion, understanding). Most importantly, events that were frequently rehearsed showed less affective fading than events that were infrequently rehearsed. For three of the four rehearsal types examined in this study, positive memories were more likely to be rehearsed than negative memories. Put another way, deliberately thinking about positive event memories helps to maintain the positive emotional content of those memories.

It appears that the act of purposefully revisiting a memory as to understand it better or to relive its emotion both increase that speed with which negative affect associated with unpleasant memories fades away and allows us to continue to enjoy the positive affect associated with our happy memories. By thinking about our bad memories for these two purposes, we are actually encouraging them to hurt less upon retrieval. However, memories aren't just for mulling. Memories are frequently shared with others. We all have our go-to anecdote that we like to share, and we find ourselves sharing our past experiences as to inform the present. And just as mulling memories impacts the present self, so does talking about them.

Telling

One of the more formal situations in which we talk about our memories is during psychotherapy. And, of course, if you are a bunch of psychologists writing about psychotherapy, you need to address the man who got everyone talking about psychotherapy: Sigmund Freud. Freud's relationship with therapy and psychology is quite complicated. While he is regarded as the father of modern psychotherapy (while he was not the first to practice verbal psychotherapy, he was the most influential), his influence in psychology has waned significantly—with *Time Magazine* asking the question on the cover of its November 29, 1993 issue if Freud's influence in psychology is dead? Freud started his career as a medical doctor in Vienna, Austria, who was interested in disorders of the brain. Initially, Freud trained in hypnosis as his main therapeutic technique but eventually rejected hypnosis in favor of more effective ways to treat nervous disorders. These new techniques involved having patients talk about their concerns (one of the reasons why Freud's patients called his form of therapy the "Talking Cure").

His techniques were groundbreaking and helped patients in ways that other types of therapy at the time could not. One of his most useful techniques was Free Association—a technique where the patient was allowed to talk freely about whatever ideas or memories occurred to them without any restrictions or censorship. Essentially the patient was encouraged to say whatever came to mind without any filter. The purpose of Free Association was to learn about the patterns of thoughts and feelings of the patient without any judgment and to get to the underlying unconscious associations within the patient that is causing psychological distress. Additionally, Freud used dream analysis in order to discover unconscious motives hidden within the contents of dreams.

While Freudian psychoanalysis is not popular anymore, it has influenced other forms of psychotherapy that are still very popular and useful. One such style is from Carl Rogers and his client-centered therapy. Client-centered therapy is very different from Freudian psychoanalysis. It focuses on the abilities and insights of the client rather than those of the therapist. In other words, the therapist does not have to uncover the clients' deep dark secrets...the client does. This style of therapy involves a relationship between the client and therapist where the client talks about their problems and the therapist empathetically listens.

Client-centered therapy allows the client to take the lead and direct the therapy. The therapist encourages the client to talk about what is bothering him and provide a context in which the client can become aware of and accept his own feelings and learn to trust his own decision making. To do this, the therapist is trained in empathetic listening (Raskin & Witty, 2007), which entails understanding what the client is saying or feeling at any given moment from the client's perspective rather than their own.

Another contemporary form of therapy is cognitive therapy. Cognitive therapy's main premise is that maladaptive thoughts affect peoples' reactions to everyday situations. For example, a person with social anxiety may have irrational thoughts of being judged and scrutinized by others. The purpose of cognitive therapy is to identify these maladaptive thoughts and replace them with more adaptive ways of thinking and coping with the real world. Returning to our example, one with social anxiety must be taught that they probably aren't being judged and scrutinized (and even if they are, it isn't the end of the world).

One of the most influential pioneers in cognitive therapy is Aaron Beck. Beck's approach is more Socratic in nature. In therapy, he leads the client through a series of questions so that the client, in turn, can use the information gained by these questions in order to gain self-insight and correct maladaptive thoughts (Beck & Weishar, 2007). In this style of therapy, the therapist takes on more of a teacher role—even assigning homework to the client to do between sessions.

While all three styles of therapy described here are different, all three have the same purpose: to help the client. While that's the main goal, each style gets there in a different way. However, all three styles do have a common and essential element: the client needs to share sensitive information. Talking is the most important part of therapy; it allows the therapist to better understand the client, direct the therapy, and encourage the client to learn what is going on inside their head. In fact, some research suggests that talking to other people can help the person who is doing the talking, the person who is listening, and the relationship between the two, specifically within the area of self-disclosure.

Self-Disclosure

Self-disclosure occurs when we share personal information about ourselves (Harvey & Omarzu, 1997). While this can occur over the course of therapy, it also occurs in far more mundane settings during our interactions. Arthur Aron and colleagues (1997) did an experiment where they had participants who were complete strangers carry out self-disclosure tasks over a 45-minute session and compared them to participants who engaged in comparable small-talk tasks. They found that the pairs that did the self-disclosure had higher post-interaction closeness than the small talk group. In other words, self-disclosure makes us feel closer to other people.

Other research on self-disclosure was conducted by Nurcan Ensari and Norman Miller (2002). They did a study to investigate how self-disclosure can help people with different world views form positive impressions of each other. Participants who self-identified as liberal had an interaction with a confederate who self-identified as conservative. The participant asked five personal questions (self-disclosure condition) or five impersonal questions. After that, the participant and confederate performed tasks where they had to work together and, afterwards, evaluate their work partner. The results showed that when the confederate self-disclosed, they had more positive evaluations from the research participant. In essence, they found that self-disclosure encourages people to like you. Perhaps someone will let Congress in on this study.

Also, self-disclosure can lead to self-reflection that makes us feel better about ourselves. Anita Kelly and colleagues (2001) did two experiments looking at how self-disclosure affects the discloser. In the first study, participants indicated that telling secrets to confidants lead to new self-insights which, in turn, lead to positive feelings. In the second study, participants were randomly assigned to write about their secrets while trying to gain new insights and were compared to a control group (who wrote about what they did the previous day). The research found that the insight group felt more positive about their secrets than the control group did about their events of the previous day. The idea is that these insights allow us to feel better about secrets that may be bothering us. In other words, talking to others (or ourselves) about our problems lets us figure out what to do about them.

Talking and the Fading Affect Bias

Self-disclosure not only makes us feel better about ourselves but has an impact on our emotions. Research by John Skowronski and colleagues in 2004 found that self-disclosure has an effect on the Fading Affect Bias (FAB). In one study, participants recalled and recorded four autobiographical memories Two events, one positive and one negative, were events that participants had frequently talked about with other people (at least ten times). The other two events (one positive and one negative) were events that had not been frequently related to others (five times or fewer). Participants rated their affect both when each event occurred and at event recall (-3 = *extremely unpleasant*; 0 = *neutral*, $+3$ = *extremely pleasant*). The results showed that the FAB was moderated by how

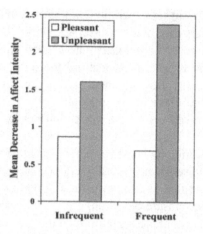

Frequency of Disclosure

FIGURE 5.1   The mean drop in affect intensity for pleasant and unpleasant events for events that were infrequently and frequently disclosed to others (adapted from Skowronski, et al., 2004).

often events had been talked about. Events that were frequently disclosed evinced a much larger FAB than events that were not (Figure 5.1).

In a second study, Skowronski and his colleague were not just interested in how often people talked about their memories but in how many people with whom they had shared their memories. In this study, participants recalled and recorded six autobiographical memories (three positive, three negative). Participants again rated their affect both when each event occurred and at event recall. In addition, participants also estimated how often they had disclosed each memory to other people. Moreover, participants were given a list of person categories (e.g., mother, friend, coach) with whom events might be discussed and were asked to circle all of the types with whom an event was shared. The results again showed that the rapid fading of negative emotion (and savoring of positive emotion) was moderated by the number of people with whom the event had been shared. That is to say, talking about an event with lots of different people led to a stronger FAB (Figure 5.2).

So far, these results suggest a link between talking and fading affect, but they do not demonstrate that talking causes fading. Perhaps people are more inclined to talk about events that had already started to fade in their emotional content and are, therefore, "safer" or less painful to talk about. In a third study, Skowronski and his colleagues were interested in establishing a causal linkage between talking about event memories and the FAB. Participants first recalled six event memories (three positive, three negative) and provided written descriptions of those events. Researchers collected the event descriptions

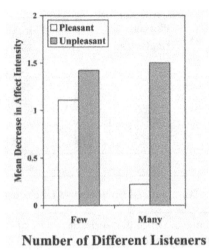

Number of Different Listeners

FIGURE 5.2   The mean drop in affect intensity for pleasant and unpleasant events for events that were shared with few and many people (adapted from Skowronski, et al., 2004).

and randomized the events into three different conditions. Participants were placed in a room with other participants and given a task that resembled speed dating.

1. Participants were told to share two of their events (one positive, one negative) with two other participants.
2. Participants were told to share two of their events (one positive, one negative) with one other participant.
3. Participants were told not to share two of their events (one positive, one negative) with anyone.

Therefore, two events were shared two times, two events were shared one time, and two events were shared 0 times.

At the end of the study, participants were asked to rate the emotional content of their memories. The results were clear; the social disclosure of the events to fellow participants had led to emotional fading. The more they had shared their events, the stronger the FAB was found to be (Figure 5.3).

So, the evidence suggests that talking about life events is beneficial in many of the same ways that thinking about them is helpful. When we describe our experiences to others, we put ourselves in a spotlight that encourages self-reflection. We are encouraged by others to accentuate the positive aspects of our lives, and we are able to put negative events into a perspective that affords emotional healing and personal growth. This is certainly the case for

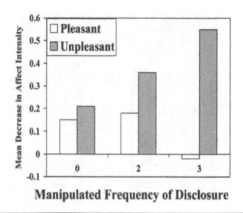

Manipulated Frequency of Disclosure

FIGURE 5.3 Experimental evidence that social disclosure of events moderates the FAB (adapted from Skowronski et al., 2004).

Pritchard. He has told his tale of sin and forgiveness to hundreds of people in settings both large and small. But for him, it is more than just the act of self-disclosure that drives him. Like many Christians, he feels the need to bear witness to the people around him. And this brings up a third kind of rehearsal, prayer. In some ways, prayer is a hybrid of thinking and talking, but it is so much more.

Praying

Praying is a lot like thinking in that is usually private. Praying is also a lot like talking in that you are sharing. Only instead of sharing with a therapist or a friend, you are sharing with a higher power. It is a combination of thinking and talking—and yet it is much more. The basic definition of prayer is individualized ritual (Janssen, de Hart, & den Draak, 1990). A ritual is a prescribed pattern of behavior. Everyone has them, from checking your cell phone first thing in the morning to brushing your teeth before going to sleep. However, not all rituals are so mundane. Religion is one area that tends to be defined by rituals. Lawson and McCauley (2002) explain how religious rituals are different from everyday rituals in five main ways: 1) they involve a deity; 2) the aim of religious rituals is to contact, identify with, or influence the deity; 3) when the rite in question has been completed, the sequence of enabling actions ends—in other words, the supplicants' work is done, and what happens next is up to the deity; 4) religious rituals can only be undertaken by members of a specific religious group—outsiders are not allowed to be involved in sacred rituals; and 5) the ritual must be exercised through special religious figures. Having established these ground rules, we will next discuss two different ways in which people reach out to their deity—communally via worship and individually via prayer.

Worship

One form of group religious ritual is worship. Sometimes referred to as "corporate prayer," worship is the public ritual of a religion that creates a common experience that forges the members of a group into a community of worshippers (Whitley, 1964). In other words, worship is what makes individuals who go to the same religious service into a congregation of people who know and are concerned with each other. Ritual helps build the sense of congregation via worship rites that are performed in a religious ceremony. Typically, they are either directly or indirectly mandated by their deity and usually involve aesthetically pleasing characteristics such as music, singing, or dancing (Spilka, 2005).

Group worship can be very meaningful. It supports courage in times of stress (Klausner, 1961), personal strength from group appeals to a higher power, and can be therapeutic (Empereur, 1987). For worship to be beneficial, the worshipper needs to understand the religious service is a ritualistic communication with themselves, others, and God (Aune, 1993). Worship fosters the social support network found in church. Social support is the emotional, informational, or material assistance provided by other people. It is encouraged by faith groups in a number of different ways: established members of a congregation tend to help new members understand the group norms of the church (informational support), they also give in a time of need (material assistance), and they can be a built in network to give affection and nurture each other (emotional support). Worship also allows people to feel interrelated to others in a similar situation. This is a rather well-known social psychological phenomenon: the idea of strength in numbers. Humans feel safer in groups and can protect and help one another in times of trouble (Baumeister & Leary, 1995).

This discussion of ritual implies a deep connection between rituals and religions but that is not as necessary as spirituality. Spirituality can be defined as a personal search for existential meaning (Doyle, 1992). This is distinct from religiosity, which involves commitment to the beliefs and practices of a particular tradition (Peteet, 1994) in that people can be high on spirituality and low on religiosity—they can be spiritual but not devoted to any specific religion. Typically, however, spirituality and religiosity are correlated.

What Is Prayer?

There are many, many different kinds of prayers, from a quick prayer of thanks before a meal or a desperate prayer for divine intervention on behalf of a sick relative. Regardless of why or how a person is praying, prayer can typically be broken down to three main parts: an introduction, a goal-directed middle, and a conclusion (Magee, 1957). The introduction involves a glorification of the target deity. This can be as simple as saying "Dear God," but can involve some form of adoration such as saying "O great and glorious God." The second part of prayer is the goal-directed middle. This is where the individual who is praying discusses the need for help and specifically what kind of help is needed (e.g., "I am sick and I need the strength to get through my surgery"). The final part of the prayer is the conclusion. This usually includes another endorsement of the power of the deity. While this is the generic formula for prayer, they can be very personalized as far as content. The main purpose of prayer is to communicate with the deity.

While there is a basic formula for prayer, the content and needs expressed by prayer mature as we grow. Long, Elkind, and Spilka (1967) found that the understanding and use of prayer goes through three stages. The first stage is called the global, *undifferentiated stage*. At this stage the understanding of prayer is very vague and typically prompted by a parent. The second stage is the *concrete differentiated stage*. For children, prayer is rather simple: it is a tool used to get something. Prayer is seen as a force that will help produce an outcome. As we grow, prayer and worship become infused with deeper meaning, which leads to the final stage, *abstract, differentiated stage*. Here, prayer becomes an external expression of an internal process—a conversation with their deity.

However, the ways in which prayer can differ extends far beyond a child praying fervently for a new toy while their parent prays fervently to become a better parent. There are many different forms of prayers, and they are complex. Some researchers (Foster, 1992) suggest 21 different forms of prayer while others (Richards & Hildebrand, 1990) define over 100 categories of prayer. In order to better understand the variety of prayers, researchers Poloma and Gallup (1991) actually created a classification system, the *Varieties of Prayer*. They identified four forms: colloquial, petitionary, ritual, and meditative. Colloquial prayer is conversational in nature and may include things such as confessions or thanksgiving. It is kind of the generic overall form of prayer. Petitionary prayer is the most widely used. It is a request form of prayer for the deity to provide what the supplicant asks for. Intercession for others, praying for others, and self-aggrandizement can also fit under petitionary prayer. Ritual prayer is ceremonial prayer. It is prayer that occurs in a pattern or has a preset statement. Prayers like "Our Father" and "Hail Mary" fit into the category of ritual prayer. Finally, meditative prayer focuses on the desire for experiential communication with a deity.

Benefits of Prayer

Prayer is a near universal phenomenon, observed in all major world religions. Whenever psychologists note universal phenomena, it triggers one very important question: WHY? And researchers have found some answers to that question (that are far more earthly and mundane than benevolent deities granting divine intervention). Prayer appears to help dealing with health issues and aids emotional adjustment to diseases. It helps stave away depressive feelings (Parker & Brown, 1982) and helps individuals cope with the stress of cardiac surgery (Saudia, Kinney, Brown, & Young-Ward, 1991), kidney transplantation (Sutton & Murphy, 1989) and being on Hemodialysis (Baldree, Murphy, & Powers, 1982). It also helps deter the use of alcohol and drugs (Shuler, Gelberg, & Brown, 1994).

It also helps people cope with life stressors. One of the main effects of prayer is tension reduction—it helps people reduce the stress and tension that they are experiencing—much like any other ritual (Elkins, Anchor, & Sandler, 1979). It is an important form of support for the elderly (Shaw, 1992) as well as parents who care for children with disabilities (Bennett, Deluca, & Allen, 1995). It also contributes to marital adjustment (Gruner, 1985). Prayer also has a positive relationship with broad variables such as life satisfaction, quality of life, general well-being, and purpose in life (Francis & Burton, 1994; Poloma, 1993; Poloma & Pendleton, 1991). In other words, prayer is a very significant aid in coping with life.

While prayer is a more active way of beseeching a deity, not everyone attempts to commune with the mystic in this manner. A related but unique way of doing so is via meditation, which will be described next.

Meditation

An offshoot of prayer is meditation. Walsh and Shapiro (2006) define meditation as "a family of self-regulation practices that focus on training attention and awareness in order to bring mental processes under greater voluntary control and thereby foster general mental well-being and development and/or specific capacities such as calm, clarity, and concentration" (pp. 228–229). Meditation may or may not be religious, and it may or may not be spiritual. There have been a number of studies that demonstrate the positive effects of mediation on various aspects of health and well-being. Shapiro, Schwartz, and

Bonner (1998) found that in an eight-week period participants using medita-tion-based stress relieving activity reported less stress and anxiety than people who did not do it. Wachholtz and Pargament (2005) conducted a study where they compared the effects of spiritual meditation with secular meditation. Par-ticipants were separated into two groups, one mediated with a spiritual mantra (God loves me) while the other group used a secular mantra (I am loved). At the end of two weeks, participants in the spiritual meditation were associated with significantly greater anxiety reduction, greater spiritual well-being, and greater ability to withstand pain than the participants in the secular meditation group. Additionally, meditation has been shown to improve physical and men-tal health. Meditation has improved stress management skills, lowered blood pressure, and lowered cholesterol (Patel, Marmot, Terry, Carruthers, Hunt, & Patel, 1985). Meditation has even been shown to extend the lives of older per-sons (Alexander, Langer, Newman, Chandler, & Davies, 1989).

Psychologists, being psychologists, have investigated ways to take these positive effects of prayer and use them in therapeutic settings. Targ and Levine (2002) compared the effects of a mind-body-spirit group intervention for women with breast cancer with a control support group. The spiritual group was taught to use meditation and other spiritual practices as a coping strategy along with the support group. While both groups demonstrated posi-tive changes in quality of life, depression, anxiety, and spiritual well-being, the spiritual group also showed an increase in spiritual integration and less avoidance behavior when coping with stress and anxiety.

Benefits of Being Prayed For

While how prayer affects people who pray may not be that surprising (there has to be a reason that so many people have been praying for so long), there is some interesting research investigating the outcomes for targets of those petitionary prayers. The results might be somewhat surprising for those who do not believe in the healing power of prayer—and maybe even to those who believe in the healing power of prayer.

While 80% of Americans believe in the power of prayer to improve the course of illness, the question does remain: does empirical research support the idea that prayer helps improve health? This was a question asked by Ran-dolph Byrd in 1988. In his study, he asked research participants to pray for 192 patients in the cardiac care unit of San Francisco General Hospital, whom gave consent to be a part of this study upon being admitted to the cardiac care unit. The participants were given the first names of the patients, their diagno-ses, and general conditions. The participants were then asked to pray for them outside the hospital. They then compared that group to 201 patients who were not prayed for at the same hospital. They then measured the number of people in four categories that denote the condition is worsening. In the control group, 16 patients required antibiotics versus 3 in the prayer group, 18 patients in the control group had a pulmonary edema versus 6 in the prayer group, 12 patients in the control group had an endotracheal intubation versus 0 in the prayer group, and 17 patients in the control group died versus 13 in the prayer group. In all four categories, the number of people who experienced the negative consequences was less in the prayer group than in the control group.

While these results can be surprising to many, there are some problems with the study. For starters, the people in the prayer group knew they were being prayed for. That could create a placebo effect; they could have been doing better because they thought something was happening to them to help them get better. In fact, not only did the patients know so did their doctors and nurses. While that may not seem like a big deal, it actually can be one. The doctors and nurses may have unintentionally treated the prayer group differently, and that may helped make a difference between the two groups.

A replication of this study was conducted by William Harris and his colleagues in 1999 in order to control for these effects. Similar to the first study, they had the people who were praying for the patients do it from a remote location. Second, they did a double-blind study. A double-blind study is one where neither the people running the experiment, nor the people in the experiment know who is in what condition. In this case, neither the patients nor the medical staff were aware of the study. Patients in a coronary care unit were randomly assigned to the prayer condition or the control condition. The people who would be praying were contacted with the first name of the patient that they had to pray for. Fifteen teams of five people prayed for each patient individually for 28 days. They were to specifically pray for "a speedy recovery with no complications" and anything else that seemed appropriate. Each patient was given a score for problems or their condition worsening ranging from one to ten. The higher the score, the worse the patient's experience was at the hospital. The prayer group (average score of 6.35) had a significantly lower score than the control condition (7.13) meaning the patients that were prayed for had significantly less problems than the control condition. This is not saying that people who are prayed for get better, but it appears that they do have an easier time dealing with what they are going through. So, when you hear a call for prayers for people who are sick in church or on Facebook, it is not a bad idea to pray; it may make their experience easier!

Spirituality and the Fading Affect Bias

Gibbons, Hartzler, Hartzler, Lee, and Walker (2014) examined the Fading Affect Bias in the context of religion and spirituality. One hundred and thirty participants were asked to retrieve four autobiographical events

(82% Christian, 9% agnostic, 4% atheist, 1% Jewish, 1% Muslim, 3% other). Two of these events, one positive and one negative, were ordinary events. Two of these events, one positive and one negative, were events that were religious or spiritual in nature. A religious or spiritual event was defined as event that included "the search for significance in ways related to the sacred" (Pargament, 1999, p. 11). To be sure, not all participants were able to retrieve these kinds of events, but the vast majority did. Participants in this study were also asked to complete a scale that assessed their overall level of spirituality. As in much of the research described in this book, participants rated how pleasant or unpleasant the events were at the time of the event and at the time of recollection. Participants also completed a survey to assess their spiritual tendencies. The Spiritual Transcendence Index is an eight-item measure that assesses cognitive, affective, motivational, and transcendent aspects of spirituality on a scale ranging from 1 (strongly disagree) to 6 (strongly agree).

The results of this study revealed that spirituality was meaningfully related to the Fading Affect Bias. Figure 5.4 shows the mean drop in affect intensity for pleasant and unpleasant events across five levels of spirituality. Participants demonstrated a strong Fading Affect Bias regardless of how spiritual they were. However, spirituality did increase the overall strength of the Fading Affect Bias. The more spiritual a person was, the less the positive emotion had faded and the more the negative emotion had faded (Figure 5.4). While this study did not directly assess the impact of prayer on fading emotion, the implications of these findings are quite tantalizing. First, the relationship between spirituality and fading emotion was evident across both

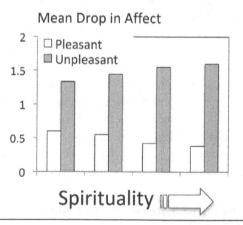

FIGURE 5.4   The Fading Affect Bias across four levels of increasing spirituality (adapted from Gibbons, et al., 2014).

everyday events and religious events. Spirituality may have influenced the emotional content for all event memories, not just ones that are religious in nature. Second, the link between prayer and spirituality seems straightforward. It is not much of a stretch to imagine that individuals high in spirituality are the same individuals prone to frequent prayer.

Thinking, talking, and praying can be truly transformative. These psychological processes are more like tidal forces altering a coastline than a gentle stream cutting through the countryside. The tide releases billions of tons of force to the eastern seaboard of the United States every second of every day. The coastline may seem unchanged but it is in a constant state of upheaval and transition. Occasionally, a hurricane might tweak a beach or erode away part of a barrier island in a dramatic fashion, but don't be fooled, the real transformation happens in the daily grind of wave activity. Likewise, the psychological processes of thought, conversation, and prayer can fundamentally alter the kind of person that one ultimately becomes. Perhaps not all at once, but they can give rise to spectacular alterations in emotion, in memory, and in character.

And that brings us back to the story of Chris Pritchard, the once-troubled young man who hatched a plan that would briefly seize the nation's attention. He has changed. He has been saved. While the emotional transformations they incur are usually not as dramatic as the one experienced by Pritchard, these processes can offer real benefits to people coping with their own emotional demons. The human capacity is there to selectively dampen the echoes of distant emotions without erasing the memories or the lessons of past events. Finally, it should be pointed out that Pritchard does not "feel good" about what happened. He can never "feel good" about his role in what transpired. And he is not without fault. He was open and sincere during a series of conversations that were undertaken during the course of writing this book.[1] His face, which remained a visage of calm and humility darkened only once, when he was asked if he had forgiven his co-conspirators, James Upchurch III and Gerald Neal Henderson, the people who had actually murdered his stepfather and attacked his mother. He lowered his gaze and admitted that he had not yet done so. Perhaps he is not yet ready. But he does feel empowered by a love that he has for his life and his Lord. He's trying to walk the path.

CHAPTER 6

A Fire Down Below

The borough of Centralia in eastern Pennsylvania has one of the most unique and tragic histories of any small town in the United States. Once a town of more than two thousand souls, the population in 2014 hovers around ten. The empty buildings and houses have been razed. The thoroughfares have been bulldozed. The ground is an uneven mix of rock, dirt, cement, and trash pitted with deep holes where the earth seems to have just collapsed. The faint outlines of sidewalks and foundations can be seen underneath a layer of dead grass and weeds. Twisted trees grow out of the earth at odd angles. There are a few streetlights—but *no streets*. Standing in the midst of the debris, it is easy to get the feeling that something terrible happened here.

Pennsylvania has been coal country since the combustible rock was discovered there and subsequently mined in the late 1700s. For the non-geologist, it is important to know that coal comes in several grades, which roughly approximates to its rigidity and carbon content. On one end of the grade is anthracite, or "hard coal." It has the highest carbon content (over 90%) of all the varieties of coal, has the fewest impurities, and burns the longest and cleanest. It is the "clean coal" that is oft bandied about in discussions of energy independence and climate change. In the middle of the grade is bituminous coal, or "soft coal." This variety of coal has much less carbon, around 70% pure, and contains a tar called bitumen, from which it gets its name. This type of coal is filled with impurities, burns faster and somewhat dirtier than anthracite. On the other end of the grade is lignite, or "brown coal." The carbon density of lignite is low, about 25%, and its tendency to retain moisture makes this coal burn the fastest and the dirtiest of all of the coals. Following Hilt's Law, a geologic rule stating that better grades of coal are found deeper in the earth, it should come as no surprise that lignite is the most plentiful form of coal and anthracite the most rare.

It was geologic good fortune that blessed this region with an abundant supply of high-quality coal. There are five major coalfields in the commonwealth of Pennsylvania, four in its eastern corridor (the Northern Anthracite Field, the Southern Anthracite Field, the Eastern Middle Anthracite Field, and the Western Middle Anthracite Field) and one vast field in its western corridor (the Main Bituminous Field). The Appalachian Mountains provide a useful landmark for helping understand how and why the coal is distributed as it is. The Appalachian Mountains are presently in geologic decline, which means that they are shrinking. Over the course of millions of years, waves of mountain building brought both fine and coarse-grained sediments onto the plain. As the mountains eroded, they did so in a rather lop-sided fashion. The coarse sediments on the western side of the mountains pooled and then settled in large clumps that produced the vast bituminous field that lies beneath a full one-third of the state. The sediments on the eastern side of the mountains were subjected to the gristmill of several glaciers and the rising and falling levels of the ocean. Subsequently, the sediment here was ground into a more fine-grained material, producing smaller pockets of anthracite beneath a porous floor of loose rock and dirt.

Anthracite was discovered in the northeastern part of Pennsylvania in the 1780s, and speculators saw an opportunity they could not pass up. Anthracite was a more efficient source of fuel than the coals that were being used at the time, and, if mined and transported in an equally efficient way, could become a source of great wealth for those with controlling interests. The speculators included wealthy individuals, such as the famous Wurt Brothers from Philadelphia and, later, the Philadelphia and Reading Coal and Iron Company and the Susquehanna Coal Company. Speculators usually started their ventures by securing inexpensive mineral rights in areas that allowed for relatively easy surface mining. Small towns would quickly spring up, with the coal and the profits flowing from the rural areas to the cities. Over the next seventy years, the amount of coal that could be easily mined from the surface shrank. There was still a great deal of coal left to be mined; the most tantalizing prize being the Mammoth Vein. The Mammoth Vein is the most prominent vein of coal in the region, reaching a maximum thickness of greater than 30 feet of pure anthracite. To truly profit, the coal companies would need two things. First, they would need the strong backs of many men to bring the coal to the surface. Second, they would have to be able to move large amounts of coal from the mines to cities like Philadelphia and New York.

After the Civil War, these needs were quickly met: The railroad came to this part of Pennsylvania along with an abundance of cheap immigrant labor, comprised mostly of Irish, Welsh, and Slavic workers. The mining companies were willing to risk the lives of these men in their pursuit of anthracite. The physical risks in mining are numerous. Collapses can crush or trap workers deep underground. Pockets of gas can overwhelm and suffocate people within seconds. A survey of the first one hundred mining fatalities in the Centralia mines, which occurred between 1870 and 1885, reveals the variety of ways in which death was a constant companion of these workers (35 killed by falling coal or rock, 25 killed by explosions, 24 crushed by equipment, 4 drowned in mudslides, 4 run over by wagons, 2 suffocated, 2 kicked by mules, 2 dropped over dead, 1 disappeared, 1 death cause not recorded).

The exploitation of the people of Appalachia by the coal industry was part of a larger set of injustices set upon poor minorities during America's painful transition during the industrial revolution. Indeed, it is important to remember that mining in the 1800s was an incredibly dangerous trade and that it paid very poorly. Moreover, workers who would dare complain or strike for better pay or safer working conditions would find themselves the target of persecution and violence. Such violence would often divide the workers against each other along ethnic lines, reinforcing prejudices brought over from Europe. The harsh conditions also created an important psychological undercurrent in the people of the region. The hardworking men who labored and died in the mines, and the families that suffered with them, developed a healthy distrust of wealthy industrialists and of the government that had enabled them. The mindset that this shared experience imparted is still evident in many of the people who reside there today.

Image © dmvphotos, 2014. Used under license from Shutterstock, Inc.

Photograph from an underground anthracite coal mine in eastern Pennsylvania.

Coal itself is dangerous and highly flammable. Anthracite is hard coal with a high carbon content, which gives it two paradoxical properties. It is very difficult to ignite, but once a fire is lit, it is nearly impossible to extinguish. Mine fires are always difficult to prevent and suppress, in large part

because of their inaccessibility. Mining companies have long used sophisticated methods to fight underground fires, which almost always involve either
degrading the fuel source or choking off the oxygen supply. Mine fires in eastern Pennsylvania, however, are something different altogether. The geology
that gave rise to the rich coalfields also made the fires in those fields particularly hard to fight. The moment they are ignited, the fires have a virtually
inexhaustible source of fuel in the rich anthracite, and the porous ground in
the region allows a continuous supply of fresh air. Once a fire starts to burn,
it may never go out. As testament to this claim, consider that in 2010, the
Office of Surface Mining reported that there were approximately one hundred
mine fires burning in the United States—nearly half of them were in the
anthracite mines of Pennsylvania.

Perhaps the most infamous of these fires resides in Centralia, Pennsylvania, which has been desiccated by an underground coal fire that started in
1962 and continues to burn to this day. The fire started accidentally when city
workers were burning trash near an open coal seam. Abandoned mine sites
have long been popular dumping grounds for trash. The seam ignited but was
quickly put out by firefighters. Or so they thought. Several days later, the fire
re-emerged. Temporary victories, in which the fire was thought extinguished,
were later found to have been short-lived. The fire would disappear for
months or even years, then suddenly re-emerge in an unexpected place. Sink-
holes would suddenly appear and begin to bellow acrid smoke. In some
places, the ground would be warm to the touch.

Three factors conspired to confound firefighting efforts in Centralia.
First, the geology of the region made the fire itself insidiously hard to locate
and fight. Because of the geology of the region, the coal seems were often
erratic, and the blaze seemed to move in directions and at speeds that were
hard to predict. In fact, it was later discovered that the fire was moving in as
many as four different directions: West, Southwest, South, and East. This
meant that much of town was in no immediate danger. Indeed, some Centra-
lians were not convinced that the fire was all that much of a risk to the town,
while others felt that their homes and lives were in grave danger. This difference of opinion often set neighbor against neighbor. Second, the mindset of
the area forged by decades of neglect and abuse at the hands of distant coal
companies and politicians meant that the townspeople had only a tenuous
sense of community upon which to fall back. In fact, the only thing they
seemed to have in common was an inherent distrust of the experts and government institutions that were best suited to put out the fire. Most of these
people were perceived as opportunistic outsiders who were trying to cause
trouble. Experts would visit the town and offer technical solutions that would
do little to quell the anxieties of the townspeople. Often, their advice would
seem condescending and contradictory. Third, the state and federal govern-

ment did not appreciate the social complexities of Centralia. They saw the problem as a technological one, and they repeatedly failed to engage the community *as a community*. Efforts to fight the inferno were subject to budgetary constraints and political squabbles. The confluence of geology, psychology, and politics meant that the efforts to extinguish the conflagration often worked against each other. In one instance, boreholes were drilled into the earth to determine the location and temperature of the fire, but these holes served to further fan the underground flames by giving them a steady supply of fresh air. In other cases, buyouts offered by the state were perceived as unfair to landowners. Government attempts to vacate the area through the use of imminent domain were also judged to be heavy-handed and one-sided.

Meanwhile, as the politics of the townspeople, experts and technicians, and government agencies played out on the surface, the fire continued to burn beneath the surface. On February 14, 1981, a single event changed everything. A twelve-year-old named Todd Domboski fell into a sinkhole one hundred and fifty feet deep that unexpectedly opened beneath his feet. As it happened, there were government officials and members of the press touring the town at the exact time of the accident. The child was saved by the heroic actions of his cousin, but the event seemed to underline the immediate dangers from the fire down below. The town's mixed feelings of anxiety, distrust, and apathy were quickly replaced by a sense of urgency and near panic in some cases. Two years later, the majority of remaining citizens took a buyout from the federal government and moved to the nearby towns of Ashland and Mount Carmel. The zip code has been revoked, and the properties have been seized through eminent domain. The remaining residents have been allowed to stay in their homes as long as they wish, but no one can move in.

What most people get wrong about the Centralia mine fire is that they believe the fire destroyed the town. It didn't.[1] The town collapsed because there was never a sense of community or shared purpose among its residents. The profits from the mines of Centralia were never reinvested in the town to create the social structures that would have given it a sense of civic identity; instead, they went to distant companies far away from this small Pennsylvania borough. By the end of World War II, the era of big coal was gone. When the fire was lit in 1962, it was twelve years after the local government in Centralia had acquired exclusive rights to the coal underneath the town. There was no longer a coal company to blame for the fire or to provide the necessary expertise to fight it. The townspeople, descendants of exploited immigrants who had learned to be wary of outsiders, were often uncivil to each other and downright hostile to strangers. Once the blaze was ignited, the town was unable to pull together and deal with its consequences.

Beneath the deserted remains of Centralia, the fire burns unabated.

T hus far, the research on the Fading Affect Bias has shown us that negative emotions fade at a rate that is substantially faster and more pronounced than positive emotions. This tendency has been documented using a number of different methods and a number of different kinds of people. This phenomenon is partly due to the natural, organic tendencies of the mind. The mind may reflect about past events, but it lives in the here and now. It is difficult for the mind to retain the emotional intensity of an event as that event becomes less and less relevant to everyday life. This is especially true for negative memories that can sap mental resources away from the tasks of the present day. But there is more going on than fading with the passage of time. The processes of thinking, talking, and praying modulate and reinforce this tendency. The inclination to selectively rehearse and reinforce positive memories, coupled with the desire to reinterpret and give meaning to negative events, means that even a slight positivity bias can be magnified many times over. Overall, this bias is beneficial to people by allowing them to move through their lives without much of the emotional baggage of painful memories. The memories remain, but the bad emotions are muted or absent or even replaced with emotions that are more desirable. Indeed, we feel comfortable stating that for most people and most events, the Fading Affect Bias reflects a basic truth about the fate of emotions in memory.

But for some people and certain events, the damaging emotions linger and continue to cause them pain. In these circumstances, neither the passage of time nor the sharing of stories is enough. For some people, the fire never goes out.

D epression, as discussed in Chapter 3, is the quintessential psychological disorder. Experienced by nearly everyone in some form at some time in life, depression can be realized in a number of ways, but it is uniformly *negative*. Every major theory of depression addresses the negativity bias that it imbues to those who suffer from this emotional disorder. There is some debate as to how much of this bias is the result of deliberate versus unconscious processes, but there is little doubt that the bias is pervasive, infecting nearly all aspects of mental life. The cognitive triad of depression, formally described by Aaron Beck in 1976, can be summarized thusly—the self has no value, the world is unfair, and the future is hopeless (or, more coarsely, "I suck, the world sucks, and the future is going to suck even worse").

The pain that is depression affords the curious researcher a means by which to examine how the mind experiences positive and negative emotions. It is possible to better understand some of the mechanisms underpinning positive and negative emotions by contrasting the experiences of those suffering from depression, and its negativity bias, to those who are not depressed. In the case of the Fading Affect Bias, which has been documented in several "normal, psychologically healthy" populations, the question is simple. Is the Fading Affect Bias present or absent in people experiencing high levels of depression?

Walker, Skowronski, Gibbons, Vogl, and Thompson (2003) examined the impact of non-clinical depression on the Fading Affect Bias. In the first study, 65 participants completed the Beck Depression Inventory. The Beck Depression Inventory produces a range of scores from 0 to 63. Higher scores are indicative of greater levels of non-clinical depression, otherwise referred to as dysphoria. Although this instrument is not a clinical assessment, it is a useful tool in identifying people who may be prone to severe episodes of depression. The scores from this inventory were used to categorize people as non-dysphoric or dysphoric. These participants were also asked to retrieve three intense positive autobiographical memories and three intense negative autobiographical memories. They were asked to rate how positive or negative the events were at the time of the event (initial affect) and how positive or negative the events were at the time of recall (current affect). Examining the difference between these two ratings showed that most events lost emotional intensity over time. Figure 6.1 presents the mean drop in affect intensity for positive and negative events for non-dysphoric and dysphoric participants. As a reminder, higher bars indicate higher levels of emotional fading. The results showed a significant Fading Affect Bias for non-dysphoric participants. Negative affect had faded significantly more than positive affect. But now look at

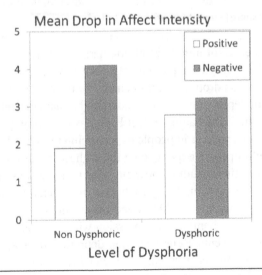

FIGURE 6.1 The mean drop in affect intensity for pleasant and unpleasant events across 2 levels of non-clinical depression (dysphoria) as assessed by the Beck Depression Inventory (adapted from Walker et al., 2003).

the dysphoric participants. Relative to their non-dysphoric counterparts, negative affect had faded *less* and positive affect had faded *more*. The Fading Affect Bias had been effectively eliminated by the presence of non-clinical depression.

The results from a second study confirmed and extended this finding. In this second study, a total of 337 participants from three universities completed the Beck Depression Inventory. The Beck Depression Inventory (BDI) scores were used to sort participants into one of five levels of dysphoria that were roughly equal in size (BDI scores of 0–2, 69 participants; BDI scores of 3–4, 62 participants; BDI scores of 5–7, 67 participants; BDI scores of 8–12, 72 participants; BDI scores of 13 and up, 67 participants). It is important to note that in this study scores ranging from 0–7 on the BDI were considered non-dysphoric. Scores ranging from 8–12 were considered mildly dysphoric. Scores at 13 and above were considered dysphoric. A few participants scored well above the mid-point of the scale. These individuals were likely clinically depressed and were discretely contacted and advised to seek immediate treatment. These participants were also asked to recall emotionally intense positive memories and emotionally intense negative memories. Again, they were asked to rate how positive the events were at the time of the event (initial affect) and at the time of recall (current affect).

The results of the second study documented the specific relationship between participants' level of dysphoria and the degree to which they expressed a Fading Affect Bias for their memories. For participants who were in any of the three non-dysphoric categories (individuals scoring 7 or less on the depression scale), negative affect faded significantly more than positive affect. That is to say, these individuals showed a robust Fading Affect Bias. This effect weakened for mildly dysphoric participants (BDI scores of 8–12), and was absent for dysphoric participants (BDI scores of 13 and up). Figure 6.2 presents the mean drop in affect intensity for positive and negative events for all 5 levels of depression. As a reminder, higher bars indicate higher levels of emotional fading. The Fading Affect Bias was evident in people not experiencing depression, weaker in people experiencing mild levels of depression, and non-existent in people experiencing the highest level of depression.

The results of these studies show findings that are consistent with most major theories of depression: A negativity bias that intensifies in lockstep with a person's level of depression. Moreover, these studies reveal what we consider to be a 'double-whammy' of depression when it comes to remembering the emotions of life events. Relative to non-depressed people, depressed people retain *more* of the negative emotions and *less* of the positive emotions associated with autobiographical memories.

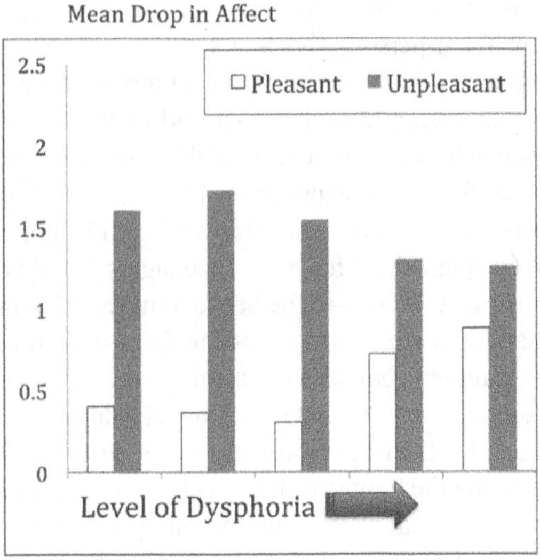

Mean Drop in Affect

FIGURE 6.2 The mean drop in affect intensity for pleasant and unpleasant events across 5 levels of non-clinical depression (dysphoria) as assessed by the Beck Depression Inventory (adapted from Walker et al., 2003).

Depression, of course, is not the only psychological illness that can influence the emotions that people associate with their personal memories. Anxiety disorders create an emotional experience that is called "threat magnification." A person who suffers from anxiety overemphasizes potential threats in their environment. They often do this because past experience has taught them, perhaps correctly, to be keenly aware of perceived dangers and to react to those perceptions quickly and aggressively. In a life or death situation, this can make a lot of sense. However, such reactions quickly become maladaptive when the threat is no longer present. Threat magnification can also occur when people are retrieving their personal event memories.

First, consider a person at the low end of the anxiety spectrum. A fairly common and relatively minor anxiety is the fear of speaking in front of others. Few individuals ever perform this task perfectly, especially in their formative years of high school and college. An individual who has retained their fear of public speaking is recalling an instance where they 'screwed up' in a public forum, such as in front of a class or on stage. That person might recall the event and experience a flush of embarrassment. Why? The event is squarely in the past and there is no obvious reason for the person to experience any emotion at all. But the event activates a present-day anxiety, and that anxiety reignites the distant memory of past humiliation. The emotion of the event itself has most likely faded, but it has been recharged with anxiety from the here and now. But for a person who is not overly prone to anxiety, a few moments pass, and the embarrassment wanes in this instance.

Now, consider an example at the other end of the anxiety spectrum. A survivor of an extremely traumatic event, such as an attempted rape or mugging, tries to recover from their experience. The event has triggered a condition known as post-traumatic stress disorder, a powerful emotional experience that sets the brain on "high alert" for potential dangers. For this individual, the threats appear to be everywhere—in the here and now *and* in the memories of past events. A shadow in the corner takes the form of a lurking intruder. A sound in the dead of night becomes a threatening voice. This person may find the memories associated with the attack extremely difficult to talk about or even contemplate, and yet, paradoxically, they may also find themselves continually re-experiencing the trauma of the event in the form of intrusive memory recollections. Time may pass, but the emotions associated with this particular experience do not seem to fade. Again, the present-day anxiety serves to maintain and even exacerbate the emotion of the traumatic event.

Walker, Yancu, and Skowronski (2014) examined the impact of anxiety on the Fading Affect Bias in three studies. They reasoned that increased levels of anxiety should disrupt the Fading Affect Bias in a fashion that is qualitatively different from the disruption caused by depression. Depression had created a negativity bias that distorted the fading affect bias by reducing the fading of negative emotion. However, the experience of anxiety is not really about increased negativity, it is about a heightened overall experience of emotion. A person prone to anxiety should experience their emotions more strongly than a person without such tendencies. Increased levels of anxiety, therefore, should reduce the perceived fading of emotions for *both* positive and negative memories.

In the first study, Walker and his colleagues assessed 98 participants using an instrument called the Depression, Anxiety, and Stress Scale (DASS). This survey asks people to read a series of statements and rate how accurately each statement describes how they have been feeling recently. The items probe the core symptoms of anxiety that include autonomic arousal, situational anxiety, and heightened levels of emotionality. Participants were divided into 3 groups that were roughly equal in size: Low Anxiety (DASS scores of 0–3; 35 participants), Moderate Anxiety (DASS scores of 4–9; 33 participants), and High Anxiety (DASS scores of 10 and above; 30 participants). For comparison purposes, here are the standard categories used when scoring the DASS: Normal (0–7), Mild Anxiety (8–9), and Moderate Anxiety (10–14). Participants were then instructed to recall five positive and five negative event memories and to provide detailed descriptions for each event. They were asked to rate how positive or negative the events were at the time of the event (initial affect) and at

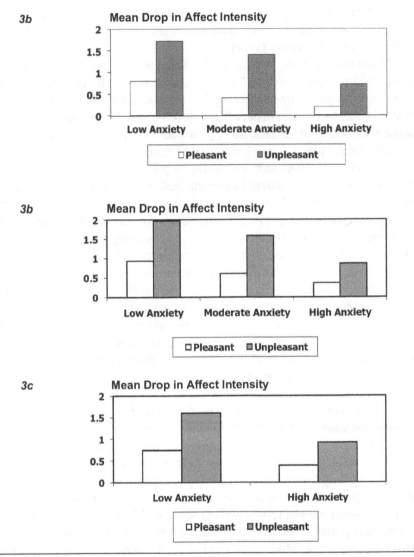

FIGURE 6.3 Change in affect as a function of event pleasantness and level of participant anxiety as assessed by the DASS (Experiment 1 [3a], and the BAI (Experiment 2 [3b], and Experiment 3 [3c]) (adapted from Walker et al., 2014).

the time of recall (current affect). Figure 6.3a presents the mean drop in affect intensity for positive and negative events for participants in the Low, Moderate, and High Anxiety groups. As a reminder, higher bars indicate higher levels of emotional fading. Participants in each anxiety group demonstrated a

Fading Affect Bias: Negative affect had faded more than positive affect. However, increased levels of anxiety were associated with less affective fading for both positive and negative events.

In the second study, Walker and his colleagues assessed 50 participants using an instrument called the Beck Anxiety Inventory (BAI). This survey is more highly regarded by researchers than the DASS that had been used in the first study, and is thought to have higher levels of validity and reliability. This score was used to place each participant into one of three groups that were roughly equal in size: Low Anxiety (BAI scores of 0–5; 17 participants), Moderate Anxiety (BAI scores of 6–13; 19 participants), and High Anxiety (BAI scores of 14 and above; 14 participants). For comparison, here are the standard categories used when scoring the BAI: Normal (0–7), Mild Anxiety (8–15), Moderate Anxiety (16–25), and Severe Anxiety (26–63). Participants were then instructed to recall two positive and two negative event memories and to provide detailed descriptions for each event. They were asked to rate how positive or negative the events were at the time of the event (initial affect) and at the time of recall (current affect). Figure 6.3b presents the mean drop in affect intensity for positive and negative events for participants in the Low, Moderate, and High Anxiety groups. Just like in the first study, participants in each anxiety group demonstrated a Fading Affect Bias. However, just like in the first study, increased levels of anxiety were associated with less affective fading for both positive and negative events.

In the third study, Walker and his colleagues employed a diary procedure. Diary procedures are more time-consuming, but they are considered more methodologically rigorous than the retrospective methods (as the memories are recorded on paper in real-time, thus eliminating some of the error inherent in our memories) used in studies 1 and 2. They assessed 25 participants using the Beck Anxiety Inventory (BAI). Each participant's score was used to place the participant into one of two groups: Low Anxiety (BAI scores of 0–11; 11 participants) and High Anxiety (BAI scores of 13–40; 14 participants). For comparison purposes, here are the standard categories used when scoring the BAI: Normal (0–7), Mild Anxiety (11–15), Moderate Anxiety (16–25), and Severe Anxiety (26–63). Participants were given five diary sheets and were instructed to keep a daily record of two unique events per day (one positive, one negative) for a period of five days. Thus, each participant was to provide a total of ten event descriptions (five positive events, five negative events). Participants rated how positive or negative each event was at the time that the event occurred (Initial Affect). After one week had passed from the date of the last event entered into the diary, participants were presented with each of their event descriptions in a testing condition. For each event, participants were asked to read each event description from their own diaries and then make a series of ratings for each event before continuing on to the next event description. One of the ratings was how positive or how negative the event was at the time of the test (Current Affect). Figure 6.3c presents the mean drop in affect intensity for positive and negative events for participants in the Low and High Anxiety groups. As in the first two studies, participants in both the Low and High Anxiety groups replicated a Fading Affect Bias. Again, increased levels of anxiety were associated with less affective fading for both positive and negative events.

The results of these experiments serve to replicate and extend the findings obtained in previous research on the Fading Affect Bias. The Fading Affect Bias robustly emerged in all studies. Moreover, in all studies the Fading Affect Bias was demonstrated regardless of the participants' level of anxiety. The results of all three experiments indicated that the Fading Affect Bias is affected by anxiety in a very particular way: Higher anxiety was associated with less affective fading for both positive events and negative events. This last result suggests that increased levels of anxiety may produce a heightened sense of arousal that serves to amplify the perceived emotional qualities of all remembered events. The net result would be that the emotions of the past would seem to fade less for anxiety-prone individuals than for their less-anxious counterparts, regardless of whether the emotion is negative or positive. This finding is consistent with research showing that anxiety-prone participants are likely to attenuate to emotionally intense stimuli.

The Fading Affect Bias is thought to be the result of healthy coping mechanisms dealing with the emotional content of event memories, emphasizing the positive aspects of life and diminishing the impact of our negative memories. The disruption of the Fading Affect Bias by depression and anxiety makes intuitive sense. Individuals prone to these disorders tend to focus on negativity (depression) or stress (anxiety). The healthy benefits experienced by "normal" people were skewed or absent in the presence of these conditions. But, let's flip the script for a moment. Can there ever be too much of a good thing? Researchers began to wonder whether it would be possible that a psychological condition could ever make the Fading Affect Bias *stronger*. One likely candidate for this prospect is the maladaptive personality trait known as narcissism.

Narcissism is the bastard child of self-confidence and entitlement. A narcissist has an inflated sense of superiority, expresses outward arrogance in thought and action, and has an insatiable hunger for the attention and adulation of others. Baumeister and Vohs (2001) characterized narcissism as an addiction to self-esteem. Originally termed megalomania (think the cartoon character Megamind), this tendency is the evil twin of humility. But the roots of narcissism are found in the same self-protective and self-enhancing mechanisms that give rise to the Fading Affect Bias. A narcissist thinks very highly of himself and often goes to great lengths to maintain their inflated sense of self. It would be reasonable to suspect that a narcissist might have an enhanced Fading Affect Bias compared to more humble individuals. After all, in order to enhance feelings of self-confidence and self-worth, they might overly boost their positive emotions while curtailing their negative emotions. This prediction is based upon a more recent conception of narcissism, which essentially describes this tendency as an excess of self-esteem.

However, another possibility exists. There is an alternative view that harkens back to the foundation of narcissistic personality disorder (Kohut, 1968). This view relies on the notion that narcissism extends beyond inflated self-esteem to the realm of a psychological condition prone to disordered patterns of thought and behavior (Twenge, 2006; Vazire & Funder, 2006). Narcissists are prone to being anti-authoritarian (non-conformists, disrespectful, disobedient). Narcissists may rebel or become deceptive and manipulative when their sense of superiority or entitlement is threatened. When their sense of self-esteem is threatened, narcissists are prone to confrontation, violence, and self-destruction (Besser & Ziegler-Hill, 2010; Vaillancourt, 2013). Collectively, these tendencies suggest that high levels of narcissism may be associated with more drawbacks than benefits. A person who is self-obsessed may fixate on their negative experiences and find it difficult to overcome the emotions associated with those events. This could produce a disruption of the Fading Affect Bias much like the disruptions caused by depression and anxiety.

Ritchie, Walker, Marsh, Hart, and Skowronski (2014) conducted three studies to examine the impact of narcissism on the Fading Affect Bias. The first study employed a diary procedure in which 26 participants were asked to record one positive and one negative event per day for five days (five positive and five negative events total). At the time that the event was recorded, participants were instructed to rate how positive or negative the event was perceived to be (Initial Affect). Participants were presented with the written descriptions of their events in a testing condition one week after the last event was recorded. For each event, participants were asked to read each event description from their own diaries and then make a series of ratings for each event before continuing on to the next event description. One of the ratings was how positive or how negative the event was at the time of the test (Current Affect). During the testing condition, participants completed the Narcissistic Personality Inventory (NPI-40; Ames, Rose, & Anderson, 2006). To complete this survey, participants read a series of 40 paired items and selected the option that best described how they thought about their own self. An example item is: "[A] I try not to be a show off" or "[B] I am apt to show off if I get the chance." Narcissistic responses are summed such that higher responses suggest higher self-reported narcissism, with the highest score being 40.

This study employed a somewhat different statistical approach. Rather than grouping participants into different groups based upon their levels of narcissism (NPI scores), the individual scores were used to predict affective fading. The research question answered by this technique is essentially the same as with the studies of depression and anxiety: Do individual differences, in this case, differences in narcissism, produce differences in the Fading Affect Bias? The answer is yes. Participants with the lowest NPI scores showed a large Fading Affect Bias. Participants with middling NPI scores didn't have any Fading Affect Bias, and participants with the very highest NPI scores actually showed a reverse Fading Affect Bias. Figure 6.4 presents the mean drop in affect intensity for pleasant and unpleasant events across five levels of narcissism. Again, higher bars indicate higher levels of emotional fading.

This study showed that high levels of narcissism disrupted the Fading Affect Bias in a way that was distinct from the effects of depression and anxiety. Like depression, higher levels of narcissism were associated with a disrupted Fading Affect Bias. Unlike depression, the highest level of narcissism showed a reversal in affective fading. For the most narcissistic of the participants, the positive emotions associated with life events faded more than the negative emotions associated with life events.

Ritchie et al. (2014) decided to see if they could replicate these findings using a larger sample. One hundred and ten students participated in this study. They included 78 women and 32 men between the ages of 18 and 41, recruited from General Psychology courses at a historically African-American university. Each participant was given twenty minutes to recall five positive events

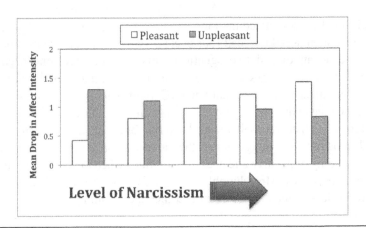

FIGURE 6.4 Mean drop in affect intensity for pleasant and unpleasant events across 5 levels of increasing narcissism as assessed by the NPI-16 (adapted from Ritchie et al., 2014).

from their own life and five negative events from their own life. Each participant was asked to describe each event in four to ten sentences and to include event details (e.g., time, location, sensory information) in the description. Participants rated each event in terms of its initial emotional experience (Initial Affect) and its current emotional value (Current Affect).

The brief narcissism inventory (the NPI-16) was administered to half of the participants *before* memory recall and to half of the participants *after* memory recall. This survey is conceptually similar to the NPI-40, with the key difference being that the highest possible score is 16 rather than 40. Participants who scored from 0–3 were classified as low in narcissism. Participants who scored from 4–6 were classified as moderate in narcissism. Participants who scored above 6 were classified as high in narcissism. The results of the second study conceptually replicated the findings of Study 1. The Fading Affect Bias was shown to be the strongest in people who were low in narcissism, reduced in people moderate in Narcissism, and absent in people high in narcissism. A more sophisticated analysis, which sought to determine at exactly what score the Fading Affect Bias collapsed, found that the Fading Affect Bias was rendered non-existent for people who scored a 10 or higher on the narcissism scale. Importantly, this second study did not replicate the reverse Fading Affect Bias found in the first study.

In the third and final study in this series, Ritchie et al. (2014) decided to examine more closely the kinds of events that participants were recalling in these studies to determine if event type could help explain narcissism's effects on the emotional content of their memories. Specifically, they decided to focus on whether the events were communal (events that focused on other people or social groups) or agentic (events that focused on the individual). In this study, 83 students from an English university participated in this study. Participants first completed the long narcissism survey (the NPI-40). Participants were then asked to recall four events: Two communal events (one positive, one negative) and two agentic events (one positive, one negative). Participants were also asked to rate the initial emotional experience (Initial Affect) and its current emotional value (Current Affect). The results showed that participants who had very high narcissism only showed a Fading Affect Bias for events that were self-focused and not for events that were more communal in nature. This suggests that the narcissists only benefit from the differential fading of positive and negative emotions when the events are focused only on themselves. More humble individuals show a robust Fading Affect Bias regardless of the kind of event that they are recalling.

Taken together, these studies reinforce the general theme of the research presented thus far in this chapter. The Fading Affect Bias is present in people who can best be described as psychologically well adjusted—that is, people who are not depressed, anxiety stricken, or overly narcissistic. Thus far, we have reviewed the effects of depression, anxiety, and narcissism on the Fading Affect Bias. Depression selectively enhances negativity and dampens positivity, creating a skewed view of reality that underscores the apathy and hopelessness of this disorder. Anxiety turns up the dial to '11' on all emotions, positive and negative, which is in accordance with the stressful state of hyper-awareness associated with this condition. The self-absorption of narcissism leads people to retain more of their negative emotions and fewer of their positive emotions, suggesting that self-centered tendencies may not be as emotionally healthy as many may think. Most people have some experience with depression, anxiety, and narcissism, and the way in which these conditions bias the mind follows a kind of intuitive, if tragic, logic. Such logic is absent when it comes to psychopathy.

The term itself conjures up the stereotypical homicidal maniac. Thankfully this macabre example is not the typical psychopath. The vast majority of psychopaths are not serial killers. They are not intrinsically violent, and they seldom cut people to pieces and drop them into the ocean in plastic wrap a la Dexter Morgan. The truth is that psychopaths are often hard to identify. Lacking the classic signs of mental illness, psychopaths are often undetected. These individuals portray many positive characteristics and make great first impressions (Healy, 1942). There is no distinct appearance or profession associated with psychopaths. They can be business owners, physicians, politicians, and even the next-door neighbors. Furthermore, many take great pains to appear normal, making it difficult to recognize them. This has come to be known as the "Mask of Sanity" (Kiehl & Buckholtz, 2010). According to Robert Hare, perhaps the world's leading authority on psychopathy, this disorder may be present in as much as 1% of the world's population. Moreover, a larger percentage of people may display some of the characteristics of psychopathy without being full-blown psychopaths.

Psychopathy is so far removed from everyday experience that a clear, concise definition of it is not readily available. Indeed, many definitions share little in common with each other, and some are even contradictory (Dutton, 2012; Healy, 1942; Hulsey, 1948). However, at its core, psychopathy seems to have three basic elements. First, psychopaths have a tendency for antisocial behavior. This tendency manifests itself in a generally uncaring attitude towards others that, in some cases, can devolve into the desire to exploit or hurt them. Second, many psychopaths have poor impulse control, which often means that they have trouble with tasks that require a great deal of planning, delay of gratification, or restraining inappropriate behaviors. They do not consider the consequences of their actions beyond the immediacy of performing those actions. Third, many psychopaths show a reduced ability to experience and express emotions or to empathize with others. This tendency shows itself through an individual's inability to fully realize or understand their own emotions or those of the people around them. This symptom is sometimes referred to as "flat affect," and it is perhaps the most chilling attribute of a psychopath. Their sense of emotion has been amputated. They can witness pain and suffering, perhaps even causing it to others, but they fail to appreciate its value.

The fact that psychopathy has been found to affect the experience and expression of emotion made it a possible candidate for influencing the Fading Affect Bias. Psychopathy should reduce an individual's overall experience of emotional intensity for their autobiographical events. For these individuals, the emotional disconnect of their condition should mute their emotional experience, particularly in the recollection of those experiences. On the surface, the initial prediction seemed obvious: Greater levels of psychopathy should be associated with greater affective fading for both positive and negative events, kind of a reversal of what was seen with anxiety. While anxiety forced people to retain their positive and negative emotions across the board, psychopathy should prevent people from experiencing much emotion at all.

Burrow, Currence, Lemus, DeBono, Crawford, and Walker (2014) examined psychopathy in 167 participants, who were sampled from two universities, an African-American university in the United States, and a predominantly Caucasian university in New Zealand. Participants completed the Levenson Self-Report Psychopathy (LSRP) scale, a survey consisting of 26 statements in which the participant, using a four point scale, rates how strongly they personally agree or disagree with each statement with 1 = strongly disagree and 4 = strongly agree. The lowest score possible for the LSRP is 26, and the highest possible score is 104. A total of 99 participants scored below the midpoint of the scale and 67 participants scored above the midpoint of the scale (a finding that, in itself, gave members of the research team pause!). Participants were asked to recall a total of ten memories, five positive and five negative, of events that were important or significant in their lives and were given twenty minutes to complete this task. They were asked to describe the memories in as much detail as possible. Participants were also asked to rate several aspects of the events such as how memorable the event was, how important it was, level of affect associated with the event for both then (Initial Affect) and now (Current Affect), and how much they have talked or thought about the event since it occurred.

Higher levels of psychopathy were associated with lower ratings of initial affect for both positive and negative events. Put another way, these results suggest that psychopaths reported that their life events were less emotional than non-psychopaths. This distortion was in the emotion that they had experienced at the time of the event. The same distortion was noted when Burrow and her colleagues (2014) examined the ratings of current affect. Higher levels of psychopathy were associated with lower ratings of current affect for both positive and negative events. The lack of emotion that psychopaths had reported for the initial event experiences had carried over to their recollection of those experiences.

Previous research on depression, anxiety, and narcissism found that these factors had altered how the affect had faded over time primarily by distorting ratings of current affect, but they did not have any effect on the initial emotional experience of the event. Psychopathy had twisted participants' perceptions of *both* the initial and current affect. But the results aren't done yet. Increased levels of psychopathy were also associated with lower memory ratings and lower ratings of event importance. Psychopaths reported that they couldn't remember what had happened to them as well as their non-psychopathic counterparts, and they indicated that those events were less important to them. This was surprising to find, particularly in a retrospective task. When people are asked to recall a subset of event memories from their lives, they generally recall memories that are both unique and important. Indeed, one of the common criticisms of autobiographical memory research is that it is really the study of "important, memorable, and emotional events," and that it often undervalues events that are less than novel.

Burrow et al.'s results were surprising but systematic. Table 6.1 summarizes the mean ratings for Initial Affect, Current Affect, Event Memory, and Event Importance for participants across five increasing levels of psychopathy, with Level 5 being the highest level. For participants past the midpoint of the psychopathy scale, their autobiographical memory systems seem to be operating in a way that is fundamentally different than any other sample this laboratory has studied to date. Their memories are less emotional both in experience and in recollection, are judged to be less important, and are remembered less vividly than the memories of ordinary individuals. These

Psychopathy Level & LSRP Scores	N	Initial Affect Intensity	Current Affect Intensity	Memory	Importance
1 (LSRP 27–41)	31	2.56	1.81	5.87	5.34
2 (LSRP 42–46)	30	2.48	1.79	5.66	5.36
3 (LSRP 47–51)	38	2.50	1.68	5.49	5.26
4 (LSRP 52–56)	33	2.38	1.63	5.52	5.31
5 (LSRP 57–80)	34	2.34	1.55	5.14	4.91

TABLE 6.1   The Mean Initial Affect Ratings, Mean Current Affect Ratings, Mean Memory Ratings, and Mean Importance Ratings for participants across 5 levels of increasing psychopathy as assessed by the LSRP. All means have been summed across positive and negative events (adapted from Burrow et al., 2014).

findings are consistent with the detachment that psychopaths often experience on a daily basis. The sentiment gleaned from such findings are perhaps best summarized in the words Albert Fish, a convicted serial killer known as 'the Bogeyman' who was executed in 1936. Convicted of three murders, and having confessed to numerous others, Fish was asked about the prospect of his impending date with the electric chair. His reply echoed his apparent disengagement from the events around him: *"I have no particular desire to live. I have no particular desire to be killed. It is a matter of indifference to me."*

Taken together, the research on the effects of depression, anxiety, narcissism, and psychopathy on the Fading Affect Bias tells a fairly consistent story. The Fading Affect Bias is present in individuals who can best be described as psychologically healthy. These people are able to employ the appropriate coping mechanisms that allow events to be put into a perspective that selectively dampens negative emotion while retaining positive emotion. In the presence of moderate levels of psychological illness, the Fading Affect Bias shows some distortion but is often still apparent. In the presence of higher levels of psychological distress, the Fading Affect Bias is further warped, in some cases resulting in its collapse. That is certainly what happened in the case of depression. Higher levels of depression led to less fading for negative emotions and more fading for positive emotions; the double whammy of depression. A similar distortion happened in the case of narcissism, suggesting that the self-absorption of this personality trait is far less beneficial than one might imagine. For the highest level of anxiety, the story was somewhat different. For these individuals, both positive and negative emotions showed evidence of less overall fading than for people who were experiencing lower levels of anxiety. Finally, participants prone to psychopathy showed that their emotional experience was fundamentally different from normal individuals. For the psychopath, the emotional experience for positive and negative events was muted, suggesting an emotional detachment unique to this condition.

Each case shows that for some individuals, the normal pattern of emotional fading present in most people can be cast asunder by flaws in the human psyche.

The legacy of Centralia is a curious one. It is one of the most famous mine fires in the history of the United States, perhaps the world. There have been many fires that have been more devastating, some of them in neighboring towns. Certainly there have been deadlier fires; for all the infamy, the fire beneath this abandoned husk of a town has not claimed a single life. Highway 61, the primary artery into town from the south, was partially destroyed by the fire, having had to be closed down and rerouted. The pavement on this stretch

'The now closed section of Highway 61
leading into Centralia, Pennsylvania.'

of road is pockmarked with deep gouges from the fire and covered with teenagers' oft profane graffiti, both of which can be seen using Google maps. It is a homage that brims with a wicked sense of humor.

And still, books have been written and documentaries have been produced focusing on this small borough. It was even the inspiration for a franchise of video games and movies bearing the name Silent Hill. In January 2014, a tour of the town yielded no smoldering pits, no harsh smell of burning coal, no obvious signs of the subterranean blaze. Perhaps the fire has burned itself out or turned downward far beneath the surface. It has been thought to be extinguished before. If it is has found the mammoth vein of anthracite, it could burn for the next five thousand years. In any case, the fire was merely the catalyst for the undoing of this little town. The townsfolk, lacking a core sense of community, fractured in the face of what should have been a simple fire. The real disaster was above ground.[2]

CHAPTER 7

Pollyanna's Revenge

It is late afternoon, after 5:00 p.m., on a chilly February day in central North Carolina. The wind is brisk and the light is starting to fade. A lone figure makes his way across a college campus's main thoroughfare. The backpack he carries is heavy, perhaps as much as 30 pounds. His gait, the rhythm of his strides and footfalls, is steady and strong but would not be characterized as normal. His forward momentum seems to be coming from a twisting motion of his hips and torso. As he approaches the stop for the shuttle, it becomes apparent that he is an older man. His chest and arms reveal evidence of physical strength that is somewhat past its peak. His face is dark brown, wide in the jaw with somewhat of a pronounced chin, and he is clean shaven. He is also wearing sunglasses, an odd choice for the time of day. Plastered on his face is a wide, friendly grin. His name is Kesho,[1] and he is a self-described Pollyanna.

Kesho was born in Cleveland, Ohio in 1964. At the time, Cleveland was still a thriving town filled with factories and jobs that provided a living wage for working-class families. There was a large African-American community in the city, and while not as large as those in cities like Chicago or Detroit, it still provided a good social network. It was the kind of town where an African-American family could make a home and set down roots. His parents welcomed the newborn Kesho into their lives, and they began the many chores of parenting. But just over a year after Kesho was born the chores associated with childcare became immeasurably harder.

Kesho developed a kidney disorder. They were producing too much protein and causing the tissues in his torso and limbs to swell. The proteins were being discharged through his urine, and the doctors thought that it would be a good idea to insert a catheter that could precisely monitor his kidneys' output over a 24-hour period. The catheter proved to be too much for the infant to withstand. Already suffering from the swollen tissues throughout his body, the child began to fuss and squirm as a result of this invasive procedure. The hospital staff, fearing that Kesho might injure himself by inadvertently pulling out the catheter, decided to immobilize the child using leg restraints. After the restraints were put firmly in place, the child was to be monitored throughout the night. But Kesho was left alone throughout the night. The staff did not check in on him like they should have. The combination of his swollen limbs and tight constraints had choked off the blood supply to both of his legs. By morning, the damage had been done. The loss of blood flow meant that the tissues in his legs began to die. Infection set in. Gangrene would be next. His legs were amputated below his knees in a last ditch effort to save his life. What should have been a simple overnight stay at the hospital altered the course of Kesho's life.

Kesho had begun walking before this incident, but he would have to learn this skill all over as he was fitted with his first pair of prosthetic limbs. He would go through at least a dozen such pairs while he was growing up. Given the point of his amputation, he spent twice the energy moving his body than most boys his age. The prosthetics, which would inevitably become ill-fitting as he aged, would sometimes rub his legs raw and cause him additional pain. Coupled with the pressure of his body weight on the small surface area of his stumps, this meant a consistent experience of pain. And of course, there was the emotional pain caused by not fitting in with his peers. Making friends was hard for him, and he found himself retreating more and more into an introverted lifestyle. If this is where the reader might expect the intervention of his loving parents to provide him with the building blocks for resilience and emotional growth, this is where Kesho's story takes an abrupt turn.

This book began with a discussion of Pollyanna's Gifts, the gifts of good moods and good times. Good moods and good times outnumber bad moods and bad times by a ratio of two to one (Walker, Skowronski, & Thompson, 2003). Many people never fully realize just how good their lives are because the mind is wired to over-value emotions and events that are infrequently experienced. Negative emotions and negative events are rare, and therefore, significantly over-valued. When negative emotions and events do occur, their effects on the mind are corrosive. Negativity hurts the mind's ability to accurately understand the world around it and to successfully solve the problems that are presented to it. Thankfully, the mind is equipped with the means to selectively dampen the emotional intensity of negative emotions while savoring the joy of positive emotions. The Fading Affect Bias, the tendency for negativity to fade faster than positivity, has been documented in numerous studies and samples around the world. The Fading Affect Bias is strengthened by the acts of thinking, talking, and praying. In retrospect, this should not be surprising, as these three acts represent the means by which most people cope with adversity. The Fading Affect Bias, however, can be disrupted by the presence of psychological abnormalities like anxiety and depression. Anxiety distorts the Fading Affect Bias by reducing the level of emotional fading for both positive and negative events. Depression seems to hurt the Fading Affect Bias most dramatically by essentially nullifying its effects.

But what does the Fading Affect Bias actually do for us? In Chapter 3, we outlined the effects of negative emotions on the individual and on the larger society. Negative emotions are taxing on the mind, taking up the mental and emotional energy that could be better spent on other tasks. Tasks that would help a person grow, expand their potential, and flourish. The Fading Affect Bias helps to create the psychological and emotional space needed to engage in these kinds of activities by selectively minimizing the negative emotions that would otherwise burden the individual. You see, while negative emotions hurt, positive emotions help.

Researchers in the area of positive psychology have documented many of the positive effects of emotions like happiness, excitement, and serenity. The findings of this field reveal that positive emotions can foster traits and qualities that can be people can use to more fully realize their potential as humans. The Fading Affect Bias allows positive emotions to do their beneficial work by minimizing negativity and allowing positivity to remain strong. This is Pollyanna's Revenge.

Broaden-and-Build Theory of Positive Emotion

Broaden-and-Build theory (BBT) is a theory that explains how positive emotions help us. Developed by Barbara Fredrickson, the main thesis of BBT is that positive emotions broaden our awareness and encourage new thoughts and actions. In other words, positive emotions broaden our awareness and that lets us build new ways of thinking and acting. As mentioned in previous chapters, more art and innovation come in times of prosperity versus time of strife.

The ideas behind BBT come from a classic paper by Fredrickson and Branigan (1998) that served to flesh out the idea that positive emotions broaden our attention and thought-action repertoires. They performed two experiments. In the first experiment participants viewed a film clip that would induce one of five emotions: Amusement (a clip of penguins), contentment (a clip of nature scenery), neutrality (a clip of colored sticks piling up), anger (a clip from the movie *Witness* where Amish people were being taunted) or anxiety (a clip from the movie *Cliffhanger* where a mountain accident occurs). Then the participants were assessed on the breadth of their visual processing through a global-local visual processing task and thought-action repertoires by asking them to list all the activities they would do in that moment (the moment where they are experiencing the emotion primed by the movie clip).

They found that participants in the amusement and contentment conditions broadened their scope of attention to a more global breadth and broadened their thought-action repertoires while the anger and anxiety conditions narrowed their thought-action repertoires. In other words, positivity gives us more possibilities of behavior while negative emotions narrow the number of different behaviors we will do. This makes sense when you look at some of the typical symptoms of depression. Depressed people tend to have a strong lack of motivation. Symptoms include staying in bed or sleeping, loss of appetite, lack of interest in hobbies, lack of interest in sex, and overall lack of motivation. Their action repertoire has become very small.

So positive emotions broaden the scope of our behavior but that's not all they do. Further work by Fredrickson (Fredrickson & Joiner, 2002) had participants complete measures of affect and coping at two different times five weeks apart. They found that initial positive affect (the affect rating at the first time recorded) predicted improved broad-minded coping *and* that initial broad-mind coping predicted increased positive affect. In other words, positive feelings lead to more broad-mindedness and broad-mindedness leads to more positive emotions. Fredrickson described this phenomenon as "upward spiraling toward emotional well-being" because the positive emotions and broad-minded coping were building the person's emotional well-being to become more and more positive.[2] This is the opposite of the downward spiral so common with illnesses such as depression and addiction. People experiencing upward spirals are doing more than enduring—they are thriving.

We discussed how positive emotions lead to new ways of thinking and behaving. Now we will discuss two seemingly contradictory ways to achieve happiness using these novel thought and behavior repertoires: Via total absorption in a task (flow) versus training yourself to objectively observe but not react to life experiences (mindfulness). After this, we will discuss Grit, the ability to maintain focus and determination in pursue of a long-term goal.

Flow

Back in the 1980s, a psychologist by the name of Mihaly Csikszentmihalyi (pronounced *chick-sent-me-high-ee*) was interested in people who get lost in their work—painters particularly. They would get so immersed in their work that they would forgo all other needs while they were working. This has happened to many people in many different fields from time to time. One of the authors of this book (Cory Scherer—CS) remembers fondly a time this happened in graduate school. One summer his adviser, John Skowronski, came down to his lab with a binder. It contained numerous pages that featured a picture of a person and a brief summary of a behavior performed by the person. Each picture was followed with a task to measure what the participant reading the binder thought and remembered about the people in the pictures. The contents of the binder were typical experimental materials for studying spontaneous trait inference (we infer traits about people based on what they do—without prompting) and spontaneous trait transference (we transfer traits from people that are being talked about ONTO the person who is talking; If I were to talk about an intelligent behavior that John did, you would transfer the trait of intelligence on to me). The author was tasked with creating a digital version of this binder.

As CS is a big, lonely nerd, this task sounded very interesting to him. He jumped into learning everything he could about the computer program and then set out to turn the binder into a computerized experiment. When recalling the story, CS remembers that John gave him the binder and instructions on Monday, July 2nd. CS started working and did not leave his office except to use the bathroom for quite a while. Quite a while turned into a couple of days. He remembers getting a phone call from his friend Jason asking him what were his plans for the day. CS told him he was going to work on his project and Jason was appalled. He told CS that he can't spend the Fourth of July in his office—he had to go out and do something. Jason gently reminded him that it already was the Fourth of July. CS had no idea. He was so caught up in the work he was doing he had little care for anything else—he doesn't remember if he ate anything or slept for those two days!

This phenomenon is what we call flow. Flow is the mental state of operation in which a person performing an activity is fully immersed in a feeling of energized focus, full involvement, and enjoyment in the process of the activity (Csikszentmihalyi, 1990). It is essentially total focus on the task at hand. When someone is in a state of flow, they are so engrossed in the activity they are doing that they lose awareness of all other things. Time, people, bodily needs such as thirst or hunger, or any other distraction are pushed to the background, and the only thing that matters is what you are doing. For example, once when one of your authors (Cory... again) was so engrossed in studying for his Ph.D. candidacy exams that he forgot that it was New Year's Eve—much to the chagrin of his brand new (and far more fun) wife.

While such total absorption in a task may sound negative, it is actually a positive experience; while in a state of flow the person feels energized and enjoys the experiences. Csikszentmihalyi and colleagues identified six factors that define the experience of flow: 1) Intense and focused concentration on the present moment; 2) Merging of action and awareness; 3) A loss of reflective self-consciousness; 4) A sense of personal control or agency over the situation or activity; 5) A distortion of temporal experience—in other words the experience of time is altered; and 6) Experience of the activity is rewarding in and of itself.

Flow doesn't happen automatically at any time. There are specific conditions that need to be met for flow to occur. Csikszentmihalyi and colleagues (2005) stated that these conditions are: 1) A person must be involved in an activity with a clear set of goals and progress. This gives the task direction and structure. 2) The task must have clear and immediate feedback. The feedback allows the person to negotiate any change in what is expected and adjust their performance, which allows them to maintain the flow state. 3) A person must have good balance between the perceived challenges of the task at hand and their own perceived skills. In other words, they must find the sweet spot of challenge and skill so they are confident that they can do the task at hand. These factors are seen as interrelated so it is combination of challenge, skill, and knowing what to do and how to do it.

Getting into a flow state is a challenge in and of itself, but maintaining the flow state is another problem entirely. There are many factors that can make flow disappear. Apathy, boredom, and anxiety are the three biggest enemies of flow. Apathy tends to occur when the challenges of the task are low and the person's skill level is low. This produces a lack of interest in the task and feelings of apathy occur. Boredom occurs when challenges are low and the skill level exceeds the task. You want to do something more challenging but you are unable to. It's like being allowed to only play with a four-piece puzzle; you will be able to master it in seconds and thus lose interest. Finally, anxiety can challenge flow. When challenges are so high that they exceed the skill level, this can cause feelings of anxiety, and when one experiences anxiety about a task that distracts the person and does not allow for the person to

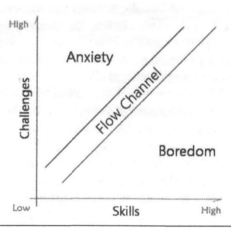

FIGURE 7.1   The experience of flow is achieved when an individual's skills are matched with the challenges of a situation. If the challenges exceed the skill set, people experience anxiety. If the challenges fall short of the skill set, people experience boredom. Adapted from Csikszentmihalyi (1990).

experience flow (Nakamura & Csikszentmihalyi, 2005). Think of a young athlete choking at the big game. While they probably frequently achieve flow while playing their sport, the anxiety associated with a high-stakes game render them incapable of getting into "the zone."

Csikszentmihalyi has also studied individual differences in the ability to experience flow. He talks about a personality type—the autotelic—who may have a greater ability of achieving flow in their lives. These people tend to be internally driven, curious, and have a sense of purpose. They are naturally inquisitive and not driven by external forces such as money, power, or fame. Research suggests that these people have a preference for situations that are challenging and encourage growth (Abuhamdeh, 2000) because these states will induce the person to enter a flow state.

There are positive consequences of achieving flow. Csikszentmihalyi (1990) suggests that people who spend more time in flow tend to be happier and more successful. Flow helps people experience more positive affect, higher life satisfaction, and better performance. After all, the experience of flow should produce intense feelings of enjoyment in the task at hand. That should make people happier and thus, have higher life satisfaction. In terms of performance, flow occurs when one is doing something and in the process of doing that something the person is mastering it. However, as one masters the task they need to have more and more challenging activities to tackle in order to maintain flow. So, essentially when you are in a flow state you are becoming more competent in the activities you are working on. There have been correlations found in flow experiences and performance in artistic and scientific creativity (Sawyer, 1992), teaching (Csikszentmihalyi, 1996) learning (Csikszentmihalyi et al., 1993) and sports (Jackson, Thomas, Marsh, & Smethurst, 2001).

Csikszentmihalyi (1990) suggests ways to apply flow in a variety of different aspects of our lives. In education, he suggests that overlearning is a key concept for attaining proficiency in academic tasks that are often perceived as daunting, such as mathematics. Overlearning is the idea of practicing a skill beyond the point of initial mastery so that the skill is practically automatic. Csikszentmihalyi believes that overlearning allows the mind to concentrate on seeing the desired work as a singular integrated action. Therefore, assignments that stretch one's skill just beyond their present capacity will lead to flow. The idea of overlearning may be used to create flow in other activities as well, such as sports. Overlearning in sports is helpful because it allows some tasks that could be perceived as challenging to become easier with a lot of practice.

Another place that flow can be useful is in the workplace. It is thought that certain tasks at work may be performed to enhance and increase flow in the workplace. Csikszentmihalyi (2003) emphasizes finding activities and spaces that are conducive to flow in the workplace and then look for and develop personal characteristics to increase experiences of flow. This can improve morale among workers by fostering a sense of greater happiness and accomplishment and better performance. In order to achieve flow in work, there needs to be three conditions: the goals for the worker are clear, feedback is immediate, and there is a balance between opportunity and capacity. The story about the author at the beginning of this section is a great example of flow from work. He understood exactly what he had to do (turn the binder into a computer program), there was a balance between opportunity and capacity (he could do it and was asked to do it), and he was provided immediate feedback (when he would have a question or concern, he would ask his adviser and he would get an immediate response regarding what was working, what was not working, and ideas on how to fix it).

Flow is also experienced during artistic pursuits. As mentioned earlier, Csikszentmihalyi started coming up with the idea of flow by watching and talking to artists. In music, there are also great examples of flow. Performers in a flow state have a heightened quality of performance as compared to when they are not in a flow state. De Manzano, Theorell, Harmat, and Ullen (2010) studied flow in music. They had pianists put in a situation that would maximize the possibility of a flow state by using piano players of high expertise and having them choose a piece of music that they played well and enjoyed playing. While the experimenters were not directly putting people in a flow state, they set up a situation where flow was most likely to occur. There was a relationship between a flow state and heart rate, blood pressure, and muscles in the face. When the pianist was in a flow state, heart rate and blood pressure decreased while facial muscles relaxed. In other words, being in a flow state puts us in a relaxed state—similar to a meditative state. During this state, the performance of the pianist improved.

Creativity

The discussion of flow and artistic endeavors lends itself to a related topic: creativity. Creativity is thinking of novel and productive ways to do things. Typically, when we think of creativity we think of artistic activities—painting, sculpting, music, acting, etc. However, this is a fairly limited view of creativity, as you can be creative in non-artistic endeavors as well. Creativity is studied in cognitive psychology, particularly in problem solving and idea generation. One area of problem solving that is of interest in cognitive psychology is that of insight. Insight is that "aha!" moment that people experience where they solve a problem or come up with an idea out of nowhere. Research suggests that people are thinking about unresolved problems and questions even when they don't consciously know it. This type of information processing occurs in the cognitive unconscious. In other words, we are thinking about things even when we do not know it. An example of such non-conscious thinking is the "tip of the tongue" phenomenon. This occurs when there is something that you are trying to remember, like a character's name on your favorite television show, and you KNOW you know it but cannot recall the name at that moment. You go through all the tricks you can think of trying to remember the person's name—heck, you can even picture the person in your mind, think of other roles the actor has played, recall the defining attributes of the character—but alas, no luck in remembering the name. So you stop thinking about it and what happens? About twenty minutes later, the name seems to pop out of nowhere. This is unconscious thinking at work. Your brain is going into overdrive searching your knowledge set finding the name while you are consciously doing other things. When the right answer is found, it is brought to your consciousness.

In cognitive psychology, there is a field that studies how to think creatively. This is called the creative cognition approach (Smith, Ward, & Finke, 1995). Creativity is a mental phenomenon that results from the application of ordinary cognitive processes. One thing that is interesting about creativity is that there is a layman's belief that creativity is somewhat innate. People are born creative and that's that. However, that's not completely true. To quote an old joke, "How do you get to Carnegie Hall? Practice, practice, practice!" If creativity is innate, practice would be an unnecessary task. However, as with any talent, even creativity gets better with practice. Practice makes perfect. As Simonton pointed out in 2000, it requires about a decade of extensive deliberate practice before a person gains world-class proficiency. Creativity comes from a well-developed skill set and a wide knowledge base. This finding has very interesting implications regarding who can do what. Shining examples of expertise and perfection in a given field aren't born, they are made. After all, it is well known that Michael Jordan—arguably the greatest basketball player of all time—was cut from his high school varsity basketball team as a sophomore. If playing basketball was an innate ability for MJ, he would have made every team he tried out for and been a standout since day one. Instead, MJ's abilities have a lot to do with the effort and dedication he had for his sport. He practiced every day. In fact, when he was with the Bulls, he would practice before practice. He had set up a group called "The Breakfast Club" who would meet at his house in the morning before going to actual practice at the Chicago Bulls training facility. This club would lift weights, perform agility drills, and of course eat a healthy breakfast before going to team practice. In other words, Michael Jordan wasn't just innately great, he was great because he worked hard at being a basketball player so that he would be the best basketball player he could be.

Mindfulness

Another individual characteristic that seems to increase well-being is mindfulness. This idea has its roots in Buddhism and has many different (yet related) definitions, but for our purposes, we will stick to definitions that come out of scientific research into mindfulness. One such definition refers to mindfulness as being in "a flexible state of mind in which we are actively engaged in the present, noticing new things and sensitive to context" (Langer, 2000). Another description of mindfulness used in the psychology literature includes "state of being attentive to and aware of what is taking place in the present" (Brown & Ryan, 2003).

Essentially, it is a state in which we don't think too hard about the past or the future. We are just existing in now, concentrating on now, and experiencing now without judging now. Just being present. Anyone who has ever ruminated over a bad break-up or awaited news of a biopsy result understands that this is easier said than done. It is also difficult to remain in the present during more mundane daily tasks (the author writing this section currently has her to-do list beside her and is waiting for a local pizzeria to open so she can place an order for her deserving research assistants). However, mounting evidence suggests that there are positive outcomes associated with engaging in mindfulness and attempting to stay in the present. Mindfulness seems to be associated with a number of positive personality traits, happy marriages, and shows potential as a therapeutic tool.

Brown and Ryan (2003) discovered that mindfulness is associated with general well-being while they were conducting research to create a scale to measure individual differences in mindfulness. While creating the Mindfulness Attentional Awareness Scale, they found that mindfulness negatively correlates measures of depression, anxiety, and neuroticism while positively correlating with self-esteem and optimism, competence, positive affect, vitality, and self-actualization. Of course, these findings were correlational data collected via survey (which does not establish that mindfulness causes all of those positive outcomes, just that they are associated with positive outcomes). However, these findings were replicated in experimental research in which participants provided real-time ratings of their emotional states several times a day over the course of two or three weeks. The real-time study also found associations between mindfulness and general, day-to-day feelings of autonomy and lower levels of negative affect. The final study in this series was the most dramatic as it studied mindfulness in cancer patients. Participants completed an eight-week long mindfulness intervention aimed at stress reduction (Kabat-Zinn et al., 1992). The research found that, compared to data collected prior to the mindfulness intervention, after the intervention, participants rated themselves as being lower in mood disturbances and stress.

Individuals who are high in mindfulness tend to have greater marital satisfaction (Burpee & Langer, 2005). This study is of particular interest to intimate relationship researchers because mindfulness was pitted against couple similarity to see which better predicted marital satisfaction. One of the leading beliefs in intimate relationship research can be summarized via the truism "Birds of a feather flock together": Happy marriages and friendships are sustained between like-minded individuals—for example, people with similar backgrounds, belief systems, and education levels. Burpee and Langer asked participants to report their individual level of mindfulness (using a different scale than the one mentioned previously, one that focuses on novelty seeking, novelty producing, flexibility, and engagement), spousal similarity, and overall marital satisfaction. Now, it is important to stress that mindfulness does not account for all marital satisfaction, but it accounted for more marital satisfaction than did other demographic variables. Additionally, while it only accounted for a small portion of marital satisfaction (8%), the current research found that similarity accounted for no marital satisfaction.

Luckily, these findings are not just good news for those amongst us who just happen to be more mindful. Of particular hopefulness within mindfulness research is the fact that mindfulness can be cultivated. Anyone who has ever tried to lose weight or quit a bad habit knows how difficult new habits can be, but it appears that mindfulness meditation can be used to increase this quality in the individual. Several different approaches to incorporate mindfulness into therapy already exist and have been evaluated for effectiveness (Baer, 2003). The Baer review contains more thorough descriptions of variations upon mindfulness therapy found here, but the overall message is that, while the research methods used in mindfulness research could be improved upon (control groups, controlling for the passage of time, blind studies, etc.), they have shown to help people with particular conditions (individuals with stressful lives, cancer patients) that require further study.

The real challenges that Kesho faced in his life were not caused by his physical disabilities; they were caused by the emotional rollercoaster ride that characterized his home life. His father was an alcoholic who was prone to both physical violence and psychological abuse. His mother, who was kindhearted and religious in her younger years, was perhaps too forgiving of her husband's inimical and unpredictable ways. His work habits were unpredictable, and his behavior at home even more so. He would spend much of his free time at local bars. He would be intoxicated several days a week, and he was fond of physical and verbal confrontations with his family. About the time that he was preparing for high school, Kesho got "the talk" that many young African-Americans get about the time of puberty. Not the sex talk. It was the talk about identity, race, and how he might be perceived by his white peers. His father emphasized caution and to never fully place his trust in his new, white friends. He did not mince words, stating that some white folk were just as likely to "stab him in the back as to help him."

The opportunities in Cleveland dried up in the mid 1970s, and his father's alcoholism was at what could have been a turning point. By this point, Kesho's father was on disability due to his exposure to asbestos during his time in the Navy. The family decided to move to Phoenix, Arizona in the hopes that a new town (and distance from old habits and acquaintances) might help Kesho's father stay sober and provide the rest of the family a chance to start fresh. The inspiration for the move was an offhand comment made by his mother, who commented that she might leave and go to someplace "like Arizona." His father abruptly replied, "good idea!" And so the family moved. This was quite a culture shock for Kesho and his family. By this time, Kesho's little brother was almost eight years old. The only time the youngsters saw other African-American children was when they went to church.

As Kesho got older, his physical strength and endurance grew. In some ways, the prosthetics had made him stronger than many of his peers. Remember, he spent more energy even doing simple things like walking. In turn, he was building up muscle mass. Although his stamina was somewhat compromised, his high activity level helped him to stay mobile. His physical prowess became apparent when he joined the wrestling team. He was strong and agile on the mat, and he earned the respect of his white teammates, although he did keep an emotional barrier between himself and them, partly because of the advice of his father and partly because of his experience as a double amputee.

After high school, Kesho had received a certificate of completion in drafting. He had learned to sketch out detailed designs, and this skill would serve him well for the next few years. He began working at a company that specialized in designing pressure suits for burn victims. People who have been horribly burned over large sections of their bodies face a number of challenges including reduced ability to fight off infections, increased sensitivity to heat, and pain. Pressure suits that fit tightly over their skin provide a layer of protection from the heat of the sun, help to keep the burn areas clean and healthy by smoothing out the affected areas, and prevent unnecessary chaffing from things like clothing. Kesho was good at his job, and he enjoyed the benefits of living on his own.

At this point in Kesho's life, his family was preparing to move again, this time setting their sights on North Carolina. His father's alcoholism had not improved with the move to Arizona, and it was thought that perhaps another move might do the trick. Kesho's boss, who was impressed with the young man's skill set, had suggested that he go to college and earn a degree in engineering. He seemed to have the aptitude and the drive, so he decided to do so. Two years later, he made the decision to follow his family to North Carolina and to attend a university in Greensboro. This decision had one drawback. To save money, he moved back in with his parents. This meant that the chaos of his family life could once again be a source of hardship. It was. His first attempt at college was a near disaster. His grades were poor, his ability to pay attention was inconsistent, and his home life was worse. His father would routinely single him out and denigrate the young man for not living up to his potential.

Kesho quit school and began a series of full-time and part-time jobs that would fill his time for the next twenty years. Many of the jobs were physically demanding. They had the effect of keeping him strong and wearing him out. He lived with his parents on and off during that time. When he was living with them, the confrontations were frequent. In one instance, he and his father began fighting in the hallways of their house. The two fell to the floor, with Kesho on top of his father. Suddenly, the anger that Kesho had felt toward his father disappeared and was replaced with sympathy and sadness. He saw him as a tired old man instead of a monster. He stood up and decided to go to work. That was a turning point in his relationship with his parents; he was now a man who was responsible for his own actions. If there was ever going to be a time for him to lose control, it would have occurred during that incident, and he now knew that he could trust himself to make wise and compassionate choices. Sadly, Kesho's father did not experience a similar moment of clarity, and he continued to struggle with his addiction for the next twenty years until his death in 2003.

Grit

The feeling of meeting a long-term, valued goal is awesome. As the authors can attest to, earning a doctorate after years of research, teaching, poverty, challenging graduate classes, and exams is exhilarating. Completion of such long-term goals (e.g., months of training in order to run a marathon, saving money for years in order to purchase your first house, putting in your twenty years in the military in order to receive a pension, parenting child, starting new business, etc.) does not happen by accident. It happens with determination, planning, self-discipline, focus, energy. It happens with grit.

Grit is the term (coined by psychologist Angela Duckworth) to describe this quality that allows a person to achieve difficult, long-term goals that require months, if not years, to achieve. These are goals that are marked by set-backs and disappointments and sacrifice. Grit is getting a lot of attention in psychology as well as non-academic circles. Duckworth was awarded a prestigious McArthur Fellowship in 2013. This award consists of $1,000,000 to pursue the recipient's area of expertise (presumably, for the betterment of our species). Duckworth was selected for this honor due to the potential grit holds for helping understand why some people are more likely to set and achieve difficult life goals than others. The hope is that with a better understanding of grit, we can encourage the non-gritty to become grittier.

Duckworth's work was inspired by working as an inner city junior high school math teacher. The school was plagued by high dropout rates. She observed that the kids who stayed in school weren't necessarily the smartest kids or the happiest kids or the most popular kids. Instead, they had qualities that allowed them to persevere despite modest backgrounds and living in dangerous neighborhoods. They were the kids who studied the most, kept their chins up when things got tough, and persisted even after failure.

Inspired by her students, Duckworth went back to graduate school in Psychology at the University of Pennsylvania. And after she earned her doctorate, she returned to junior high school to study eighth graders. This led to one of the early research publications in the grit literature (Duckworth & Seligman, 2005). This article actually predates the coining of the term *grit*, and instead studied one important facet of grit: self-discipline. Over the course of two separate studies, Duckworth followed eighth graders from the beginning to the end of an academic year. At the beginning of the year, she collected extensive data about the students, including their IQs, impulsiveness, self-control, and ability to delay gratification. They also measured behaviors that influenced academic success, including the amount of time spent watching television, completing homework, school absences, and performance on standardized exams.

The relationship between self-discipline and final GPA was twice as big as the relationship between IQ and final GPA ($r = .32$, which is a moderate correlational relationship vs. $r = .67$, which is a strong correlational relationship). Additionally, of the eight academic variables collected (first marking period GPA, final GPA, spring achievement test, selection to a competitive high school, absences, time spent on homework, time spent watching TV, time of day homework is begun), kids high in grit watched significantly less television, were significantly more likely to attend school, and spent more time working on homework assignments. Meanwhile, IQ was unrelated to these three important factors to success.

A more recent article also studied academic success, but this study didn't just look at typical American junior high schoolers. The participants in this study were young people that made it to the Script's National Spelling Bee in Washington, D.C. (Duckworth, Kirby, Tsukayama, Bernstein, & Ericsson, 2011). Duckworth and her colleagues asked Bee participants questions regarding their preparation for the Bee. Specifically, they asked the participants how much time they devoted to three different methods of preparation: 1) leisure reading in order to build vocabulary and familiarity with how words are spelled, 2) being quizzed by another person, and 3) solitarily learning and memorizing words. They also asked spelling bee participants how much they enjoyed the three forms of preparation. Duckworth and her colleagues found that the students enjoyed solitary learning the least. The researchers also found that solitary learning was the greatest predictor (of the three factors listed) of performance in the spelling bee. So which kids win the Spelling Bee? Kids who display grit by sticking to a lonesome study routine that isn't particularly pleasant but yields success.

But grit isn't just useful for understanding high-achieving teenagers. Research has found that grit can predict which men stay married and which men get divorced. Eskreis-Winkler, Shulman, Beal, & Duckworth (2014) found that men with higher levels of grit are 17% more likely to stay married than men who are lower in grit. This finding did not apply to women (which is an interesting research finding in and of itself). However, it does demonstrate that when it comes to maintaining a marriage, it appears that the willingness to apply one's self to the long-term commitment to another person is important to success (at least for men).

Kesho is an embodiment of grit. He found steady work and was able to move out and live on his own for much of the next two decades. Then, in 2005, things changed again. On the heels of his father's death came more bad news. He suffered an injury that rendered him incapable of staying at his current job in a warehouse. At 45 years of age, Kesho found himself with few alternatives. He moved in with his mother. After four years of work in retail and human services, he decided to give college a serious try. At first, his grades were shaky, like before. But many other things were different. He was more mature, and he found himself identifying more with his instructors, who were usually closer to his own age than his fellow students. The work ethic that had been instilled in him over twenty years of effort began to serve him well in this new academic setting. With the absence of his father's drinking, he found that he could focus for longer periods of time on his studies. He was able to rely upon his younger brother, with whom he described his relationship as "tight," for social support and words of encouragement. And so, he continued. His grades improved and the academic acknowledgements soon followed. He made the Dean's list for two semesters. He graduated from college in 2013. Something he had been striving for, in his heart and in his head, for more than twenty years.

Kesho's story is not a tale that ends with a dream job, the promise of true love, or a winning lottery ticket. The truth is the story is not over yet. Kesho is a double amputee who is now struggling with a new ailment. The dark sunglasses that he wears are a means for him to deal with a heightened sensitivity to light brought on by diabetes. He is also a 51-year old black man with a college degree who is presently unemployed. Technically, he is one of the long-term unemployed people often referred to in business reports on the struggling U.S. economy. And still he has hope. He realized that his transformation that began in 2009 would not lead to overnight success. It would be more like a ten-year plan that includes normalizing his relationship with his family, earning his degree, coping with his diabetes, and finding a career path. When asked why he didn't just decide to live off the government for the rest of his life, his reply was quick and crisp. "That would be giving up. I have found that when I give up, I fail 100% of the time."

This book began with the observation that most people misunderstand the term *Pollyanna*. They believe that a Pollyanna is a person who is always happy, always positive, and completely oblivious to the harsh realities of the world. A Pollyanna is sheltered from the experiences of hardship, pain, and suffering. A Pollyanna is naïve to the point of ignorance. But if the case of Kesho proves anything, it is that a Pollyanna does not live a sheltered life free from negative experiences. A Pollyanna is not willfully ignorant of pain. A Pollyanna experiences it, copes with it, and puts it into perspective. A Pollyanna does not allow the pain to linger any longer than it has to, lest it become an obstacle that prevents them from moving forward. A Pollyanna is happy to have had those experiences and to learn the lessons that have allowed them to persevere. A Pollyanna is constantly focused on making a better tomorrow. Like Kesho.

CODA

by Rich Walker

I am standing, near as I can figure, in the exact spot when Ken McElroy was killed in Skidmore, Missouri. I look at the ground, half expecting to see the man's blood still staining the pavement. Over the past three days, I have criss-crossed the county, visited the courthouse in Maryville, and chatted up a few people around several of the small nearby towns. I have stood at McElroy's grave in St. Joseph. Something is bothering me this morning. My first thought is the time of day. My flight leaves in a few hours from Kansas City. I should be leaving soon so that I can have plenty of time to return the rental car and clear security. But I have more than enough time to get there. It must be something else. Something about this trip has me unsettled. I allow my mind to wander.

The interviews I had scheduled did not quite pan out like I had hoped. People who were willing to talk on the phone seemed to stay quiet when I met them in person. I understand. I am an outsider and Skidmore is a small town, much smaller than it was in the 1980s. The last census put the population at just under 300, but it feels smaller. Desolate. Like an old man biding its time, marking the days off the calendar until it finally dies. This town has seen more than its share of violence and tragedy since the days of Ken McElroy. On April 11, 2001 Branson Perry, a young man just 20 years old, went missing after he went outside to return a set of jumper cables to the garage. No clues for law enforcement, no resolution for the family. In 2004, Bobbie Jo Stinnett a young pregnant woman was found murdered; she had been butchered and her child taken from her womb. Bobbi Joe's daughter will grow up to learn that her entrance into this world was marked by the violent and senseless death of her mother. There is no emotional recovery from something like that. My mind pauses as if it fleetingly sensed something. I continue to think.

I think back to my interview with Chris Pritchard, the born-again Christian who spent two decades in prison after plotting to murder his mother and stepfather. His answers were all sincere, his honesty seemed boundless, and he offered up no excuses for his actions or the consequences they wrought. I detected only one weakness in the spiritual armor that protected his soul. And it was a big one. He hasn't forgiven his co-conspirators. He hasn't even talked to them. The ones who actually carried out the crime and per his directions killed his stepfather and caved in the skull of his mother. He has now dedicated his life to the church and to help people who are transitioning from prison back to society, but one could argue that he still has much to learn about the Christian ideals of forgiveness. One could go so far as to say that Pritchard was fooling himself. The emotional probe I had sent into my brain detected something, and this time the feeling was not quickly receding.

Doubt. Maybe I was fooling myself with all of the research, the data collection, the talks at conferences, and the endless cycle of writing and revising academic papers and scholarly book chapters. I was trained to be a rigorous social scientist. A skeptic. What am I doing writing a book about positive psychology, about the boon of positive life events, and the ability of humans to demonstrate resilience in the face of hardship? I should be writing about the harshness of reality, about how unfair it is, and about how people are prone to their worst predilections.

The paved streets of Skidmore are covered in mud from tractors and pickups that have come in from the fields caked in thick layers of black and brown. I start the car and put it in reverse. My left front tire catches a big piece of mud and spins for a second before it catches the pavement. I aim the car south down 113 and out of town. The doubt in my mind simmers as I drive. I cross the Nodaway River and spot something to my right on a farm road skirting the edge of a field. A large red-tail hawk, an adult female based on her size and coloration, is feasting upon a dead opossum. I slow my car and then bring it to a stop, expecting her to fly off at any moment. But she doesn't. She eyes my car for several seconds and steps back towards the bloody carcass. She drags it away from the road in several sharp, hopping tugs. That's when I spot her wing, bent at an odd angle and dragging the ground. The injury looks several days old, and it is almost certain that she can't fly. She will probably be dead within a few weeks. This could very well be her last meal. I stay and watch her for several minutes, allowing me to take her beauty and to appreciate her valiant struggle in the face of certain death.

My mind continues to wander. During the course of writing this text, I have met some interesting people. For various reasons, their stories were not included. I had a lengthy conversation with a survivalist wanna-be, a pot-bellied man who shifted uncomfortably in his seat when we talked. He talked about his dis-satisfaction with the government and repeatedly stated that he would be prepared when "it hit the fan." He had a stockpile of food and weapons in a safe place. Across the room, his teenage daughter was busy texting on her phone and giving the devastating headshakes and eye-rolls that adolescent girls are wont to do. For all of his conviction, it was clear that she wasn't buying any of it. During a lull in the conversation, she chimed in that she was going to college in the upcoming year. The man's eyes brightened with pride. I queried her intended major. She replied "interior design." I studied his face for a moment, his eyes had softened and he was smiling. He was sending his daughter to college for interior design. Not to be a doctor or an engineer, professions that might find some agency in the post-apocalyptic hellscape he had described to me, but to be an *interior designer*. And then it occurred to me— he hadn't completely succumbed to the gloom and doom he had been spewing. He was hopeful in spite of himself. That interview ended abruptly when I asked a question that used the phrase "chicken little."

My mind switches gears to a gang member I talked with on three occasions in my car. He was a member of the Crips. He was a tall, muscular, African-American man in his early twenties. His skin was emblazoned with several tattoos, one of which I photographed with my phone so I could verify the legitimacy of his gang affiliation. There was the distinct aroma of marijuana on his person during one of our conversations. But that is where the stereotype ends and the reality sets it. He did not seem aggressive or "thuggish." He had a child, a little boy that he dressed in North Carolina blue. He worked at a "big box store" for his primary source of legitimate income. Yes, he did deal weed, but he stayed clear from violence and the hard drugs. With no way to verify that claim, I took him at his word. He also offered this tidbit of wisdom that stuck with me. The real threat to gang activity was not the possibility of being arrested by the police or the potential of violence from rival gangs. The real threat was simply people doing good for each other. It was the steady stream of church activity buses that rolled through the neighborhood he worked. Volunteers driving through backstreets and blind alleys would stop and ask people if they needed a place to stay or a hot meal. They would coax them off the street, at least for the night, taking away some of his best customers. What stopped him from recruiting more gang members? Again, the police and rival gangs had little to do with it. In his view, most kids aren't cut out for the criminal life. Football and basketball take his best recruits. That does not diminish the seriousness of gang activity, but it does offer a straightforward solution to help stem the tide. Engage the youth in positive activity. Give them hope. Those interviews ended when his cell phone number was changed, and I was no longer able to reach him.

My mind has returned to the present. I am back in my rented car watching the hawk dig into her meal, occasionally chirping with what sounds like satisfaction. I think of my wife; she and I work with injured hawks and owls and have found our place in this world caring for these magnificent creatures. I think of my students, who drive me crazy, but most of whom are smart and energetic. I think of my colleagues—friendly, supportive, and as helpful as you could hope. The pangs of doubt that had seemed so strong a few minutes ago have faded. They have been replaced with something more hopeful and yet somehow more realistic.

My mind is quiet, and I begin to see the connections between the stories, the data, and the theory. Perhaps I am having a brief experience of Flow. The bully who met his fate at the hands of vigilante assailants, the ex-convict who found salvation, the teacher who persevered in his class after a tragedy, the last remaining residents of a forsaken town, the double-amputee going back to college, and even the hawk standing before me—they are all part of a larger story. The struggles of life and death face every person and every creature on earth. To meet these inevitabilities head on with courage, tenacity, and hope is the only choice that makes sense. Resilience, be it in the form of creativity or mindfulness or just grit and determination, is the adaptive response. Perhaps the research on fading emotion that I have done with my friends and colleagues tells part of that story. I think it does. The fact that I am part of that story, as both a person and as a scholar, gives me comfort and strength.

I take one more look at the injured hawk crouching defensively over her meal. During my fugue, she had drawn up her good wing to shelter the carcass from prying eyes, a behavior known as mantling. I glance in the mirror at the outskirts of Skidmore, then put my car back in gear and pull away. A few scattered pieces of mud fall away from the undercarriage as I pick up speed.

Endnotes

Introduction

1. Jonah Lehrer. "Depression's upside." February 25, 2010. This article can be found at the following website: http://www.nytimes.com/2010/02/28/magazine/28depression-t.html?pagewanted=all&_r=0.

2. Joshua Kendall. "Madness made them great." June 25, 2013. This article can be found at the following website: http://www.slate.com/articles/health_and_science/science/2013/06/business_success_from_mental_illness_steve_jobs_henry_heinz_and_est_e_lauder.html.

3. Jennifer Brown. "12 shot dead, 58 wounded in Aurora movie theater during Batman premier." July 21, 2012. This article can be found at the following website: http://www.denverpost.com/news/ci_21124893/12-shot-dead-58-wounded-aurora-movie-theater.

Chapter 1

1. The World Database of Happiness. http://www1.eur.nl/fsw/happiness.

Chapter 2

1. Indeed, we are respectful fans of the works of both of these individuals. Ehrenreich has written remarkable texts, most notably *Nickeled and Dimed*, which highlights the plight of the working poor who struggle in the margins of society. Shermer wrote one of the best books on skepticism, *Why People Believe Weird Things*. Both texts are commonly used in college classrooms. However, we feel that in attacking the questionable claims of some authors, an entire area has been inappropriately maligned.

Chapter 3

1. We would like to thank Harry N. MacLean for his e-mail correspondence regarding the story of Ken McElroy and for the use of the photograph in this chapter. This tale is more fully described in Harry N. MacLean's 1988 book *In broad daylight: A murder in Skidmore, Missouri*.

2. We would like to thank Dr. Jeffrey Sable, Christian Brothers University, for reviewing a draft of this chapter and providing useful comments on the physiological aspects of emotion.

3. Dr. Howard Barnes passed away in 2013. He is missed.

Chapter 4

1. We could like to sincerely thank Dr. Joseph Peterson for his willingness to pro-
    vide us with essential details related to the February 14, 2008, shooting at
    Northern Illinois University. Our thoughts are with him, the students in his
    charge that day and their families, and all people who are touched by tragedy
    that results from gun violence.

Chapter 5

1. We would like to thank Chris Pritchard for taking the time to talk personally
    with Rich Walker about his life and his spiritual journey. We wish him well.

Chapter 6

1. We would like to extend our sincere thanks to Dr. Harold Aurand for his help
    in providing much of the historical background on Centralia and for providing
    a tour of the vicinity.

2. The definitive work on the social collapse of Centralia is detailed in *The
    real disaster is above ground: A mine fire and social conflict* by J. Stephen
    Kroll-Smith and Stephen Robert Couch, 1990. Lexington, KY: University
    Press of Kentucky.

Chapter 7

1. Kesho is a pseudo-name used to shield this individual's identity. Kesho is a
    Swahili word that means "tomorrow."

2. We would like to point out that some of Barbara Fredrickson's work has been
    sharply criticized. Specifically a 2005 paper she published with Marcial Losada
    which claimed to have found the "positivity ratio" that would lead to happiness
    and flourishing. We share the skepticism offered in such claims. Indeed, upon
    learning of this criticism, we removed all discussion of the positivity ratio from
    this text. As we stated in Chapter 2, we do not believe in a "golden ticket" to
    happiness, but we do believe that positive emotions have value. For a more
    complete discussion, see Brown, N., Sokal, A. D. & Friedman, H. L. (2013).
    The complex dynamics of wishful thinking: The critical positivity ratio. *Ameri-
    can Psychologist, 68*, 801-813. For Fredrickson's response, see Fredrickson,
    B. L. (2013). Updated thinking on positivity ratios. *American Psychologist, 68*,
    814–822.

REFERENCES

Introduction

de Becker, G. (1997). *The gift of fear*. New York: Dell.

Dutton, K. (2012). *The wisdom of psychopaths: What saints, spies, and serial killers can teach us about success.* New York: Scientific American/Farrar, Straus and Giroux.

Herbert, G. (1651/1910). *The English poems of George Herbert.* Cambridge, UK: Cambridge University Press. Reprint edition (December 13, 2010).

Porter, E. H. (1913/2009). *Pollyanna: The first glad book.* Republished by CreateSpace Independent Publishing Platform (November 9, 2009).

Reece, C. L. (1995). *Pollyanna plays the game.* Uhrichsville, OH: Barbour Publishing.

Chapter 1

Andrews, F. M., & Withey, S. B. (1976). *Social indicators of well-being: America's perception of life quality.* New York: Plenum.

Bernstein, A. E. (2005). The contributions of Marcel Proust to psychoanalysis. *Journal of the American Academy of Psychoanalysis and Dynamic Psychiatry, 33*(1), 137–48.

Berntsen, D. (1996). Involuntary autobiographical memories. *Applied Cognitive Psychology, 10,* 435–454.

Chwalisz, K., Diener, E., & Gallagher, D. (1988). Autonomic arousal feedback and emotional experience: Evidence from the spinal cord injured. *Journal of Personality and Social Psychology, 54,* 820–828.

Frijters, P., Johnston, D., & Shields, M. (2011). Happiness dynamics with quarterly events data. *Scandinavian Journal of Economics, 113,* 190–211.

Diener, E., Ng, W., Harter, J., & Arora, R. (2010). Wealth and happiness across the world: Material prosperity predicts life evaluation, whereas psychosocial prosperity predicts positive feeling. *Journal of Personality and Social Psychology, 99,* 52–61.

Lüdtke, O., Roberts, B. W., Trautwein, U., & Nagy, G. (2011). A random walk down university avenue: Life paths, life events, and personality trait change at the transition to university life. *Journal of Personality and Social Psychology, 101,* 620–637.

Myers, D. G., & Diener, E. (1995). Who is happy? *Psychological Science, 6,* 10–19.

North, R. J., Holahan, C. J., Moos, R. H., & Cronkite, R. C. (2008). Family support, family income, and happiness: A 10-year perspective. *Journal of Family Psychology, 22*(3), 475–483.

Scheier, L. M., Botvin, G. J., & Miller, N. L. (1999). Life events, neighborhood stress, psychosocial functioning, and alcohol use among urban minority youth. *Journal of Child & Adolescent Substance Abuse, 9,* 19–50.

Suefeld, P., & Eich, E. (1995). Autobiographical memory and affect under conditions of reduced environmental stimulation. *Journal of Environmental Psychology, 15,* 321–326.

Thompson, C. P., Skowronski, J. J., Larsen, S., & Betz, A. (1996). *Autobiographical memory: Remembering what and remembering when.* New York: Lawrence Erlbaum Associates.

Veenhoven, R. (2000). The four qualities of life: Ordering concepts and measures of the good life. *Journal of Happiness Studies, 1,* 1–39.

Wagenaar, W. A. (1986). My memory: A study of autobiographical memory over six years, *Cognitive Psychology, 18,* 225–252.

Waldfogel, S. (1948). The frequency and affective character of childhood memories. *Psychological Monographs, 62,* Whole No. 291.

Walker, W. R. (2014). Sampling autobiographical experiences via text messaging. Unpublished manuscript.

Chapter 2

Aeschylus. *Oresteia – Agamemnon, The Libation Bearers, and The Eumenides.* Grene, D. & Lattimore, R. (Eds.) Chicago: University of Chicago, 1953.

Aesop. (2007). The boy who cried wolf. In D.L. Ashliman (Ed.), *Aesop's Fables* (pp. 102–116). New York: Penguin Group.

Byrne, R. (2006). *The secret.* New York: Atria Books.

Diener, E., & Diener, C. (1996). Most people are happy. *Psychological Science, 7*(3), 181–4.

Drucker, P. F. (1973). *Management: Tasks, responsibilities, practices.* New York: Harper & Row.

Dunn, E., & Norton, M. (2012). Don't indulge. Be happy. Opinion Page. *The New York Times,* Sunday July 7, 2012.

Ehrenreich, B. (2009). *Bright-Sided: How positive thinking is undermining America.* New York: Metropolitan Books.

Festinger, L., Riecken, H. W., & Schachter, S. (1956). *When prophecy fails.* Minneapolis: University of Minnesota Press.

Gigerenzer, G. (2007). *Gut feelings: The intelligence of the unconscious.* New York: Viking Press.

Gilbert, D. T., & Ebert, J. E. J. (2002). Decisions and revisions: The affective forecasting of changeable outcomes. *Journal of Personality and Social Psychology, 82*, 503–514.

Gilbert, D. T., Lieberman, M. D., Morewedge, C. K., & Wilson, T. D. (2004). The peculiar longevity of things not so bad. *Psychological Science, 15*, 14–19.

Hyatt, M. S. (1998). *The millennium bug: How to survive the coming chaos.* Washington D.C.: Regnery Publishing.

Jamison, K. R. (1993). *Touched with fire: Manic depressive illness and the artistic temperament.* New York: The Free Press.

Jaensch, E. R. (1929). *Grundformen menschlichen Seins.* Berlin: Otto Elsner.

Kuran, T., & Sunstein, C. R. (1999). Availability cascades and risk regulation. *Stanford Law Review, 54*, No. 4.

Krugman, P. (2008*). The return of depression economics and the crisis of 2008.* New York: W.W. Norton.

Lemieux, P. (2003). Following the herd. *Regulation, 26*(4), 16–21.

McKenzie, C. & Nelson, J. (2003). What a speaker's choice of frame reveals: Reference point, frame of reference, and framing effects. *Psychonomic Bulletin & Review, 10*(3): 596–602.

Myers, D. G. (2000). The funds, friends, and faith of happy people. *American Psychologist, 55*, 56–67.

Shermer, M. (1997). *Why people believe weird things: Pseudoscience, superstitions, and other confusions of our time.* New York: W.H. Freeman and Co.

Shermer, M. (2009, December 18). Kool-Aid psychology: Optimism versus realism. *Scientific American, 302*, 39.

Treanor, J. (July 6, 2012). Serious Fraud Office to investigate Libor manipulation, *The Guardian.* Retrieved July 10, 2012.

Twenge, J. M. (2009). Generational changes and their impact in the classroom: Teaching Generation Me. *Medical Education, 43*, 398–405.

Twenge, J. M., & Campbell, S. M. (2008). Generational differences in psychological traits and their impact on the workplace. *Journal of Managerial Psychology, 23*, 862–877.

Twenge, J. M., Konrath, S., Foster, J. D., Campbell, W. K., & Bushman, B. J. (2008). Egos inflating over time: A cross-temporal meta-analysis of the Narcissistic Personality Inventory. *Journal of Personality, 76*, 875–901.

Voltaire (1959) [1759]. Bair, Lowell. ed. *Candide.* New York: Bantam Dell.

Von Restorff, H. (1933). The effects of field formation in the trace field. *Psychological Research, 18*(1): 299–342.

Wells, B. E., & Twenge, J. M. (2005). Changes in young people's sexual behavior and attitudes, 1943–1999: A cross-temporal meta-analysis. *Review of General Psychology, 9*, 249–261.

Chapter 3

Alloy, L. B., & Abramson, L. Y. (1979). Judgment of contingency in depressed and nondepressed students: Sadder but wiser? *Journal of Experimental Psychology: General, 108*, 441–485.

Beck, A. T. (1967). *Depression: Clinical, experimental, and theoretical aspects.* New York: Hoeber. Republished as *Depression: Causes and treatment.* Philadelphia: University of Pennsylvania Press.

Beck, A. T., Rush, A. J., Shaw, B. F., & Emery, G. (1979). *Cognitive therapy of depression.* New York: Guilford.

Beaver, K. M., Vaughn, M. G., Delisi, M., & Wright, J. P. (2008). Anabolic-androgenic steroid use and involvement in violent behavior in a nationally representative sample of young adult males in the United States. *American Journal of Public Heath, 98*(12), 2185–2187.

Bodenhausen, G. V., Sheppard, L., & Kramer, G. P. (1994). Negative affect and social perception: The differential impact of anger and sadness. *European Journal of Social Psychology, 24*, 45–62.

Bora, E., Fornito, A., Pantelis, C., & Yücel, M. (2011). Gray matter abnormalities in Major Depressive Disorder: A meta-analysis of voxel based morphometry studies. *Journal of Affective Disorders, 138*, 9–18.

Boyd-Wilson, B. M., Walkey, F. H., McClure, J., & Green, D. E. (2000). Do we need positive illusions to carry out plans? Illusion: and instrumental coping. *Personality and Individual Differences, 29*(6), 1141–1152.

Carson, R. C., Hollon, S. D., & Shelton, R. C. (2010). Depressive realism and clinical depression. *Behaviour Research and Therapy, 48*, 257–265.

Chapell, M. S., Blanding, Z. B., Silverstein, M. E., Takahashi, M., Newman, B., Gubi, A., & McCann, N. (2005). Test anxiety and academic performance in undergraduate and graduate students. *Journal of Educational Psychology, 97*(2), 268–274.

Cheung-Blunden, V., & Blunden, B. (2008). The emotional construal of war: Anger, fear, and other negative emotions. *Peace and Conflict: Journal of Peace Psychology, 14*(2), 123–149.

Damasio, A. (1994). *Descartes' error: Emotion, reason, and the human brain.* New York: Putnam.

Dalgleish T., Williams J. M. G., Golden A.-M. J., Barnard P. J., Au-Yeung C., et al. (2007). Reduced specificity of autobiographical memory and depression: The role of executive processes. *Journal of Experimental Psychology: General, 136*(1), 23–42.

Dobson, K. S., & Franche, R. L. (1989). A conceptual and empirical review of the depressive realism hypothesis. *Canadian Journal of Behavioral Science, 21,* 419–433.

Dobson, K. S., & Pusch, D. (1995). A test of the depressive realism hypothesis in clinically depressed subjects. *Cognitive Therapy and Research, 19,* 41–50.

Fu, T., Koutstaal, W., Fu, C. H. Y., Poon, L., & Cleare, A. J. (2005). Depression, confidence, and decision: Evidence against depressive realism. *Journal of Psychopathology and Behavioral Assessment, 27,* 243–252.

Fuster, J. M. (2008). *The prefrontal cortex* (4th ed.). London: Academic Press.

Harmon-Jones, E., & Peterson, C. K. (2009). Supine body position reduces neural response to anger evocation. *Psychological Science, 20,* 1209–1210.

Hembree, R. (1988). Correlates, causes, effects, and treatment of test anxiety. *Review of Educational Research, 58*(1), 47–77.

Howell, L. L., Carroll, F. I., Votaw, J. R., Goodman, M. M., & Kimmel, H. L. (2007). Effects of combined dopamine and serotonin transporter inhibitors on cocaine self-administration in rhesus monkeys. *Journal of Pharmacology and Experimental Therapeutics, 320*(2), 757–765.

Johnson, S. (2010). *Where good ideas come from: A natural history of innovation.* New York: Penguin.

Joiner, T. E., Kistner, J. A., Stellrecht, N. E., & Merrill, K. (2006). On seeing clearly and thriving: Interpersonal perspicacity as adaptive (not depressive) realism (or where three theories meet). *Journal of Social and Clinical Psychology, 25*(5), 542–564.

Joormann, J., Teachman, B., & Gotlib, I. H. (2009). Sadder and Less Accurate? False memory for negative material in depression. *Journal of Abnormal Psychology, 118,* 412–417.

Kaiser, D. (2011). Why fear is your friend. Retrieved from *www.Lifehack.org,* June 7.

Kruesi, M. J., Hibbs, E. D., Zahn, T. P., et al. (1992). A 2-year prospective follow-up study of children and adolescents with disruptive behavior disorders. *Archives of General Psychiatry, 49,* 429–435.

Lerner, J. S., & Tiedens, L. Z. (2006). Portrait of the angry decision maker: How appraisal tendencies shape anger's influence on cognition. *Journal of Behavioral Decision Making, 19,* 115–137.

Ludwig, A. (1995). *The price of greatness: Resolving the creativity and madness controversy.* New York: The Guilford Press.

MacLean, H. N. (1988). *In broad daylight: A murder in Skidmore, Missouri.* New York: Harper and Row.

MacLeod, C., Mathews, A., & Tata, P. (1986). Attentional bias in emotional disorders. *Journal of Abnormal Psychology, 95*(1), 15–20.

Mahl, G. F. (1949). Effect of chronic fear on the gastric secretion of HCl in dogs. *Psychosomatic Medicine, 11*(1), 30–44.

Marcus, G. F. (2008). *Kluge: The haphazard construction of the human mind.* Boston: Houghton Mifflin.

Minsky, M. (1997). *The society of mind.* New York: Simon and Schuster.

Mitchell, K. J., Livosky, M., & Mather, M. (1998). The weapon focus effect revisited: The role of novelty. *Legal and Criminological Psychology, 3,* 287–303.

Moore, M. T., & Fresco, D. (2007). Depressive realism and attributional style: Implications for individuals at risk for depression. *Behavior Therapy, 38,* 144–154.

Moss, M. (2009). Design hates a depression. Retrieved from www.observatory. designobserver.com, January 6, 2009.

Msetfi, R. M., Muphy, R. A., Simpson, J., & Kornbrot, D. E. (2005). Depressive realism and outcome density bias in contingency judgments: The effect of the context and intertrial interval. *Journal of Experimental Psychology: General, 134,* 10–22.

Msetfi, R. M., Murphy, R. A., & Simpson, J. (2007). Depressive realism and the effect of intertrial interval on judgments of zero, positive, and negative contingencies. *The Quarterly Journal of Experimental Psychology, 60,* 461–481.

Munafò, M. R., Durrant C., Lewis G., & Flint J. (2009). Gene X environment interactions at the serotonin transporter locus. *Biological Psychiatry, 65*(3), 211–219.

Nabar, M., & Nicholas, T. "Uncertainty and Innovation During the Great Depression" Harvard Business School. January 14, 2010.

Orobio de Castro, B., Veerman, J. W., Koops, W., Bosch, J. D., & Monshouwer, H. J. (2002). Hostile attribution of intent and aggressive behavior: A meta-analysis. *Child Development, 73,* 916–934.

Raes, F., Hermans D., Williams J. M. G., & Eelen, P. (2006). Reduced autobiographical memory specificity and affect regulation. *Cognition & Emotion, 20,* 402–429.

Reynolds, M. (2011). Want to change—get angry! Psychology Today Online, January 1. http://www.psychologytoday.com/blog/wander-woman/ 201101/want-change-get-angry

Risch N., Herrell R., Lehner T., et al. (2009). Interaction between the serotonin transporter gene (5-HTTLPR), stressful life events, and risk of depression: a meta-analysis. *Journal of the American Medical Association, 301*(23), 2462–2471.

Seipp, B. (1991). Anxiety and academic performance: A meta-analysis of findings. *Anxiety Research, 4*, 27–41.

Share, A. (2012). Fire in the West Parts 1 and 2. Retrieved from www. americanforests.org.

Shiota, M. N., & Kalat, J. W. (2012). *Emotion.* Belmont, CA: Wadsworth.

Valzelli, L., & Bernasconi, S. (1979). Aggressiveness by isolation and brain serotonin turnover changes in different strains of mice. *Neuropsychobiology, 5*, 129–135.

Van der Does, A. J. W. (2001). The effects of tryptophan depletion on mood and psychiatric symptoms. *Journal of Affective Disorders, 64*, 107–119.

Virkkunen, M., Nuutila, A., Goodwin, F. K., & Linnoila, M. (1987). Cerebrospinal fluid monoamine metabolite levels in male arsonists. *Archives of General Psychiatry, 44*, 241–247.

Woollett, K., & Maguire, E. A. (2011). Acquiring "the knowledge" of London's layout drives structural brain changes. *Current Biology, 21*, 2109–2114.

Chapter 4

Adams, D. (1980). *The restaurant at the end of the universe.* London: Pan Books.

Berntsen, D. (1996). Involuntary autobiographical memories. *Applied Cognitive Psychology, 10*, 435-454.

Bonanno, G. A. (2004). Loss, trauma, and human resilience: Have we underestimated the human capacity to thrive after extremely adverse events? *American Psychologist, 59*, 20–28.

Bonanno, G. A., Ho, S. M. Y., Chan, J. C. K, Kwong, R. S. Y., Cheung, C. K. Y., Wong, C. P. Y., & Wong, V. C. W. (2008). Psychological resilience and dysfunction among hospitalized survivors of the SARS epidemic in Hong Kong: A latent class approach. *Health Psychology, 27*, 659–667.

Bonanno, G. A., & Mancini, A. D. (2008). The human capacity to thrive in the face of extreme adversity. *Pediatrics, 121*, 369–375.

Bonanno, G. A., Rennicke, C., & Dekel, S. (2005). Self-Enhancement among high-exposure survivors of the September 11th terrorist attack: Resilience or social maladjustment? *Journal of Personality and Social Psychology, 88*, 984–998.

Bonanno, G. A., Wortman, C. B., Lehman, D. R., Tweed, R. G., Haring, M., Sonnega, J., Carr, D., & Neese, R. M. (2002). Resilience to loss and chronic grief: A prospective study from pre-loss to 18 months post-loss. *Journal of Personality and Social Psychology, 83*, 1150–1164.

Cason, H. (1932). The learning and retention of pleasant and unpleasant activities. *Archives of Psychology, 134*, 1–96.

Comblain, C., D'Argembeau, A., & Van der Linden, M. (2005). Phenomenal characteristics of autobiographical memories for emotional and neutral events in older and younger adults. *Experimental Aging Research, 31,* 173–189.

Freud, S. (1915/1957). Repression. In J. Strachey (Ed. & Trans.), *The standard edition of the complete psychological works of Sigmund Freud* (Vol. 14, pp. 143–158). London: Hogarth Press.

Freud, S. (1937/1964). Constructions in analysis. In J. Strachey (Ed. & Trans.), *The standard edition of the complete psychological works of Sigmund Freud* (Vol. 23, pp. 255–269). London: Hogarth Press.

Galea, S., Ahern, J., Resnick, H., Kilpatrick, D., Bucuvalas, M., Gold, J., & Vlahov, D. (2002). Psychological sequelae of the September 11 terrorist attacks in New York City. *New England Journal of Medicine, 346,* 982–987.

Galea, S., Vlahov, D., Resnick, H., Ahern, J., Ezra, S., Gold, J., et al. (2003). Trends of probably post-traumatic stress disorder in New York City after the September 11th terrorist attacks. *American Journal of Epidemiology, 158,* 514–524.

Gibbons, J. A., Lee, S. A., & Walker, W. R. (2010). The fading affect bias begins within 12 hours and persists for 3 months. *Applied Cognitive Psychology, 25*(4), 663–672.

Hartnett, J. L., & Skowronski, J. J. (2010). Affective forecasts and the Valentine's Day shootings at NIU: People are resilient, but unaware of it. *The Journal of Positive Psychology, 5*(4), 275–280.

Holmes, D. (1970). Differential change in affective intensity and the forgetting of unpleasant personal experiences. *Journal of Personality and Social Psychology, 3,* 234–239.

Kravitz, L. (2002). 'Yesterday is Gone.' Released November 11, 2002. Virgin Records.

Landau, J. D., & Gunter, B. C. (2009). "Don't worry; you really will get over it": Methodological investigations of the Fading Affect Bias. *The American Journal of Psychology, 122*(2), 209–217.

Loftus, E. F., & Pickrell, J. E. (1995). The formation of false memories. *Psychiatric Annals, 25,* 720–725.

Nesselroade, J. R., Stigler, S. M., & Baltes, P. B. (1980). Regression toward the mean and the study of change. *Psychological Bulletin, 88*(3), 622–637.

Pavlov, I. P. (1927). *Conditioned Reflexes: An Investigation of the Physiological Activity of the Cerebral Cortex. Translated and Edited by G. V. Anrep.* London: Oxford University Press.

Ritchie, T. D., Batteson, T. J., Bohn, A., Crawford, M. T., Ferguson, G. V., Schrauf, R. W., Vogl, R. J., & Walker, W. R. (in press). A pancultural perspective on the fading affect bias in autobiographical memory. *Memory.*

Ritchie, T. D., Skowronski, J. J., Hartnett, J., Wells, B., & Walker, W. R. (2009). The fading affect bias in the context of emotion activation level, mood, and personal theories of emotion change. *Memory, 17*, 428–444.

Schrauf, R. W., & Hoffman, L. (2007). The effects of revisionism on remembered emotion: the valence of older, voluntary immigrants' pre-migration autobiographical memories. *Applied Cognitive Psychology, 21*, 895–913.

Stoeber, J., & Janssen, D. P. (2011). Perfectionism and coping with daily failures: Positive reframing helps achieve satisfaction at the end of the day. *Anxiety, Stress, & Coping, 24*, 477–497.

Taylor, S. E. (1991). Asymmetrical effects of positive and negative events: The mobilization-minimization hypothesis. *Psychological Bulletin, 110*, 67–85.

Thompson, C. P., Skowronski, J. J., & Betz, A. L. (1993). The use of partial temporal information in dating personal events. *Memory and Cognition, 21*, 352–360.

Walker, W. R., Skowronski, J. J., & Thompson, C. P. (2003). Life is pleasant— and memory helps to keep it that way! *Review of General Psychology, 7*, 203–210.

Walker, W. R., Skowronski, J. J., Gibbons, J. A., Vogl, R. J., & Thompson, C. P. (2003). On the emotions that accompany autobiographical memories: Dysphoria disrupts the fading affect bias. *Cognition and Emotion, 17*, 703–724.

Walker, W. R., Vogl, R. J., & Thompson, C. P. (1997). Autobiographical memory: Unpleasantness fades faster than pleasantness over time. *Applied Cognitive Psychology, 11*, 399–413.

Chapter 5

Alexander, C. N., Langer, E. J., Newman, R. I., Chandler, H. M., & Davies, J. L. (1989). Transcendental meditation, mindfulness, and longevity: An experimental study with the elderly. *Journal of Personality and Social Psychology, 57*, 950–964.

American Psychiatric Association. (2013). *Diagnostic and statistical manual of mental disorders* (5th ed.). Arlington, VA: American Psychiatric Publishing.

Aron, A., Melinat, E., Aron, E. N., Vallone, R. D., & Bator, R. J. (1997). The experimental generation of interpersonal closeness: A procedure and some preliminary findings. *Personality and Social Psychology Bulletin, 23*, 363–377.

Aune, M. B. (1993). "But only say the word": Another look at Christian worship as therapeutic. *Pastoral Psychology, 43*, 145–157.

Baldree, K. S., Murphy, S. P., & Powers, M. J. (1982). Praying. *Nursing Research, 31*, 107–112.

Baumeister, R. F., & Leary, M. R. (1995). The need to belong: Desire for interpersonal attachments as a fundamental human motivation. *Psychology Bulletin, 117*, 497–529.

Beck, A. T., & Weishar, M. (2007). Cognitive therapy. In R. J. Corsini & D. Wedding (eds.). *Current psychotherapies* (8th ed.). Belmont, CA: Brooks-Cole.

Bennett, T., Deluca, D. A., & Allen, R. W. (1995). Religion and children with disabilities. *Journal of Religion and Health, 34*, 301–312.

Byrd, R. C. (1988). Positive therapeutic effects of intercessory prayer in a coronary care unit population. *Southern Medical Journal, 81*, 826–829.

Diagnostic and Statistical Manual of Psychiatric Disorders, Fourth Edition (DSM-IV) 309.81 Posttraumatic Stress Disorder.

Dickens, C. (1860). *Great Expectations.* Chapman & Hall, London.

Dostoevsky, F. (1917). *Crime and Punishment.* New York: P.F. Collier & Son.

Doyle, D. (1992). Have we looked beyond the physical and psychosocial? *Journal of Pain and Symptom Management, 7*, 302–311.

Elkins, D. Anchor, K. N., & Sandler, H. M. (1979). Relaxation training and prayer behavior as tension reduction techniques. *Behavioral Engineering, 6*, 81–87.

Empereur, J. L. (1987). Liturgy as humanizing or as sacred. In J. L. Empereur (Ed.), *Worship: Exploring the Sacred* (pp. 85–96). Washington D.C.: Pastoral Press.

Ensari, N., & Miller, N. (2002). The out-group must not be so bad after all: The effects of disclosure, typicality, and salience on intergroup bias. *Journal of Personality and Social Psychology, 79*, 861–875.

Fiske, S. T. (1992). Thinking is for doing: Portraits of social cognition from daguerreotype to laserphoto. *Journal of Personality and Social Psychology, 63*, 877–889.

Foster, R. J. (1992). *Prayer: Finding the heart's true home.* San Francisco: Harper.

Francis, L. J., & Burton, L. (1994). The influence of personal prayer on purpose in life among Catholic adolescents. *Journal of Beliefs and Values, 15*, 6–9.

Gibbons, J. A., Hartzler, J., Hartzler, A., Lee, S., & Walker, W. R. (2014). Religious coping moderates the Fading Affect Bias across religious and non-religious events. Paper presented at the 2014 meeting of the Midwestern Psychological Association, Chicago.

Green, D. (Director). (1992). *Honor Thy Mother.* [TV Movie] United States: MCA Television, Point of View Productions.

Gruner, L. (1985). The correlation of private, religious devotional practices and marital adjustment. *Journal of Comparative Family Studies, 16,* 47–59.

Harris, W. S., Gowda, M. Kolb, J. W., Strychacz, C. P., Vacek, J. L., Jones, P. G., Forker, A., O'Keefe, J. H., & McCallister, B. D. (1999). A randomized, controlled trial of the effects of remote intercessory prayer on outcomes in patients admitted to the coronary care unit. *Archives of Internal Medicine, 1959,* 2273–2278.

Harvey, J. H., & Omarzu, J. (1997). Minding the close relationship. *Journal of Personality and Social Psychology, 41,* 866–888.

Janssen, J., de Hart, J., & den Draak, C. (1990). Praying as individualized ritual. In H. G. Heinbrock, & H. B. Boudewijnse (eds.), *Current studies on rituals: Perspectives for the Psychology of Religion* (pp. 71–85). Amsterdam: Rodopi.

Kelly, A. M., Klausas, J. A., vonWeiss, R. T., & Kenny, C. (2001). What is it about revealing secrets that is beneficial? *Personality and Social Psychology Bulletin, 27,* 651–665.

Klausner, S. Z. (1961). The social psychology of courage. *Review of Religious Research, 3,* 63–72.

Lawson, E. T., & McCauley, R. N. (2002). The cognitive representation of religious ritual form: A theory of participants' competence with religious ritual systems. In I. Pyysianen & V. Anttonen (Eds.), *Cognitive Approaches in the Cognitive Science of Religion* (pp. 153–176). New York: Continuum.

Lawson, E. T., & McCauley, R. N. (2002). *Bringing ritual to mind.* Cambridge, UK: Cambridge University Press.

Long, D., Elkind, D., & Spilka, B. (1967). The child's conception of prayer. *Journal for the Scientific Study of Religion, 6,* 101–109.

Magee, J. (1957). *Reality and prayer: A guide to the meaning and practice of prayer.* New York: Harper & Brothers.

McGinnis, J. (1992). *Cruel doubt.* New York City: Pocket.

Paloutzian, R. F. (1996). *Invitation to the psychology of religion* (2nd ed.). Boston, MA: Allyn & Bacon.

Pargament, K. (1999). The psychology of religion and spirituality? Yes and no. *International Journal for the Psychology of Religion, 9,* 3–16.

Parker, G. B., & Brown, L. B. (1982). Coping behaviors that mediate between life events and depression. *Archives of General Psychiatry, 39,* 1386–1391.

Patel, C. Marmot, M. G., Terry, D. J., Carruthers, M., Hunt, B., & Patel, M. (1985). Trial of relaxation in reducing coronary risk: Four year follow up. *British Medical Journal, 290,* 1103–1106.

Pennebaker, J. W., Kiecolt-Glaser, J. K., & Glaser, R. (1988). Disclosure of traumas and immune function: Health implications for psychotherapy. *Journal of Consulting and Clinical Psychology, 56,* 239–245.

Petrie, K. J., Booth, R. J., Pennebaker, J. W., Davison, K. P., & Thomas, M. G. (1995). Disclosure of trauma and immune response to a hepatitis B vaccination program. *Journal of Consulting and Clinical Psychology, 63,* 787–792.

Peteet, J. R. (1994). Approaching spiritual problems in psychotherapy: A conceptual framework. *Journal of Psychotherapy Practice and Research, 3,* 237–245.

Pew Trust (April, 2011). State of recidivism: The revolving door of America's prisons. Full report at http://www.pewstates.org/research/reports/state-of-recidivism-85899377338.

Poloma, M. M. (1993). The effects of prayer on mental well-being. *Second Opinion, 18,* 37–51.

Poloma, M. M., & Gallup, G. H. Jr. (1991). *Varieties of prayer: A survey report.* Philadelphia: Trinity Press International.

Poloma, M. M., & Pendleton, B. (1991). The effects of prayer and prayer experiences on measures of general well-being. *Journal of Psychology and Theology, 19,* 71–83.

Raskin, N. J., & Witty M. (2007). Person-centered therapy. In R. J. Corsini & D. Wedding (eds.). *Current Psychotherapies* (8th ed.). Belmont, CA: Brooks-Cole.

Richards, C., & Hildebrand, L. (1990). *Prayers that prevail.* Tulsa, OK: Victory House.

Ritchie, T. D., Skowronski, J. J., Wood, S. E., Walker, W. E., Vogl, R. J., & Gibbons, J. A. (2006). Event self-importance, event rehearsal, and the Fading Affect Bias in autobiographical memory, *Self and Identity, 5,* 172–195.

Roberts, H. W. (1995). *Pastoral care through worship.* Macon, GA: Smith & Helwys.

Routledge, C., Arndt, J., Wildschut, T., Sedikides, C., Hart, C. M., Juhl, J., Vingerhoets, A. J. J. M., & Schlotz, W. (2011). The past makes the present meaningful: Nostalgia as an existential resource. *Journal of Personality and Social Psychology, 101,* 638–652.

Salinger, J. D. (1961). Franny and Zooey. New York: Little, Brown, & Company.

Saudia, T. L., Kinney, M. R., Brown, K. C., & Young-Ward, L. (1991). Health locus of control and helpfulness of prayer. *Heart and Lung, 20,* 60–65.

Seligman, M. E. P., & Csikszentmihalyi, M. (2000). Positive Psychology: An introduction. *American Psychologist, 55,* 1–14.

Seligman, M. E. P., Steen, T. A., Park, N., & Peterson, C. (2006). Positive Psychology progress: Empirical validation of interventions. *American Psychologist, 60,* 410–412.

Shapiro, S. L., Schwartz, G. E., & Bonner, G. (1998). Effects of mindfulness-based stress reduction on medical and premedical students. *Journal of Behavioral Medicine, 21,* 581–599.

Shaw, R. J. (1992). Coping effectiveness in nursing home residents. *Journal of Aging and Health, 4,* 551–563.

Shuler, P. A., Gelberg, L., & Brown, M. (1994). The effects of spiritual/religious practices on psychological well-being among inner city homeless women. *Nurse Practitioner Forum, 5,* 106–113.

Simoneaux. V. (Director). (1992). Cruel Doubt [TV Movie]. United States: NBC Productions, Susan Baerwald Productions.

Skowronski, J. J., Gibbons, J. A., Vogl, R. J., & Walker, W. R. (2004). The effect of social disclosure on the affective intensity provoked by autobiographical memories. *Self & Identity, 3,* 285–309.

Spilka, B. (2005). Religious practice, ritual and prayer. In Paloutzian, R. F., & Park, C. L. (eds.). *Handbook of the psychology of religion and spirituality,* New York: Guilford.

Spilka, B., Hood, R. W., Jr., Hunsberger, B., & Gorsuch, R. L. (2003). *The psychology of religion: An empirical approach* (3rd ed.). New York: Guilford Press.

Sutton, T. D., & Murphy, S. P. (1989). Stressors and patterns of coping in renal transplant patients. *Nursing Research, 38,* 46–49.

Targ, E. F., & Levine, E. G. (2002). The efficacy of a mind-body-spirit group for women with breast cancer: A randomized controlled trial. *General Hospital Psychiatry, 24,* 238–248.

Wachholtz, A. B., & Pargament, K. I. (2005). Is spirituality a critical ingredient of mediation? Comparing the effects of spiritual meditation, secular meditation and relaxation on pain sensitivity and endurance. *Journal of Behavioral Medicine, 28,* 369–384.

Walker, W. R., Skowronski, J. J., Gibbons, J. A., Vogl, R. J., & Ritchie, T. D. (2009). Why people rehearse their memories: Frequency and relations to the intensity of emotions associated with autobiographical events. *Memory, 17,* 760–773.

Walsh, R., & Shapiro, S. L. (2006). The meeting of meditative disciplines and western psychology: A mutually enriching dialogue. *American Psychologist, 61,* 227–239.

Whitley, R. (1964). *Religious behavior.* Englewood Cliffs, NJ: Prentice-Hall.

Wildschut, T., Sedikides, C., Arndt, J., & Routledge, C. (2006). Nostalgia: Content, triggers, functions. *Journal of Personality and Social Psychology, 91,* 975.

Chapter 6

Ames, D. R., Rose, P., & Anderson, C. P. (2006). The NPI-16 as a short measure of narcissism. *Journal of Research in Personality, 40*, 440–450.

Baumeister, R. F., & Vohs, K. D. (2001). Narcissism as addiction to esteem. *Psychological Inquiry, 12*, 206–210.

Beck, A. T. (1976). *Cognitive therapy and emotional disorders.* New York: International Universities Press.

Besser, A., & Zeigler-Hill, V. (2010). The influence of pathological narcissism on emotional and motivational responses to negative events: The roles of visibility and concern about humiliation. *Journal of Research in Personality, 44*, 520–534.

Burrow, A., Currence, N., Lemus, D., DeBono, A. E., Crawford, M. T., & Walker, W. R. (2014). Psychopaths view autobiographical memories as less memorable, important, and emotional than normal individuals. *International Journal of Humanities and Social Science, 7*(4), 1–9.

Dutton, K. (2012). *The wisdom of psychopaths: What saints, spies, and serial killers can teach us about success.* New York: Farrar, Straus and Giroux.

Healy, W. (1942). Review of 'The mask of sanity, an attempt to reinterpret the so-called psychopathic personality.' *The Journal of Abnormal and Social Psychology, 37*(1), 139–141.

Hulsey, C. (1948). The concept of the psychopath. *American Journal of Orthopsychiatry, 18*(2), 297–308.

Kiehl, K. A., & Buckholtz, J. W. (2010). Inside the mind of a psychopath. *Scientific American Mind*, September/October, 22–29.

Kohut, H. (1968). The psychoanalytic treatment of narcissistic personality disorders: Outline of a systematic approach. In *The search for the self* (Vol. 1). New York: International Universities Press.

Kroll-Smith, J. S., & Couch, S. R. (1990). *The real disaster is above ground: A mine fire and social conflict.* Lexington, KY: The University Press of Kentucky.

Ritchie, T., Walker, W. R., Marsh, S., Hart, C., & Skowronski, J. J. (2014). Narcissism distorts the fading affect bias in autobiographical memory. Unpublished manuscript.

Twenge, J. M. (2006). *Generation me: Why today's young Americans are more confident, assertive, entitled and more miserable than ever before.* New York: Free Press.

Vaillancourt, T. (2013). Students aggress against professors in reaction to receiving poor grades: An effect moderated by student narcissism and self-esteem. *Aggressive Behavior, 39*, 71–84.

Vazire, S., & Funder, D. (2006). Impulsivity and the self-defeating behavior of narcissists. *Personality and Social Psychology Review, 10*, 154–165.

Walker, W. R., Skowronski, J. J., Gibbons, J. A., Vogl, R. J., & Thompson, C. P. (2003a). On the emotions that accompany autobiographical memories: Dysphoria disrupts the fading affect bias. *Cognition and Emotion, 17*(5), 703–723.

Walker, W. R., Yancu, C. N., & Skowronski, J. J. (In press). Trait anxiety reduces affective fading for positive and negative autobiographical memories. *Advances in Cognitive Psychology.*

Chapter 7

Abuhamdeh, S. (2000). The autoelic personality: An exploratory investigation. *Unpublished manuscript.* University of Chicago.

Baer, R. A. (2003). Mindfulness training as a clinical intervention: A conceptual and empirical review. *Clinical Psychology: Science and Practice, 10*, 125–143.

Brown, K.W., & Ryan, R. M. (2003). The benefits of being present: Mindfulness and its role in psychological well-being. *Journal of Personality and Social Psychology, 84*, 822–848.

Burpee, L. C., & Langer, E. J. (2005). Mindfulness and marital satisfaction. *Journal of Adult Development, 12*, 43–51.

Csikszentmihalyi, M. (1990). *Flow: The Psychology of Optimal Experience.* New York: Harper & Row.

Csikszentmihalyi, M. (2003). *Good business: Leadership, flow, and the making of meaning.* New York: Penguin.

Csikzentmihalyi, M., Abuhamdeh, S., & Nakamura, J. (2005). Flow. In A. Elliot. (Ed.), *Handbook of competence and motivation.* New York: The Guilford Press, 598–698.

de Manzano, O. Theorell, T., Harmat, L., & Ullen, F. (2010). The psychophysiology of flow during piano playing. *Emotion, 10*, 301–311.

Duckworth, A. L., Kirby, T. A., Tsukayama, Bernstein, H., & Ericsson, K. A. (2011). Deliberate practice spells success: Why grittier competitors triumph at the National Spelling Bee. *Social Psychology and Personality Science, 2*, 174–181.

Duckworth, A. L., & Seligman, M. E. P. (2002). Self-discipline outdoes IQ in predicting academic performance of adolescents. *Psychological Science, 16*, 939–944.

Fredrickson, B. L., & Branigan, C. (2005). Positive emotions broaden the scope of attention and thought-action repertoires. *Cognition and Emotion, 19*, 313–332.

Fredrickson, B. L., & Joiner, T. (2002). Positive emotions trigger upward spirals toward emotional well-being. *Psychological Science, 13*, 172–175.

Jackson, S. A., Thomas, P. R., Marsh, H. W., & Smethurst, C. J. (2001). Relationship between flow, self-concept, psychological skills, and performance. *Journal of Applied Sport Psychology, 13,* 129–153.

Kabat-Zinn, J., Massion, A. O., Kristeller, J., Peterson, L. G., Fletcher, K. E., Pbert, L., Lenderking, W. R., & Santorelli, S. F., (1992). Effectiveness of a mediation-based stress reduction program in the treatment of anxiety disorders. *American Journal of Psychiatry, 149,* 936–943.

Langer, E. J. (2000). Mindful learning. *Current Directions in Psychological Science, 9*(6), 220–223.

Nakamura, J., & Csikszentmihalyi, M. (2001). Flow theory and research. In C. R. Snyder, E. Wright, & S. J. Lopez (Eds.), *Handbook of Positive Psychology*. London: Oxford University Press, 195–206.

Nakamura, J., & Csikszentmihalyi, M. (2005). The concept of flow. *Handbook of Positive Psychology*. London: Oxford University Press, 89–105.

Sawyer, K. (1992). Improvisational creativity: An analysis of jazz performance. *Creativity Research Journal, 5,* 253–263.

Simonton, D. K. (2000). Creativity: Cognitive, personal, developmental and social aspects. *American Psychologist, 55,* 151–158.

Smith, S. M., Ward, T. B., & Finke, R. A. (1995). The creative cognition approach: Cognitive processes in creative contexts. In S. M. Smith, T. B. Ward, & R. A. Finke (Eds.), *The creative cognition approach*. Cambridge, MA: MIT Press.

Walker, W. R., Skowronski, J. J., & Thompson, C. P. (2003). Life is good—and memory helps to keep it that way! *Review of General Psychology, 7,* 203–210.